APPROACHES TO THE WELFARE STATE

APPROACHES TO THE WELFARE STATE

Pranab Chatterjee

NASW PRESS

National Association of Social Workers
Washington, DC

Jay J. Cayner, ACSW, LSW, *President*
Robert H. Cohen, JD, ACSW, *Executive Director*

Linda Beebe, *Executive Editor*
Nancy A. Winchester, *Editorial Services Director*
Wendy Almeleh, *Copy Editor*
Louise R. Goines, *Proofreader*
Sheila Holzberger, Wolf Publications, *Typesetter*
Bernice Eisen, *Indexer*

All the maps in this book were drawn with MacGlobe software by Brøderbund; the exhibits and bar diagrams with DeltaGraph Professional for Macintosh software by DeltaPoint, Inc.; and the flowcharts with MacFlow for Macintosh software by Mainstay.

Library of Congress Cataloging-in-Publication Data
Chatterjee, Pranab
    Approaches to the welfare state / Pranab Chatterjee.
        p.   cm.
    Includes bibliographical references and indexes.
    ISBN 0-87101-262-6 (pbk. : alk. paper)
    1. Welfare state.   I. Title.
HV31.C383   1996
361.6'5--dc20
                          95-50668
                              CIP

Printed in the United States of America

To Manu

Father to five-year-old son:

"Remember son, a begging man has no dignity."

Son: "Right, Dad! No dignity!"

(A few minutes of silence.)

Son: "Dad . . . ?"

Father: "Yes?"

Son: "A begging tiger has no dignity!"

Father: "Well, son, tigers don't beg."

Son: "They do, too, when they get old, have no teeth, and can't hunt . . ."

Manu Chatterjee (private conversation, 1977)

CONTENTS

LIST OF FIGURES, TABLES, AND MAPS
xiii

PREFACE
xvii

ACKNOWLEDGMENTS
xxi

PART 1: THE PARAMETERS OF THE WELFARE STATE
1

WELFARE: THE BASIC CONCEPTS
3
What Is Social Welfare?   3
What Is Social Welfare Policy?   13
Social Welfare, Social Welfare Policy, and the Welfare State:
Key Concepts and Taxonomies   18
Concluding Observations   21
References   23

2

INFRASTRUCTURE OF THE WELFARE STATE
27
The Infrastructure   28
Contradictions in the Intellectual Foundations   37
References   41

3

THE WELFARE STATE IN A WORLD SYSTEM
45

The World System   45
Trends in the Three Worlds   49
Impact of the 1980s on the World System   60
Welfare Infrastructure in the World System   67
Questions about Welfare Infrastructures   78
References   80

PART 2: THREE COMPETING THESES ABOUT THE WELFARE STATE

4

WELFARE IS AN IDEOLOGICAL COMPROMISE: 1
87

What Is Ideology?   87
History of Sociological Perspectives   95
Ideology and Social Welfare   103
Whose Ideology?   108
Ideology: Cause or Justification?   109
References   110

5

WELFARE IS AN IDEOLOGICAL COMPROMISE: 2
115

On Reasons and Justifications   115
On Entire Systems and Subsystems   116
Conclusions   129
References   132

6

WELFARE IS A CAMOUFLAGE FOR CLASS, GENDER, OR INTEREST-GROUP CONFLICT: 1
137

What Is Conflict?   137
Parties to Conflict   139
Theories of Conflict   141

Conflict and Social Welfare: Five Propositions   150
References   151

7

WELFARE IS A CAMOUFLAGE FOR CLASS, GENDER, OR INTEREST-GROUP CONFLICT: 2
155

Thesis 1: Welfare Is a Camouflage for Community-Level Conflicts   155
Thesis 2: Welfare Is a Camouflage for Organizational-Level Conflicts   159
Thesis 3: Welfare Is a Camouflage for Ethnic Conflicts   162
Thesis 4: Welfare Is a Camouflage for Interest-Group Conflicts   163
Thesis 5: Welfare Is a Camouflage for International Conflicts   178
Conflict and the Welfare Infrastructure   180
References   183

8

WELFARE IS A BY-PRODUCT OF INDUSTRIALIZATION: 1
187

What Is Industrialization?   187
Groups That Sponsor Industrialization   202
Paradigms of Industrialization   212
Ontological Issues in the Paradigms   222
Industrialization and Social Welfare: 10 Theses   227
References   227

9

WELFARE IS A BY-PRODUCT OF INDUSTRIALIZATION: 2
233

The 10 Theses   233
The Three Worlds in the 21st Century   250
References   251

PART 3: SUMMARY AND CONCLUSIONS

10

APPROACHES TO THE WELFARE STATE: WHO IS RIGHT?
257

The Welfare State: Points of Agreement and Dispute   258
The Welfare State: Who Is Right?   261
Concluding Remarks   270
References   271

11

VISIONS OF THE WELFARE STATE: WHAT IS RIGHT?
273
Is There a Surplus?   273
The Moral Foundation   275
The Political Foundation   277
The Legal Foundation   277
The Scientific Foundation   279
Conclusion   279
References   282

GLOSSARY
283

INDEX
297

ABOUT THE AUTHOR
311

LIST OF FIGURES, TABLES, AND MAPS

FIGURES

Figure 1-1. Pryor's Concepts of Transactions in Society 5

Figure 1-2. Types of Allocations 7

Figure 1-3. A Model for Progressive Social Welfare 14

Figure 1-4. A Model for Regressive Social Welfare 15

Figure 1-5. Offe's Model of Relationships between the Market Economy and the Welfare State 17

Figure 2-1. The Infrastructure of the Welfare Society 28

Figure 2-2. The Infrastructure of the Welfare Society: Payers 29

Figure 2-3. The Infrastructure of the Welfare Society: Types of Transfer 31

Figure 2-4. The Infrastructure of the Welfare Society: Transfer Agents 33

Figure 2-5. The Infrastructure of the Welfare Society: Recipients 34

Figure 2-6. The Infrastructure of the Welfare Society: Providers 35

Figure 2-7. The Infrastructure of the Welfare Society: Limits on Transfer 38

Figure 3-1. Population of Selected Countries in the Three Worlds: 1991 54

Figure 3-2. Per Capita GNPs of Selected Countries in the Three Worlds: 1991 55

Figure 3-3. Growth in the GNPs of Selected Countries in the Three Worlds: 1990–91 57

Figure 3-4. Female Life Expectancy in Selected Countries in the Three Worlds: 1991 58

Figure 3-5. Population per Hospital Bed in Selected Countries in the Three
          Worlds: 1991 59

Figure 3-6. Percentage of the GNPs for Education in Selected Countries in
          the Three Worlds: 1991   61

Figure 4-1. Four Ways of Viewing Ideology and Social Welfare   109

Figure 5-1. Ideology as the Reason for Social Welfare   116

Figure 5-2. Ideology as Justification for Social Welfare   116

Figure 6-1. Conflict as an Intermediary between Two Orders   138

Figure 7-1. The Beneficiaries of Conflict in a Welfare State   165

Figure 7-2. The Beneficiaries of Conflict in a Welfare State: Revised
          View   166

Figure 7-3. Six Ways of Defining a Child-Assistance Policy   168

Figure 7-4. Seven Ways of Defining an Aged-Assistance Policy   169

Figure 7-5. Seven Ways of Defining Health, Mental Health, and Corrections
          Policy   172

Figure 7-6. Seven Ways of Defining Income Maintenance or Assistance
          Policy   173

Figure 7-7. Conflicts in the Welfare Infrastructure   181

Figure 8-1. A Model of the Kuznets Curve   192

Figure 8-2. Sources of U.S. Income: 1993   199

Figure 8-3. Expenditures of the U.S. Welfare State: 1993   200

Figure 8-4. The Technology Base of the Three Worlds   203

Figure 8-5. Insiders and Outsiders in Transfer Activity, with Children (the
          Junior Generation) as Outsiders   210

Figure 8-6. Insiders and Outsiders in Transfer Activity, with Children (the
          Junior Generation) as Insiders   211

Figure 9-1. Variations in the Welfare State   235

Figure 10-1. Approaches to the Welfare State: 1   264

Figure 10-2. Approaches to the Welfare State: 2   265

Figure 11-1. The Moral Foundations of the Welfare Community and the Wel-
          fare State   278

TABLES

Table 1-1. Units of Social Organization in Transfer Activity 11

Table 3-1. Welfare Trends in the Three Worlds 62

Table 3-2. Social Welfare Provisions in Four First World Countries 71

Table 3-3. Social Welfare Provisions in Four Second World Countries 75

Table 3-4. Social Welfare Provisions in Four Third World Countries 79

Table 3-5. Comparison of 11 Variables in the Welfare States 80

Table 4-1. Components of Four Ideologies 90

Table 5-1. Four Ideologies Discussed by George and Wilding 122

Table 5-2. Model of Nine Ideologies of Help 127

Table 5-3. Ideologies of Help: Role of the State and the Market 130

Table 6-1. Attributes of Fordism and Post-Fordism 149

Table 8-1. Key Attributes of Two Economies 190

Table 8-2. Human Development Indices in Industrial and Nonindustrial Countries 195

Table 8-3. Social Security Expenditures as a Percentage of the GDP of Industrial and Nonindustrial Countries: 1985–90 197

Table 8-4. Health Care Expenditures as a Percentage of the GDP of Industrial and Nonindustrial Countries: 1990–91 198

Table 8-5. Sponsors of Industrialization, Their Ideologies, and the Consequent Directions of the Welfare State 205

Table 9-1. Gould's Comments on Pierson's Hypotheses about the Welfare State 239

Table 9-2. Intended and Unintended Consequences of the Welfare State: The Structural Functionalist View 241

Table 9-3. The Functions of Poverty in First World Countries 242

Table 9-4. Characteristics of Prefisc and Postfisc Welfare States 244

Table 9-5. Natural Experiments in Social Development in the Third World: 1945–85 248

Table 9-6. Natural Paired Experiments in Social Development between Second and Third World Countries: 1945–85 248

MAPS

Map 3-1. The Third World (Nonaligned Nations) in 1964 47

Map 3-2. The First World in 1992 50

Map 3-3. The Second World in 1992 51

Map 3-4. The Third World in 1992 52

PREFACE

T he study of the welfare state is like the proverbial story of six blind people examining an elephant. In that story, each person, after having felt one part of the elephant, declared that the animal looked like a rope (the tail), a pillar (one leg), a tube (the trunk), a stake (the tusk), a corrugated ceiling (the abdomen), or a banana leaf (the ear). All six were correct in their perceptions but incorrect in their description of the animal. Like the six blind people who explored the elephant, scholars often end up studying only a part of the welfare state. The economist has one perception of the phenomenon; the social worker and the moral philosopher, another; the sociologist and the political scientist, yet another; and the organizational behaviorist, still another. Their perceptions are informative but incomplete.

However, there is one difference in this analogy. The six blind persons studied a *tame* elephant (it had to be tame to allow the six people to intrude on it), so their experiences teach us nothing about a *must* (the Hindi word for raging) elephant. Often, the welfare state is more like a must than a tame elephant, roaming and running about every which way in a large territory. The perspectives of the somewhat blind social scientists of various disciplines are often tame and static views of a sometimes *must* and dynamic entity.

The economists, who were asked by Harry Truman to be one-armed policy advisers,[1] inform us about the feasibility of a welfare state and about the economic efficiency of different types of welfare states. They tell us that a society must have a baseline production process and that this process must be continuous over time if the welfare state is to be viable. However, they are not well equipped to teach us how the resources that are produced should be distributed. John Stuart Mill taught them that.

The moral philosophers, some of them card-carrying economists, inform us about whether there should be a welfare state at all and, if so, who should be the right and proper claimants of it. From Adam Smith and Karl Marx to John Rawls and Robert Nozick, moral philosophers have argued about what the state should or should not do, what the family should or should not

---

[1] Truman once asked a group of distinguished economists for advice so he could formulate economic policies for the United States. The group told him: "Well, Mr. President, on the one hand, you could do this. On the other, you could do that!" Truman replied: "What I really need is a one-handed economist!"

do, what should or should not be done with the operation of the market, and who should or should not have entitlements in the distribution of income.

The social workers, when not busy arguing with the ghost of Abraham Flexner (who pronounced in 1915 that social work was not really a profession) or seeking solidarity among themselves with medical metaphors, inform us that more and more welfare should be provided that is less and less means tested and that increased state spending, managed by welfare administrators, is the only way to solve social problems. They are close to the Marxian notion of distribution, but it is not politically correct for them to acknowledge this fact because increasingly they are also in favor of the Invisible Hand (Adam Smith's metaphor for the market) compensating them for their diagnosis and treatment of all social ailments.

The sociologists, who for years were busy building models, found that by the end of the 20th century, both the state and the market were giving parties to which they were not invited. While trying to decide whether to seek an alliance with social workers (and lose face) or with organizational behaviorists (with whom they have no leg to stand on), they inform us that the welfare state is social stratification by another name. Furthermore, they tell us that various groups in this stratification matrix are in an elliptical orbit around the state but are held together by a centripetal force.

The psychologists, who were invited to the parties given by both the market and the state, are in a good mood. Nobody has asked them to give their opinions about the welfare state and, as far as they are concerned, no member of their profession should even make eye contact with persons who ask about it. If approached by pushy questioners who want to know about the welfare state, they have a one-liner ready: "It destroys incentive, which we have long called motivation!"

The political scientists have been busy on two fronts: being political with legal scholars, so they know firsthand what entitlements are, and being empirical about voting behavior, so they know how entitlements come about. When asked about their alliance with the legal profession, they, too, have a one-liner ready: "Politics has long made strange bedfellows!" When asked about the impact of voting behavior on the welfare state, they offer another one-liner: "The higher the number of people voting, the more the welfare state benefits!" When asked how this idea applies to the elites, who are few in number and, consequently, have a low voting capacity (but high benefits), they inform us: "Whereas most voters vote in only *one* place, the members of the elite vote in *many* places!"

The organizational behaviorists have come up in the world, from their humble origins in sociology (reading Max Weber and Edgar Schein) and social psychology (reading Kurt Lewin and Howard Stein) to the posh environs of the business schools. Not only are they invited to the parties given by the state and the market, but they get called first about their availability for such parties. They inform us that the welfare state originates from transformational leadership, but after its birth can be run with transactional leadership. When a crisis occurs, the welfare state may be subjected to options, from restructuring to rethinking. The problem of the welfare state, they tell us, is basically a management problem.

In short, it seems that social workers approach the study of the welfare state by examining its structure, programs, scope, and inherent dilemmas, whereas social scientists from other disciplines, such as economics, sociology, and political science, study the emergence of the welfare state in several technopolitical contexts. Furthermore, there appear to be three distinct orientations to the study of social welfare policy: (1) social welfare policies are a function of a society's conflicting values and ideologies (the position of most social workers and some social scientists), (2) social welfare policies are a camouflage for inherent class, gender, and interest-group conflicts in a society (the position of Marxists, conflict theorists, and feminist theorists), and (3) social welfare policies are a function of the technological bases of a society (the position of most social scientists). In this book, I explore the development of the welfare state from these various positions and, at the end (chapter 10), construct a visual model that puts these positions in perspective for a multidisciplinary audience. I leave it to the reader to judge whether I have been a fair or biased referee.

ACKNOWLEDGMENTS

The idea for this book began in the mid-1970s, when I was asked to teach a course at Case Western Reserve University on theories of social welfare and social justice. I am grateful to my colleagues Edward Mullen, Merl C. Hokenstad, Jr., Richard L. Edwards, Darlyne Bailey, and Marvin Rosenberg, who supported my efforts to develop and teach this course. I am also grateful to Shanti Khinduka and Joyce Everett for their support of the idea that the experiences from this course could be translated into a book. The advice and comments of Anthony R. C. de Crespigny (of the United Kingdom) were invaluable. I am wiser because of the advice of Professor P. K. Saha, who told me: "Write the book in Anglo-Saxon English." I am not only thankful for my wife Marian's tolerance during the writing of the book but wiser still from trying to follow her admonishment: "Write the book in plain English!"

And I am forever indebted to my students, some of whom continued to discuss the contents of the course on theories of social welfare with me long after the semester was over. The following students from this group stand out in my mind: Craig Boitel, Mark Chapin, Il-Sub Choi, Julian Chow, Katherine Dunlap, Riad Hamzawi, Judy and Harvey Hilbert, Jongsook Kim, Elmer Martin, Jr., Michael Melendez, John Meyers, Lenore Olsen, Margie Rodriguez, Ann Roy, Peter Stoddard, Barbara Wester, Joyce White, and Paz Zorita. I am especially indebted to Paz because of her convictions about the limits of the welfare state, a view I happen to share. If the ideas of this book seem relevant and useful, then the persons named here made that possible. If there are problems or the ideas are poorly developed, I am solely responsible.

Part 1

THE PARAMETERS OF THE WELFARE STATE

Part 1 consists of three chapters. In chapter 1, I define concepts, such as social welfare, social welfare policy, and the welfare state; trace their origin in the Western world; and review the known taxonomies of the welfare state. Chapter 2 examines the infrastructure of the welfare state using a model that shows the relationships between the ideological and technopolitical bases of society and the groups that pay for social welfare and trace the relationships among these payors, the transfer agent, the recipients, and the providers of in-kind services. This model is then used throughout the book as a framework for understanding the various dimensions of the welfare state. In chapter 3, I explore the worldwide systematic variations in the nature of the welfare state that are due to ideologies, economic bases, and historical configurations.

1

Welfare: The Basic Concepts

Alms are the result on the one hand of a moral idea about gifts and wealth and on the other of an idea about sacrifice. Generosity is necessary because otherwise Nemesis will take vengeance upon the excessive wealth and happiness of the rich by giving to the poor and the gods.

Mauss, *The Gift*

What Is Social Welfare?

The term *social welfare* is popularly understood as cash or in-kind payments to persons who need support because of physical or mental illness, poverty, age, disability, or other defined circumstances. Often the provider of such support is some form of governmental body, although in many cases, it is a voluntary organization, a church body, an occupational guild, or another nongovernmental group.

Scholars who study social welfare sometimes distinguish between economic welfare and noneconomic welfare (Moon, 1977; Rothenberg, 1961; Rowley & Peacock, 1975). *Economic welfare* refers to an individual's well-being as a function of income, holdings, tax status, and other such indicators, whereas *noneconomic welfare* refers to a person's well-being with respect to biological, spiritual, emotional, and normative conditions. Thus, persons with low income and holdings are likely to be in poor health (both mental and physical) and may need support from government or nongovernment bodies. In such cases, the lack of economic welfare may lead to poor noneconomic welfare. For the most part, such distinctions are popular among economists.

Other scholars differentiate between social welfare and other forms of welfare (Chatterjee, 1985; Gil, 1970; Gilbert & Specht, 1974; Plant, 1988; Rein, 1970; Rochefort, 1986; Rohrlich, 1971). Rochefort, for example, suggested that social welfare often means a society's system of provisions for its members who are in need in which the society protects not only these members but itself from these members. This point was emphasized by

3

Goode (1967) in "The Protection of the Inept." It seems, then, that social welfare often means more than the economic well-being of individuals, but includes the idea of protecting individuals in need as well as protecting society from individuals in need.

Individuals in need, however, are seen as belonging to groups that are identifiable by society. One formal definition of social welfare is as follows:

> Social welfare is a *transfer system* through which *allocations* of goods and services are made to individuals and groups through a given *unit of social organization,* such as the family, the church, the guild, the state, or the corporate group, under *a set of rules and with a set of reciprocal roles.* . . . In this definition of social welfare, there are four components: (a) a transfer system (through which allocations are made); (b) allocations; (c) a given unit of social organization; and (d) a set of rules. (Chatterjee, 1985, p. 27)

These four components of social welfare are discussed next.

TRANSFER SYSTEM

Pryor (1977) suggested that there are two types of transactions in society: those that take place under a transfer system and those that take place under an exchange system. A transfer system is a one-way transaction, in which income, wealth, or some other item is transferred from one party to another and there is no identifiable recompense to the party that originated the transfer. An exchange system is a two-way transaction, where one party provides some goods or services to another and, in turn, is recompensed for doing so.

A transfer can be of two types: transfer by source and transfer by centricity. *Transfer by source* refers to the status of the provider and the recipient. If a well-to-do person or group is the provider and a person or group of modest means is the recipient, then the transfer may be called a *progressive transfer.* The reverse of a progressive transfer is called a *regressive transfer.* Progressive and regressive transfers may occur between age cohorts (from young adults and middle-aged persons to young children or aged people, or vice versa), between groups that occupy different positions in a socioeconomic hierarchy (from middle-class and working-class people to poor people, or vice versa), and between those who are and are not in the labor force. Thus, taxing wealthy people to make welfare payments to low-income or poor families is a form of progressive transfer, whereas taxing working-class or poor people to support higher education (which benefits middle-class people) is a form of regressive transfer. When a transfer situation cannot be identified as either progressive or regressive, it is called a *neutral transfer.* Thus, taxing families in a community that is somewhat even in socioeconomic composition to support a school system is neutral transfer since it is a transfer from one socioeconomic class to the same socioeconomic class. However, it is a progressive transfer when it is seen as a transfer from one generation to another.

    Transfer by centricity, in turn, can be of two types. When it refers to the situation in which a transfer from one party or group to another goes through a central collection or clearing agent (for example, a designated person in a group or a central government in a nation), it is called *centric transfer.* When it refers to the absence of a central agent in the transfer situation, it is called a *noncentric transfer* (Stark, 1995).

    Exchange is also of two types: market exchange and nonmarket exchange. *Market exchange* refers to a transaction by the rules of supply and demand, and *nonmarket exchange* refers to a transaction by social norms and emotional bonds. See Figure 1-1 for a graphic representation of Pryor's ideas about transfer and exchange.

Figure 1-1.

Pryor's Concepts of Transactions in Society

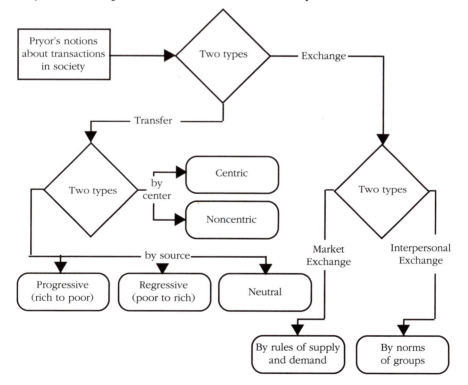

Transfer may take one of the following two forms: social insurance and welfare. *Social insurance* refers to transfer to a group of recipients for whom some form of transfer has taken place in the past. *Welfare* refers to transfer to a group of people who have made no contributions to the transfer process in the past. Both terms are variants of transfer. The term social insurance can be somewhat confusing, because it is often confused with the word "insurance." *Insurance* is a commodity one purchases at the marketplace (like life insurance, car insurance, or disability insurance), and the seller pays the purchaser a previously agreed-on sum if and when the purchaser encounters a specified calamity. Social insurance, on the other hand, is often a transfer process where the state collects specified amounts from people in the labor force and distributes the money to certain categories of people (the aged, the unemployed, the ill, and so on). The understanding is that when people leave the labor force, either temporarily or permanently, owing to aging, loss of employment, illness, or other such specified reasons, they too will receive transfer payments from those remaining in the labor force.

ALLOCATIONS

Allocations can be understood at two levels. The first level is when the goods or services being transferred (regardless of whether they are centric or noncentric or progressive or regressive) are either in cash or a cash equivalent or in kind. The second level involves whether the transfer goes directly to the recipient or to a third party who provides certain goods and services to the recipient. For brevity, I refer to the first level as cash versus kind and to the second level as direct versus indirect (see Figure 1-2 for the various kinds of allocations).

Cash versus Kind

Cash may be transferred to recipients in two ways: through checks or money or through tax credits or tax deductions. In-kind transfer occurs when the agent of transfer (such as a government) either employs a group or develops an organization to provide certain services or purchases those services from independent providers. These services may include health care, housing, training or education, personal advice or counseling, and protection (often known as protective services).

Direct versus Indirect

All cash transfers are direct transfers, since the transactions take place between the recipients and the centric agents. Groups and organizations that are employed by the transfer agents to provide services are involved in direct transfer. On the other hand, independent providers that are

Figure 1-2.

Types of Allocations

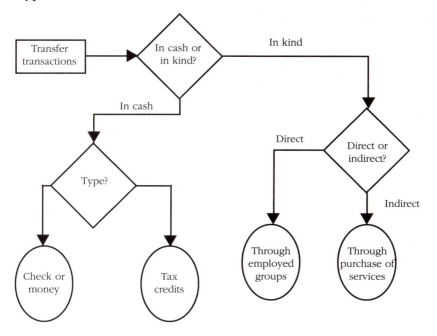

reimbursed by the transfer agents are involved in indirect transfers. Such reimbursements may be called *third-party payments*. Not all third-party payments take place in the transfer sector, however. Many third-party payments also take place in the exchange sector (see Figure 1-1), as is the case when persons who purchased insurance policies through market exchange receive certain goods or services.

In-cash transfers are also called *income supplement* or *income maintenance* plans, and in-kind transfers may include such services and artifacts as subsidized (the recipient does not procure them from market exchange) health care (including mental health care) or housing. Sometimes, social services or legal services may also be included in the latter category.

Transfers (either in kind or cash) can be *comprehensive* (administered by one set of offices or agencies) or *diversified* (administered by many agencies or offices). They can also be *universal* (a basic floor of income and services provided to all, regardless of social position or economic status) or *means tested* (available only to those of a specific social position or economic status). Sometimes, transfers may be *indexed* so as not to exceed a lifestyle attainable by earning a minimum possible wage or some other standard; at other times, they are set by another formula.

Often transfers are aimed at children or persons who are sick (including those who are mentally ill and disabled), unskilled (unemployable), or unemployed. In some settings, transfers are planned for all five categories, but in others, transfers are aimed at various forms of overlap of these categories (such as children of unskilled parents) or to those who meet further qualifications (such as aged persons who have a history of labor force participation). A source of controversy is whether transfers to these categories of persons should be universal or means tested or be reduced to *zero transfers* (meaning none at all).

UNIT OF SOCIAL ORGANIZATION

Social welfare as a transfer system often requires a social organization—a social structure, such as the family, church, community, tribe, clan, state, or guild, each of which has different types of members. In all forms of social organization, the recipients and providers of transfers are bound by some rule of membership.

Family

The family, especially the extended family, is perhaps the oldest and most primitive form of social organization. Families range in structure from single parent to nuclear (two parent) to several types of extended families and may also vary on a continuum from patriarchal to matriarchal.

In this social unit, transfers (usually income transfers) take place from the young adult and middle-aged members to the very young and aged members. Transfers, in the form of inheritance, may also be made from the aged members to the middle-aged members, in which case they are transfers of wealth. Seen from a different perspective, transfers within the family take place between those who are attached to the labor force and those who are not or between those who are healthy and those who are ill or have a disability. In any case, within-family transfers may be centric (go through a central agent like a patriarch or matriarch) or noncentric (are transactions between two family members).

In most societies, the family is the first-line provider of transfers to individuals in need. In some societies (like most societies in Africa and Asia), it is the only provider of transfers. Hereafter, for convenience, I refer to a family that provides such transfers as the *welfare-providing family*.

The Church

The church (in the generic sense, including the temple, the mosque, or any other community around a place of worship) is another social organization that is often engaged in transfer. Depending on the church's mission, history, ideological origins, and prosletizing zeal, transfer may take place from the church as an organization to individuals or families in need or from key members of the church to persons in need. In such cases, the transfers are either centric or noncentric. Also depending on the church's mission, history, and so forth, the recipients may be members of the church or outsiders whom the church may consider potential members.

In many societies, the church is the second-line provider of transfers to persons in need. Hereafter, I refer to the church as a transfer agent as the *welfare church*.

The Community

The term *community* may mean different things to different people. It may mean an aggregate of several or many families who are bound by geography; ethnic, tribal, or clan loyalties; or religious or linguistic identities. In *tribal societies,* these boundaries of geography, ethnicity, tribe, clan, religion, and language are the same (Kottak, 1979). In *agricultural societies,* they may overlap, and, consequently, rules of transfer may develop in one community but not in another. Most agricultural societies are patriarchal, and rules of transfer evolve within ethnoreligious, ethnolingual tribal groups. When the concept of a state exists, rules of transfer may still continue within these communal boundaries (Martin & Voorhies, 1975). The *welfare community* is much like the welfare church, and in many societies is the second-line provider of transfers to persons in need.

The State

The state may evolve as a large territorial and political unit of governance in many agricultural societies, but is often not engaged as an agent of transfer. However, it becomes an agent of centric transfer in most industrial societies (Kottak, 1979; Rimlinger, 1971). Furthermore, in industrial societies, earlier (and historically evolved) welfare churches and welfare communities are likely to continue in some form or fashion. In addition, guilds, collective-bargaining organizations (like labor unions), and voluntary organizations usually develop to perform certain types of transfers (Pryor, 1977). Often these guilds, unions, and voluntary organizations can be identified as parochial or secular. Thus, in industrial societies, two different sectors are frequently engaged in transfer activity: those carried on under state, or public, auspices and those undertaken with private leadership.

In industrial societies, the state is the last-line provider of transfers. For many in industrial societies, however, it is the only provider because the family, the church, and the community are unable to do so. I refer to this type of state as *the welfare state* and argue that its development started, for the most part, in the Western world (North America and Europe) owing to industrialization and the separation of church and state.

SOCIETY

A *welfare society* is a social order that includes the welfare family, the welfare community, the welfare church, and the welfare state. It is based on institutions (the family, the polity, the economy, and religion) that promote social welfare. In other words, it is a social order where the efforts of all the institutions are devoted to promoting human well-being. Welfare state, welfare community, welfare churches, and welfare family are subsets of a welfare society.

Table 1-1 presents a summary of the units of social organization that are involved in transfer activities. The term *provider* is often used to denote the designee of the transfer agent. Such providers may be voluntary secular agencies, voluntary sectarian agencies, state bureaucracies, independent or group practitioners, and so on. Furthermore, they may be involved in in-kind direct or indirect transfers, as shown in Figure 1-2.

SET OF RULES

The last component of social welfare is a set of rules. These rules involve five domains:

1. *Membership of the recipient.* Is this person a member of the family (as in a welfare-providing family) or a member of the church or the community (as in a welfare church or welfare community) or a citizen of the state (as in a welfare state)? At times, nonmembers or noncitizens are eligible to be recipients, but there must be special provisions to include them.
2. *Vulnerability.* Is the recipient seen as a person who is likely to become a victim or an embarassment to everybody or prone to develop more problems or dangerous to himself or herself? Often this vulnerability is understood within the cultural standards of a specific time and place. Griswold (1994, p. 93) called it "the cultural construction of social problems."
3. *The deserving status of the recipient.* Most cultures set up, either explicitly or implicitly, an order of preference for certain recipients over others. For example, in some cultures, blind persons or soldiers who have been disabled in a war or workers with work-

Table 1-1. Units of Social Organization in Transfer Activity

UNITS OF SOCIAL ORGANIZATION	WHERE FOUND	HOW TRANSFER IS DONE
Welfare-providing family, with rules of membership First-line provider	Almost everywhere	Centric transfer through a patriarch or a matriarch Noncentric transfer between two family members Transfer may take place within extended or nuclear families
Welfare church, with clear rules of of membership Second-line provider	Almost everywhere	Centric transfer through the church hierarchy Noncentric transfer among member families Centric or noncentric transfer from the church hierarchy or member families to outsiders (some of whom may be potential members)
Welfare community, with some rules of membership Second-line provider	Almost everywhere	Centric transfer through the community hierarchy Noncentric transfer among member families Centric or noncentric transfer to outsiders at times
Welfare state, with rules of citizenship Public–private divisions Parochial–secular divisions Last-line provider and sometimes the only provider	Industrial societies	Centric transfer through state hierarchies (bureaucracies) Noncentric transfer from welfare churches and welfare communities to those in need Noncentric transfer from voluntary organizations to those in need

related injuries are preferred recipients, and able-bodied mental patients or poor persons may be seen as nonpreferred recipients.

4. *The allocation as a right or a gratuity.* Is the allocation an entitlement, which the recipient has the right to receive, or charity, which may be given or withdrawn according to the whim of the donor?

5. *The process by which one becomes a transfer agent.* In the family, who does the transfer: the patriarch, the matriarch, or a designee of either one? In the church or in the community, should the transfer agents be the church elders, the community leaders, or their agents? If their agents, how should the agents be selected? In the state, how should such agents be chosen? Should they be required to have special training, knowledge, skill, and perhaps a license? Should there be a hierarchy among these agents? Should the state's charge to these agents be to move the recipients from the transfer situation to a market-exchange situation?

The Role of the Market

For the most part, social welfare is society's way of managing (often with some kind of infrastructure) persons or groups who are not or cannot be participants in the process of market exchange, such as those who are poor, young, disabled, aged, chronically ill, or mentally retarded. Some authors (see, for example, Beeghley, 1988; Ulmer, 1969) have argued that not all transfers flow to persons who are poor or young, or disabled. In fact, they have noted, certain types of both in-cash and in-kind transfer flow to those who are rich, middle class, or working class, as well as to other active participants in the market exchange. Such transfers are either not called social welfare (Beeghley, 1988; Pohlmann, 1990) or are seen as an extended form of welfare "not for the poor alone" (Kahn & Kamerman, 1977) or as "welfare for the well-to-do" (Tullock, 1983). Examples of welfare for the well-to-do include social security benefits to affluent elderly people, price supports to certain manufacturers or farmers, housing subsidies or low-interest housing loans to middle-class persons, state-supported higher education to middle-class students, and tax write-off schemes for wealthy people. Seen from this perspective, certain types of social welfare are *progressive* (the transfer flows from the well-to-do to those who are not or from those who are successful in the marketplace to those who are not), others are *regressive* (the transfer flows either uniformly from everyone to those who are privileged and successful in the marketplace or from those who are less privileged and out of the market-exchange arena to those who are engaged in market exchange), and still others are *neutral* (see Figure 1-1).

Wealth versus Income Transfer

For the most part, the types of allocations shown in Figure 1-2 are done by *income transfer*. That is, a part of the income of those who are in the marketplace is transferred to those who are not (as in progressive social welfare), or a part of the income of all people is transferred to those who are relatively privileged (as in regressive social welfare).

Participation in the marketplace requires the possession of certain resources. Beeghley (1988) contended that those at the top of a social hierarchy (the upper class in industrial societies) usually own wealth (the means of production) and use wealth to obtain their income. Those in the middle of the social hierarchy (the middle and working classes in industrial societies) have knowledge and skills and use them to obtain income. Those at the bottom of the social hierarchy (poor people and others without any of these resources) have only unskilled labor or nothing at all with which to obtain income. It may be argued that both progressive and regressive social welfare involve income transfer, whereas prolonged forms of regressive social welfare may lead to the transfer of wealth (the accumulation of more wealth at the top).

The transfer of wealth may also occur when a society loses a war or the technological base of a society changes from one type to another, leading to changes in the composition of the top of the social hierarchy. Figures 1-3 and 1-4 present models of the progressive and regressive forms of social welfare, respectively.

WHAT IS SOCIAL WELFARE POLICY?

Hill (1993), an eminent British writer on welfare policy, noted that it is not possible to separate social policy from economic policy because both involve the redistribution of income. He also suggested that the study of social policy or welfare policy cannot be value free and therefore should be examined as arguments advanced both from the political and ideological Left and Right. Marshall (quoted in Gilbert & Specht, 1974, p. 3), another British writer, called welfare policy "the policy of governments with regard to action having a direct impact on the welfare of citizens by providing them with services or income." Titmuss (1969, p. 42), who educated an entire generation of British scholars on the subject, defined welfare policy as "provisions by collectivities" to deal with various "states of dependency." In the United States, Kahn (1979) pointed to the tension between redistribution, which would foster equality, versus limited and earmarked aid to unfortunate and handicapped persons, which would maintain the present inequalities.

Figure 1-3.

A Model for Progressive Social Welfare

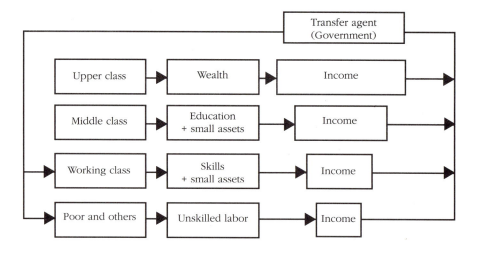

Gilbert and Specht (1974, p. 5) suggested that "social welfare is that pattern-ing of relationships which develops in society to carry out mutual support functions." Thus, the objective of welfare policy is this *patterning* for mutual aid. Tropman (1989) argued that the understanding of welfare policy means the understanding of seven value conflicts or dilemmas: (1) What mixture of work and leisure should be allowed? (2) What mixture of right versus gratuity is to be permitted? (3) Should the provisions made be adequate or equitable? (4) What types of dependence does the society permit to be reduced? (5) Should the benefits be targeted to the individual or to the person's family? (6) Should the making of welfare policy be secularized or not? (7) Should wel-fare policy be carried out under public or private auspices?

Karger and Stoesz (1994) defined social welfare policy as "a subset of social policy," leading to cash and in-kind benefit structures. They added that social welfare policy emerges as responses to social problems that are often guided by certain dominant values and that these values are at the core of American ideologies.

Most of the works on social welfare policy just cited were written by persons from the social work profession. In the social sciences, another trend is seen. Instead of examining the various realms of social welfare policy, social scientists examine the reasons for and the economic contexts of the emergence of the welfare state. For example, Goodin (1988, pp. 20–22) suggested that

Figure 1-4.

A Model for Regressive Social Welfare

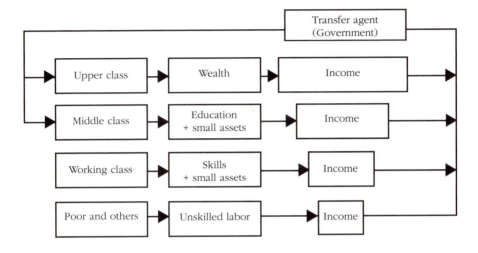

the welfare state is set in the context of a market economy. The function of the welfare state is . . . . to modify the play of market forces in various limited respects. Its function is not to supplant the market altogether. . . .

The welfare state strives to produce a post-fisc distribution of certain goods and services that is preferable to the pre-fisc one. In a planned economy, by contrast, all outcomes are the outcomes of planning. . . .

An important feature of the welfare state is that it limits its provision to certain basic needs. The substance of these needs varies from society to society, of course. But what remains relatively constant across all societies is the recognition of a category of "needs" separate from that of "mere wants."

Goodin then outlined the basic aims of social welfare policy: (1) to respond to those who are affected by the failure of the market and (2) to safeguard the market.

Offe (1984) expanded on the relationship between the market economy and the welfare state by suggesting the following four scenarios:

1. The expanding private sector economy generates a tax base for "growth dividend" out of which welfare state transfers and services can be financed.

2. The provision of skills, health care, peaceful industrial relations, "built-in" demand stabilizers, etc., generates
the necessary input for market economy and supports its
further expansion.

3. Labor-saving technical change, capital flight, domestic demand gap, etc., undermine prospects for long-term
full employment on which [the welfare state] is premised.

4. The excessive tax burden and crowding-out effect of
state budget deficits lead to . . . disincentives to invest,
employ, and work; and [the welfare state] causes labor
market rigidities and "immoralist" attitudes.

In this schema, the first two scenarios are what is termed *supportive* of the
welfare state, and the third and fourth are termed *antagonistic* to the welfare
state. Figure 1-5 outlines them.

Elaborating on some of Offe's ideas Esping-Andersen (1990) stated
that the development of the welfare state can be understood from three
dimensions: (1) the roles of the state and the market in making allocations,
(2) the impact of the welfare state on society's hierarchies, and (3) the process by which certain allocations become entitlements. He then proposed
three types of welfare states (which he called three "worlds of welfare capitalism"): the liberal regimes (Australia, Canada, Great Britain, and the United
States), the social democratic regimes (the Scandinavian countries), and the
conservative-corporate regimes (Austria, France, Germany, Italy, and Holland). In the liberal regimes, the trend is toward "intervention" with groups
facing market failure, whereas in the other two regimes, the trend is toward
"prevention," so that vulnerable groups are spared the impact of market
failure.

There are some major differences between the positions of social
workers and those of social scientists who have studied social welfare policy.
Social workers emphasize that variations in social welfare policies are due to
differences in the values and ideologies of given societies (Gilbert & Specht,
1974; Karger & Stoesz, 1994; Tropman, 1989). Social scientists, however, are
divided into three main camps. The first camp (see, for example, Barry, 1990;
George & Wilding, 1976) agrees more or less with the position of social
workers. The second camp (Esping-Andersen, 1990; Goodin, 1988; Offe, 1984;
Rimlinger, 1971; Schumpeter, 1950; Wilensky, 1975) contends that the variations are due to the technoeconomic bases and market fluctuations within
and around given societies. The third camp suggests that social welfare
policies are a camouflage for inherent class and interest-group conflicts in
society (Bernstein, 1968; Corrigan & Leonard, 1979; Gough, 1980; Levine,

Figure 1-5.

Offe's Model of Relationships between the Market Economy and the Welfare State

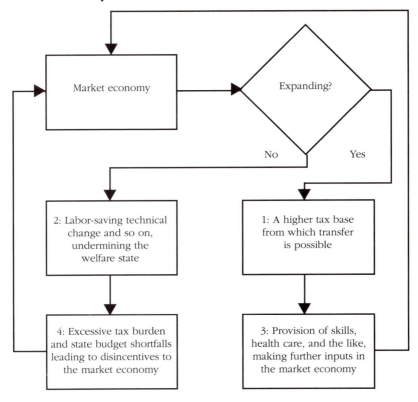

1988; Piven & Cloward, 1971; Pohlmann, 1990). In sum, there seem to be three orientations to the study of social welfare policy:

1. Social welfare policies are a function of the conflicting values and ideologies of a society (the position of most social workers and some social scientists).
2. Social welfare policies are a camouflage for inherent class and interest-group conflicts in a society (the position of most conflict theory-oriented social scientists and some feminist theorists).
3. Social welfare policies are a function of the technological bases of society (the position of most social scientists).

I discuss the first orientation in chapters 4 and 5; the second, in chapters 6 and 7; and the third, in chapters 8 and 9. In chapter 10, I speculate whether any of these orientations is correct.

In chapter 2, I present the key ideas that explain social welfare policies. These are ideas about different types of providers and recipients of social welfare.

SOCIAL WELFARE, SOCIAL WELFARE POLICY, AND THE WELFARE STATE: KEY CONCEPTS AND TAXONOMIES

KEY CONCEPTS

At this point, it is important to clarify several key concepts. A *welfare society* is a social order that includes the welfare family, the welfare community, the welfare church, and the welfare state. It is based on institutions (the family, the polity, the economy, and religion) that promote social welfare. To put it differently, it is a social order in which the efforts of all institutions are devoted to promoting human well-being.

Social welfare is an abstraction that refers to one-way transactions (or transfers or nonmarket exchange). It is the process by which some part of income is transferred from the producers of income to others. The recipients of social welfare may be poor or others who are not capable of market exchange.

Social welfare policy is the ensemble of concrete plans by which social welfare is implemented. At times, some of these plans may be in conflict with each other.

In the *welfare family* (present in almost all family structures), income is transferred from those who earn the income to those who do not. When individuals or families are unable to earn an income through market exchange, organized church or community groups (the *welfare church* or the *welfare community*) may transfer income to them from other church or community members. In many countries, either the family, the church, or the community cannot or does not perform transfer functions. In such nations, sometimes the state performs such transfers, in which case it is called the *welfare state.*

The welfare state is a modern phenomenon whereas the welfare family, welfare church, and welfare community are ancient institutions. There are often many types of efforts by welfare churches and welfare communities in a welfare state: both *private* (welfare church or welfare community) and *public* (welfare state). Furthermore, all forms of welfare church activities are *sectarian,* and all nonsectarian private efforts, coupled with all public efforts, are *secular.*

From the perspective of the state or the nation as a whole, the welfare state is often engaged in centric transfers, whereas churches, communities, and families undertake noncentric transfers. Viewed from the perspective of the community or the church, transfers by church or community authorities are centric transfers, whereas all other transfers are noncentric.

SOME TAXONOMIES

It is clear that social welfare, social welfare policy, and the welfare state are closely related concepts. Several scholars have studied the variations within each concept and then traced their distribution over time and among nations. This section describes the different taxonomies of these concepts.

Social Welfare

Given my belief that social welfare is a form of transfer, there seem to be three ways to understand the variations in social welfare. The first two ways—that social welfare can be progressive, regressive, or neutral and centric or noncentric—have already been discussed. The third way to study welfare is to determine whether it is item focused or comprehensive. In item-focused social welfare, only one type of transfer—income, health care, child care, housing, or protection from some vulnerability—takes place at one time. In contrast, in comprehensive social welfare, several items are transferred to a given person or population at one time and perhaps through the same agent.

In short, social welfare can be examined in one or several dimensions at a time. For example, one can determine that a given system has a tendency to develop regressive, centric, and item-focused social welfare.

Social Welfare Policy

There are three popular taxonomies of social welfare policy. The first taxonomy, introduced by Wilensky and Lebeaux (1958), divides social welfare policy into two types: *residual* and *institutional*. In the residual type, it is assumed that social welfare policy applies only to those who cannot be supported by the family or market system, whereas in the institutional type, it is believed that social welfare is the first-line defense against calamities in an industrial society. Wilensky and Lebeaux suggested that the residual type was more prevalent in the United States before 1929 and that since then, the country has followed a middle course between the two types of policies.

The second taxonomy, developed by Wolins (1967), distinguishes between policies in which the recipients' status depends on membership in a church or a state or an *acceptable deviance*. In the former, the recipient is entitled to certain goods and services by virtue of his or her membership, whereas in the latter, the recipient is in a socially unacceptable role (such as being a poor person with a physical disability), but the "deviance" can be tolerated. In contrast, being an able-bodied poor person would be considered a form of *unacceptable deviance* and hence the person would not merit the provisions of goods or services under the policy.

The third taxonomy was offered by Marshall (1964). It categorizes recipients of social welfare as having one or more of three different forms of rights: civil rights, social rights, and political rights. Those with civil rights are guaranteed certain behavioral patterns by the state, and these are the traditional civil rights enacted by the U.S. Bill of Rights of 1793 (the right to vote, the right to freedom of speech, and the like). Those with social rights are guaranteed certain basic goods and services (such as a minimum income or a basic health care package). It is possible for groups to have none of these rights, only one of these rights, or both types of rights. However, it is the availability of political rights that makes the availability of the other two rights feasible, as Grønbjerg (1977) found in an empirical study of the 50 U.S. states.

The Welfare State

There seem to be about seven classification systems of the welfare state. The first two taxonomies focus on the nature of the elites who usher in industrialization in a given society. For example, Kerr, Dunlop, Harbison, and Myers (1964) suggested that a nation's labor policy and welfare policy are forged by the type of elites (in that nation) who introduce industrialization. These elites are members of the middle class, dynastic leaders, colonial administrators, revolutionary intellectuals, and nationalist leaders. It is the industrializing elites who set the cultural rules by which the nature of the welfare state is determined. The United States during the late 19th and early 20th centuries is an example of industrialization by the middle class. Saudi Arabia is an example of industrialization by dynastic leaders. India before 1947 is an example of industrialization by colonial administrators, and after 1947 (the year of India's independence from the British) represents industrialization by nationalist leaders. And China after 1948 represents industrialization by revolutionary intellectuals.

The second taxonomy, offered by Rimlinger (1971), is similar to that of Kerr et al. (1964). Rimlinger also proposed that the industrializing elites set the nature of the welfare state. He listed three types of elites: liberal (comparable to the middle class), patriarchal (comparable to the dynastic leaders and colonial administrators), and collectivistic (comparable to revolutionary intellectuals and nationalist leaders). These elites set the tone by which the wage-labor contract in the marketplace is defined, and this definition, in turn, influences the nature of the welfare state. In chapter 9 I discuss Rimlinger's thesis in greater detail.

The third and fourth taxonomies, developed by the British writers George and Wilding (1976) and Pinker (1979), suggest that the ideologies of a nation's elites define the nature of a welfare state. George and Wilding, for example, stated that the British welfare state (and the U.S. one as well) is a compromise between four types of elite ideologies: anticollectivism, reluctant collectivism, Fabian socialism, and Marxism. Pinker modified this typology to indicate that a welfare state reflects a compromise between three ideologies: classical individualism, Marxism and its derivates, and mercantile collectivism. In chapter 5 I discuss this thesis in greater detail.

The fifth and sixth taxonomies, suggested by Mishra (1984), represent a historical progression in some countries. Mishra's first taxonomy distinguishes the ideological pull of the elites: (1) those with free-market ideologies (individualism in George and Wilding's and Pinker's taxonomies), (2) those with socialist ideologies (akin to Fabian socialism and the different types of Marxism), and those in a centrist position between the two (comparable to mercantile collectivism). Mishra's second taxonomy emerged from economic theory, in which earlier forms of the welfare state were identified as the differentiated welfare state (DWS) and the integrated welfare state (IWS). The DWS is based on the economic theories of Keynes (1936) and Beveridge (1945), and the economy is regulated from the demand side, whereas the IWS is based on post-Keynesian theories, and the economy is regulated by both the demand and the supply sides. In the DWS, social welfare institutions are relatively autonomous, but in the IWS, they are interdependent with the economy.

The seventh taxonomy, proposed by Esping-Andersen (1990), involves three types of welfare states—liberal, social democratic, and conservative-corporate—which, as was mentioned earlier, Esping-Andersen termed "the three worlds of welfare capitalism." Orloff (1993) noted that liberal welfare states in this typology are comparable to welfare states with residual social welfare policies, whereas both social democratic and conservative-corporate welfare states are closer to welfare states with "institutional" policies. In chapter 9 I discuss both Mishra's and Esping-Andersen's theses in greater depth, and chapter 7 covers the ideas of Orloff.

CONCLUDING OBSERVATIONS

The concept of social welfare is an ancient one. Just about all the great religions incorporate the concept in one way or another (Choi, Martin, Chatterjee, & Holland, 1978) and designate the roles of providers and recipients, which may be called social welfare policy. The efforts to dignify poor people in the Bible, concepts of *Yishuv* among the Jews, *danadharma* (religion is charitable compassion) in Hinduism, and *zakat* (the obligation of the privileged to support the nonprivileged) in Islam are examples of social welfare policy in the welfare community and the welfare church.

The concept of the welfare state, that is, positioning social welfare institutions at the state level, seems to have been devised in imperial Germany in the mid-19th century (Rimlinger, 1971) and to have spread to the countries of western Europe, North America, and Australia. Almost all these countries are democracies with a clear separation of church and state, are highly industrialized, and have well-developed market economies.

The concept of the welfare state has been tried in the current and former Communist countries as well. This trend started in the Soviet Union after the Bolshevik Revolution in 1917 and eventually spread to the countries of Eastern Europe, Cuba, and China. These countries also had a clear separation of church and state but close ties between the state and the Communist Party. Only a part of these economies were industrialized under central planning, and the countries did not have market economies. It seems that these countries had an easy time introducing social welfare institutions but a difficult time sustaining them.

In addition, the concept of the welfare state seems to be emerging in the Pacific Rim countries of Taiwan, South Korea, Hong Kong, and Singapore (Japan went through a similar developmental phase earlier) (Berger, 1986). These countries have undergone massive industrialization since the 1970s, have strong market economies, and a separation of church and state.

In the rest of the world, the welfare state has not yet emerged. Almost all these countries, with the possible exception of those in the Gulf region, have not undergone massive industrializaton. In the Middle East, between Iran and Pakistan, the concept of the welfare church is still common, and there is no separation of church and state. In India, there is a precarious separation of church and state, lopsided industrialization, and a mixed or partly controlled economy. In much of Latin America, the Catholic Church has a strong influence on the affairs of the state, and the welfare church and welfare community are more prevalent than the welfare state. In most of Africa, south of Egypt and north of South Africa, the tribal base can be thought of as the welfare church or the welfare community. There has been no massive industrialization, no welfare state (except in Egypt and South Africa), and little separation of the community (in this case, the tribal community) and the state (Dixon, 1987a, 1987b; Hokenstad, Khinduka, & Midgley, 1992).

In short, the welfare state is of recent origin (about 150 years old) in Australia, North America, and western Europe and is emerging in the Pacific Rim. In the rest of the world, ancient institutions—the welfare family, welfare community, and welfare church—are prevalent.

REFERENCES

Barry, N. (1990). *Welfare*. Minneapolis: University of Minnesota Press.

Beeghley, L. (1988). *The structure of social stratification in the United States*. Boston: Allyn & Bacon.

Berger, P. (1986). *The capitalist revolution*. New York: Basic Books.

Bernstein, B. J. (1968). The New Deal: The conservative achievements of liberal reform. In B. J. Bernstein (Ed.), *Towards a new past: Dissenting essays in American history* (pp. 263–288). New York: Pantheon Books.

Beveridge, W. H. (1945). *Full employment in a free society*. New York: W. W. Norton.

Chatterjee, P. (1985). Origins of social welfare policy and models of help. *Social Development Issues, 9*, 27–46.

Choi, I., Martin, E., Chatterjee, P., & Holland, T. (1978). Ideology and social welfare. *Indian Journal of Social Work, 39*, 139–160.

Corrigan, P., & Leonard, P. (1979). *Social work practice under capitalism*. London: Macmillan.

Dixon, J. E. (Ed.). (1987a). *Social welfare in Africa*. London: Croom-Helm.

Dixon, J. E. (Ed.). (1987b). *Social welfare in the Middle East*. London: Croom-Helm.

Esping-Andersen, G. (1990). *The three worlds of welfare capitalism*. Princeton, NJ: Princeton University Press.

George, V., & Wilding, P. (1976). *Ideology and social welfare*. Boston: Routledge & Kegan Paul.

Gil, D. (1970). A systematic approach to social policy analysis. *Social Service Review, 44*, 411–426.

Gilbert, N., & Specht, H. (1974). *Dimensions of social welfare policy*. Englewood Cliffs, NJ: Prentice Hall.

Goode, W. (1967). The protection of the inept. *American Sociological Review, 32*, 5–19.

Goodin, R. E. (1988). Reasons for welfare: Economic, sociological, and political—but ultimately moral. In J. D. Moon (Ed.), *Responsibility, rights, and welfare: The theory of the welfare state* (pp. 19–54). Boulder, CO: Westview Press.

Gough, I. (1980). *The political economy of the welfare state*. London: Macmillan.

Griswold, W. (1994). *Cultures and societies in a changing world*. Thousand Oaks, CA: Sage Publications.

Grønbjerg, K. (1977). *Mass society and the extension of welfare*. Chicago: University of Chicago Press.

Hill, M. (1993). *Understanding social policy*. Oxford, England: Basil Blackwell.

Hokenstad, M. C., Khinduka, S. K., & Midgley, J. (Eds.). (1992). *Profiles in international social work*. Washington, DC: NASW Press.

Kahn, A. J. (1979). *Social policy and social services*. New York: Random House.

Kahn, A., & Kamerman, S. (1977). *Not for the poor alone*. New York: Harper & Row.

Karger, H. J., & Stoesz, D. (1994). *American social welfare policy*. New York: Longman.

Kerr, C., Dunlop, J. T., Harbison, F. H., & Myers, C. A. (1964). *Industrialism and industrial man*. New York: Oxford University Press.

Keynes, J. M. (1936). *The general theory of employment, interest, and money*. New York: Harcourt, Brace.

Kottak, C. P. (1979). *Cultural anthropology*. New York: Random House.

Levine, R. (1988). *Class struggle and the New Deal*. Lawrence: University of Kansas Press.

Marshall, T. H. (1964). *Class, citizenship, and social development*. Garden City, NY: Doubleday.

Martin, K., & Voorhies, B. (1975). *Female of the species*. New York: Columbia University Press.

Mauss, M. (1967). *The gift*. New York: W. W. Norton.

Mishra, R. (1984). *The welfare state in crisis*. New York: St. Martin's Press.

Moon, M. (1977). *The measurement of economic welfare*. New York: Academic Press.

Offe, C. (1984). *Contradictions of the welfare state*. Cambridge, MA: MIT Press.

Orloff, A. S. (1993). Gender and the social rights of citizenship. *American Sociological Review, 58,* 303–328.

Pinker, R. (1979). *The idea of welfare*. London: Heineman.

Piven, F. F., & Cloward, R. (1971). *Regulating the poor: The functions of social welfare*. New York: Random House.

Plant, R. (1988). Needs, agency, and welfare rights. In J. D. Moon (Ed.), *Responsibilities, rights, and welfare*. Boulder, CO: Westview Press.

Pohlmann, M. (1990). *Black politics in conservative America*. New York: Longman.

Pryor, F. L. (1977). *The origins of the economy*. New York: Academic Press.

Rein, M. (1970). *Social policy*. New York: Random House.

Rimlinger, G. (1971). *The welfare state and industrialization in Europe, America, and Russia*. New York: John Wiley & Sons.

Rochefort, D. A. (1986). *American social welfare policy*. Boulder, CO: Westview Press.

Rohrlich, G. (1971). Social policy and income distribution. In R. Morris (Ed.-in-Chief), *Encyclopedia of social work* (15th ed., Vol. 2, pp. 1385–1386). New York: National Association of Social Workers.

Rothenberg, J. (1961). *The measurement of social welfare*. Englewood Cliffs, NJ: Prentice Hall.

Rowley, C., & Peacock, A. (1975). *Welfare economics: A liberal restatement*. New York: John Wiley & Sons.

Schumpeter, J. (1950). *Capitalism, socialism, and democracy*. New York: Harper & Row.

Stark, O. (1995). *Altruism and beyond: An economic analysis of transfers and exchanges within families and groups*. New York: Cambridge University Press.

Titmuss, R. M. (1969). *The gift relationship*. London: George Allen & Unwin.

Tropman, J. E. (1989). *American values and social welfare*. Englewood Cliffs, NJ: Prentice Hall.

Tullock, G. (1983). *Welfare for the well-to-do*. Dallas: Fisher Institute.

Ulmer, M. J. (1969). *The welfare state, USA*. Boston: Houghton Mifflin.

Wilensky, H. (1975). *The welfare state and equality*. Berkeley: University of California Press.

Wilensky, H., & Lebeaux, C. (1958). *Industrial society and social welfare*. New York: Russell Sage Foundation.

Wolins, M. (1967). The societal function of social welfare. *New Perspectives: The Berkeley Journal of Social Welfare, 1,* 1–18.

2

INFRASTRUCTURE OF THE WELFARE STATE

> The repute of generosity has three evils: it can corrode the
> man who has this repute; it can harm the man who admires
> this generosity if he imitates it ignorantly; it can erode who-
> ever receives generosity if he knows the giver.
>
> Shah, *The Way of Sufi*

C hapter 1 outlined the basic concepts of social welfare. This chapter
covers some related concepts, indicated by the following questions:

1. What are the *sources* (hereafter called payers) from which income (or payments for in-kind services) is transferred to the recipients?
2. In the welfare state, how many *types of transfer* (from the payer
   to the recipient) are common?
3. Who are the commonly designated *transfer agents,* and what
   functions do they serve?
4. What are the *categories of recipients?* Are they distinct or overlapping entities?
5. Who are the *providers* (of in-kind services)? How are they different from the payers?
6. What are the *limits on transfer,* if any?
7. What ideas *prescribe* transfer, and what ideas legitimate it?

These seven questions are summarized in the model of the infrastructure of the welfare state presented in Figure 2-1. This model is used
throughout this book to evaluate almost all paradigms of the welfare state.

Figure 2-1 shows four types of players in interaction within the
context of an econotechnological foundation. The interactions, called transactions, are possible because of four major prescriptive or antecedent factors: (1) the location of a nation within a world system, (2) the various
ideological traditions of the elites of a nation, (3) the inherent conflicts and
contradictions faced by a nation, and (4) a nation's ability to industrialize its
economic and technological bases (see the bottom of Figure 2-1). These
four factors are examined in chapters 3–9. The remainder of this chapter is
devoted to developing the model presented in Figure 2-1 and discussing
each item in detail.

Figure 2-1.

The Infrastructure of the Welfare Society

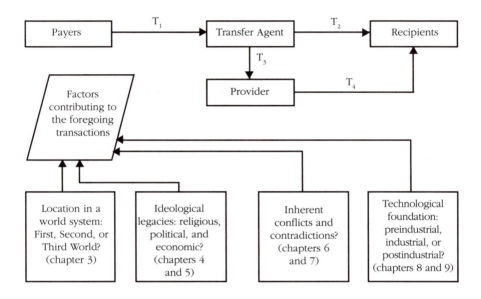

THE INFRASTRUCTURE

Figures 2-1 through 2-7 represent a comprehensive model of the welfare society, of which the welfare state is an integral and important part. A welfare society has several types of payers, transfer agents, providers, and recipients. When the transfer agent is the state, it is understood as the welfare state.

THE PAYERS

In the modern welfare society, there are four ways to conceptualize the payers from whom the transfer process begins: (1) a voluntary–involuntary dimension, (2) a social class or socioeconomic-status (SES) dimension, (3) a public–private dimension, and (4) a corporate–individual dimension. These four categories are not mutually exclusive and may overlap (see Figure 2-2).

Gilbert and Specht (1974, p. 141) observed that "the term voluntary social services is frequently used to refer to those supported by funds obtained 'voluntarily' through private contributions rather than 'involuntarily' through the tax systems." The involuntary payer means the taxpayer, and the money paid in the form of taxes goes to provide income or to pay for such services as health care or housing. Karger and Stoesz (1994, p. 463) defined

Figure 2-2.

The Infrastructure of the Welfare Society: Payers

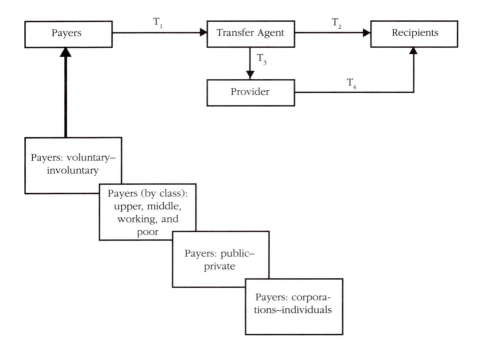

"the voluntary sector" as "that part of the mixed welfare economy consisting of private, nonprofit agencies."

Voluntary payers are usually distributed in the workforce, and local communities develop a social organization of fundraising for nonprofit agencies that provide recreational, emergency shelter, counseling, and other social services. The voluntary payments made to these efforts are usually tax deductible by the payers. The social organizations that are engaged in voluntary fundraising, called the United Appeal, Red Feather, or Community Fund Drive, or the like, are popular in the United States. The U.S. voluntary sector is also dominated by large businesses.

The voluntary payers are grouped by their places of employment or business, which act as collection agents for the payers' donations. Because these firms compete with each other to collect the most money, the voluntary payers often face a great deal of social pressure from their peers and superiors to make large donations, so the firms will look good in the community.

In addition to the demands for donations at their places of employment, voluntary payers who attend church receive requests for donations from their churches, and part of these donations become transfer payments through church-related welfare services.

These transfers from voluntary payers make the existence of the welfare community (discussed in chapter 1) possible. Such a welfare community can provide services that supplement the basic services provided by involuntary transfers. O'Connell (1993) observed that in the United States, voluntary payers with incomes under $10,000 a year gave a much higher share of their incomes than did those with incomes of $50,000 to $100,000 in 1992.

In the second categorization, payers are classified according to SES. In this mode of organization, the payers are grouped in a hierarchy, with upper-class payers at the top, followed by middle-class payers, working-class payers, and then poor or lower-class payers at the bottom. Although class or SES is an important analytic category of conflict theorists and Marxist scholars, it is by no means unique to them; conservative social scientists (see Banfield, 1971) also use it. Beeghley (1988) has showed that class is an important factor in looking at voluntary gifts and tax burdens. In chapters 6 and 7, I present some theoretical positions about the social class of payers and its impact on social welfare policy.

The third dimension of payers is the public–private one. In this context, private may mean money donated voluntarily by individuals, foundations, nonprofit organizations, and so on. Sometimes specific programs for a target population can be developed by matching public and private funds; the private portion comes from the voluntary donations, whereas the public portion comes from what has been collected by the state as a transfer agent.

The fourth dimension of payers is corporations versus individuals. Here, a transfer agent may collect involuntary payments from both individuals and their employer corporations. Social security taxes in the United States are one example of this type of transfer.

TYPES OF TRANSFER

Chapter 1 discussed two categories of transfer: centric versus noncentric and progressive (to less privileged persons or groups) and regressive (to privileged persons or groups). Here, I add another category: transfer Types 1 to 4, outlined in Figure 2-3.

The analysis of the differences among Type 1, Type 2, Type 3, and Type 4 transfers is an important foundation for understanding social welfare policy and the functioning of the welfare state. The following are some possible scenarios in relation to these types of transfer:

Scenario 1. The payers are middle- or working-class voluntary contributors, and the transfer agent is a metropolitan community-based annual fund drive. The transfer agent decides to keep a certain amount as fundraising costs for its own use, and this amount is deducted from T_1. Thus, the recipients get the amount of T_1–T_2. This is a case of noncentric transfer, from

Figure 2-3.

The Infrastructure of the Welfare Society: Types of Transfer

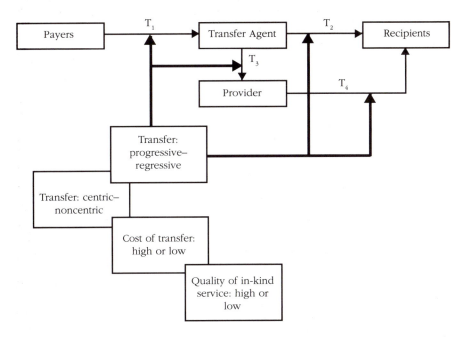

voluntary payers to recipients. What percentage of T_1 should the transfer agent receive: 10 percent, 20 percent, or more? Questions like this are often posed regarding the delivery of voluntary social welfare and social services in welfare states.

Scenario 2. The payers are involuntary working- or middle-class payers, and the transfer agent is the state. In a question similar to the one in scenario 1, what percentage of T_1 is the state allowed to keep for its costs? Can the state transfer a part of T_1 to some other expense category in its budget, rather than to the recipients?

Scenario 3. As in scenario 2, the payer is an involuntary middle- or working-class payer. The recipient needs dental care, and the state as the transfer agent decides to pay the dentist (a provider) for this care (a form of third-party payment). What percentage of T_1 can the transfer agent keep to cover its costs? What happens if the dentist's services to the recipient (T_4) is not equivalent to T_3? Furthermore, is T_3 always (or most of the time) higher than the amount (say T_5) that the recipient would have paid the dentist? Are there bookkeeping costs involved? Do third-party payments usually lead to the escalation of costs in the welfare state? Also, because the dentist is not directly accountable to the recipient, does the recipient get inferior or incompetent services? Would it be desirable for the transfer agent to set up an organization in which the dentist is employed by the transfer agent and another organization to monitor or supervise the dentist's delivery of services? Does the decision to employ the dentist lead to lower costs but increased bureaucratization and possibly to the recruitment of dentists with poor training?

It is clear that the simple four lines in Figure 2-3, called T_1, T_2, T_3, and T_4, help one understand some of the basic dilemmas in social welfare policy and the welfare state. They lead to the following important questions:

1. What percentage of the transfer should the transfer agent keep?
2. Is the third-party payment system a better device than state bureaucracies with employees?
3. Are in-kind transfers paid for by the transfer agent inferior to services obtained by simple market transfer?

TYPES OF TRANSFER AGENTS

Chapter 1 ended with the observation that the idea of the family, the community, and the church as transfer agents is ancient and that the idea of the state as the transfer agent is of recent origin. The idea of the collective-bargaining body (like a labor union or a professional association) and the corporation as transfer agents is perhaps even newer. Chapters 4 and 5 elaborate on the role of the state as transfer agent. Figure 2-4 is a graphic representation of the different types of transfer agents.

CATEGORIES OF RECIPIENTS

Most modern welfare societies have seen a substantial increase in the category of recipients. Figure 2-5 presents a heuristic category of recipients.

In any welfare system, recipients who were payers at one time or other are likely to have more political clout than are those who were not. For example, persons who are retired from the workforce and who have paid social security taxes for a long time have more political power than do those who have never worked or have worked in marginal jobs from time to time.

In general, people who are defined as "vulnerable" are likely to be recipients. However, vulnerability is a subjective cultural definition and can be defined differently in different times and places. For example, Aries (1962), Eliade (1975), and Bronfenbrenner (1972) described how cultures define who is a child and develop social control measures for "protecting" children, and Sommerville (1982) discussed how the modern industrial states of the West came to define children as a vulnerable population.

Children can also be seen as a society's asset because among them are the future leaders of the society. Supporting children, protecting them,

Figure 2-4.

The Infrastructure of the Welfare Society: Transfer Agents

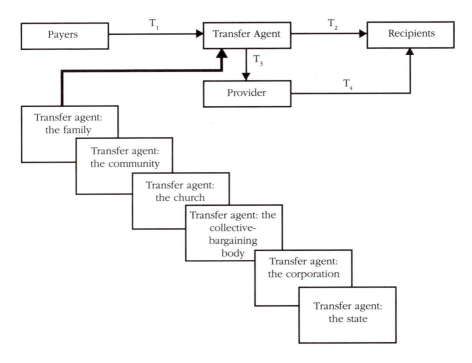

and preparing them for a good future is an investment in the future. This concept of investing in the future has also been applied to another category of recipients, categorized as "protected entrepreneurs": powerful individuals and corporations who have failed in the marketplace and have asked for and received large amounts of transfers. These protected entrepreneurs justify their receipt of transfers by contending that supporting them is also an "investment in the future" and that without such support, many jobs and sources of income for a significant number of persons in the society would disappear.

Once protected entrepreneurs are thought of as vulnerable, transfer begins to reach society's powerful insiders from the upper and middle classes. Thus, the concept of vulnerability can be applied to groups like children, mothers of children without much support, and people who are disabled or chronically ill, on the one hand, and upper-class captains of industry and their middle-class agents, on the other hand. Larson (1977) argued that most professionals, such as lawyers, business managers, and chartered accountants, are from the middle class but act as agents of the upper class.

Figure 2-5.

The Infrastructure of the Welfare Society: Recipients

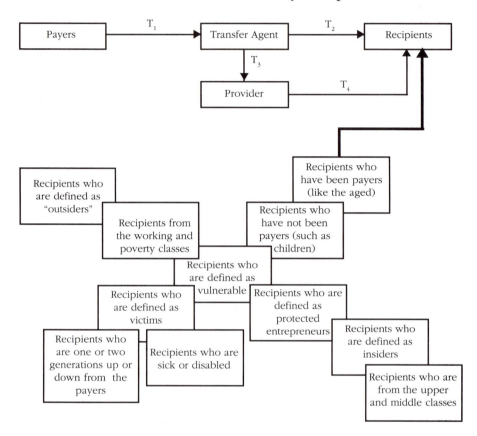

Victimization (by illness, age, lack of education or skills, or other factors) creates another category of recipients. Again, people, such as those who have been in an industrial accident, become victims who have been payers, and in many settings would be preferred to victims who were born into poverty and have not been payers. The latter category, often children of transgenerationally poor persons, are also considered outsiders by some welfare states.

PROVIDERS

Often the term *provider* means a person, group, or organization that has the necessary skills to provide important in-kind services (ranging from health, dental, mental health, housing, protective services, education, to legal services) to recipients. The dentist in scenario 3 (Types of Transfer), for example, is a provider, whether he or she has a solo or a group practice. The dentist is a provider because he or she is paid by the transfer agent, not by the recipient of the service. The modern welfare state has many types of providers, discussed next (see also Figure 2-6).

Providers as employees. The transfer agent has the option of employing the providers of services. To do so, the transfer agent must set up career tracks for providers of health, dental, mental health, and protective care; rent, purchase, or build houses; and develop job slots for teachers and lawyers. Once these career tracks, job slots, or housing inventories are in place, then the transfer agent needs to build an organization, often in the classic Weberian bureaucratic style (Weber, 1946), to develop inventories and accountability. Further organization building may be required to oversee quality assurance. Thus, employing the providers often means building large and impersonal organizations or, as Lipsky (1980) called them, "street-level bureaucracies."

Providers as independent contractors. The second option may be to develop contracts with a number of independent providers. In this case, the

Figure 2-6.

The Infrastructure of the Welfare Society: Providers

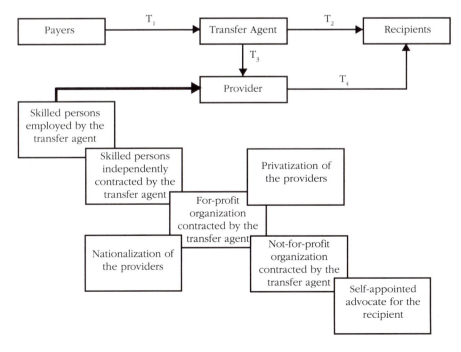

transfer agent "purchases" a volume of services from the providers by paying them a fee for providing services to the recipients. This option initially seems more attractive and less expensive than the first option. However, this type of purchase of services is difficult to monitor or supervise, and it is even more difficult to ensure that even-quality services are provided in each case. In some ways, this option is subject to misuse by unscrupulous providers who may bill the transfer agent at inflated rates. Policing the entire purchase-of-services scheme, over time, sometimes proves more costly than the first option (of employing the providers).

Providers as for-profit or nonprofit groups. Two other types of providers are common, both of which are found in the private or voluntary sectors. They are commercial for-profit firms and nonprofit organizations. For example, the transfer agent may contract with a commercial firm (also called a for-profit organization) to provide nursing home services to certain recipients. The transfer agent may also hire a nonprofit nursing home (which may have been started by private efforts and later supported by a community fund drive) for the same purpose. The transfer agent's choice of one of these two organizations that provide the same service may depend on a combination of economic and political considerations.

Sometimes these economic and political considerations may lead to one of two types of social movements: a push (1) to nationalize (that is, buy, otherwise acquire, or annex) the service provider, leading to the formation of another street-level bureaucracy (Lipsky, 1980) or (2) to privatize (that is, encourage the development of an entire industry that bids to provide the services on a fee-for-service basis). During the administration of Ronald Reagan in the United States and the administration of Margaret Thatcher in England in the 1980s, the trend toward privatization was strong.

Apart from the economic and political motifs driving the privatization or nationalization movements, the issues of efficiency and quality control are also important. Nationalization often means the development of vast and impersonal bureaucracies, and privatization means encouraging the opening of a new set of markets. Should there be provisions for some form of regulation of these markets? Should the pricing in these new markets be done by the rules of demand and supply, according to classic economics, or should the government or the transfer agent engage in some arbitrary price-fixing?

Another player that has an impact on the provider–recipient relationship is the self-appointed advocate for the recipient. Such advocates can be individuals or organizations (either commercial firms or nonprofit organizations). Such advocacy may originate from professional social workers (or nonprofit social work agencies) who may use advocacy to legitimate their roles in society. Or it may come from commercial firms or law firms, whose reasons for such advocacy may also be similar to those of professional social workers because they gain visibility, increase their share in some segmented market, or gain other political advantages.

LIMITS ON TRANSFER

By *limits on transfer,* I mean rationing the income, goods, or services the recipient gets. In market exchange (see Figure 1-1, chapter 1), rationing occurs according to the rules of supply and demand. If one has limited skills or capital, then one also has limited income. If one has limited income, then one has limited power to purchase goods and services. The market, or the Invisible Hand, as Adam Smith (1776/1963) put it, engages in rationing.

In the transfer sector, there are also rationing devices that control the amount of income, goods, and services that flow to the recipient, hereafter referred to as "limits on transfer" (see Figure 2-7).

Like market rationing, transfer is also rationed. Lipsky (1980) noted that street-level bureaucracies use queuing, creaming, and hiding certain benefits from recipients as methods of rationing. Coulton, Rosenberg, and Yankey (1981) showed how some recipients come to be preferred or favored, how all recipients may be awarded an equal share unrelated to their individual needs, or how some persons (such as the protected entrepreneurs discussed earlier) are allowed to receive transfers to "protect" the society.

To this list, I add such devices as co-payment systems and requirements for recipients to perform services (as was done in the programs of the Works Progress Administration of the administration of Franklin D. Roosevelt in the United States during the Great Depression of the 1930s) in exchange for transfer.

One or more of these rationing devices can also be found in many health care settings, legal clinics, public housing arrangements, or public schools. When the state or the transfer agent does not design these rationing devices, they seem to emerge automatically in the bureaucracies that are built to deliver the services.

CONTRADICTIONS IN THE INTELLECTUAL FOUNDATIONS

The idea of the welfare state, its desirability, and its format have been debated passionately by several English and American scholars since the latter part of the 18th century. Adam Smith and Bernard Mandeville argued (see Barry, 1990, pp. 16–20) that an unhindered operation of the market system is the best way to provide welfare to all. (The views of M. Friedman, 1962, a modern-day economist, seem to be close to this position.) Jeremy Benthum added that a market system that produces "maximal happiness of the maximal number" is the best system, and Edwin Chadwick, Benthum's secretary, observed that "the danger of indiscriminate welfare payments was that they must have a tendency to encourage individuals to become welfare claimants: a good or service provided at zero price will attract an infinite demand" (quoted in Barry, 1990, p. 26).

Figure 2-7.

The Infrastructure of the Welfare Society: Limits on Transfer

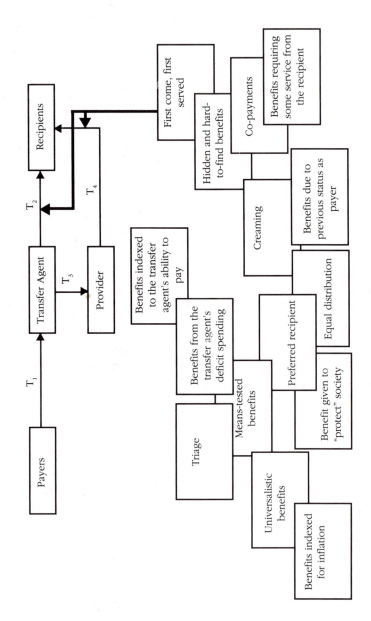

These 18th and 19th century pro-market English thinkers were known as "liberal" thinkers about the political economy of welfare. (In contrast, in the United States, liberal political philosophy has come to mean support of state intervention and state spending to accomplish certain ends.) To this, the voice of John Stuart Mill was a challenge:

> The laws and conditions of the production of wealth, partake of the character of physical truths. There is nothing optional or arbitrary in them. This is not so with the distribution of wealth. That is a matter of human institution only. (Mill, 1848, cited in Barry, 1990, p. 31)

With Mill, then, production or wealth building can be studied using scientific ideas. However, distribution (which makes welfare possible) cannot be studied scientifically because it is a moral or normative issue. The state is required to take a position in this moral issue, and Mill's observation implies that it should take a pro-welfare position.

Concern with the concept of *liberty* brought in other scholars, who took positions between the market and the state ends of the continuum. One such 20th century scholar was Hobhouse (1922, 1964), who advocated a minimum income for all (not just for poor people), a need-based distribution, ways of controlling idlers, and the importance of reciprocity between the recipient, the transfer agent, and the payer. In essence, he believed, the state is required to deliver *liberty* (or freedom) and *justice,* and it cannot do so without a minimum, need-based income.

However, the provision of a minimum, need-based income, Hobhouse thought, should not mean that individuals who can participate in a market economy and choose not to do so should be allowed to become dependent on welfare. At issue was whether the state's obligation to facilitate the operation of a free market is in conflict with the state acting as a parent-surrogate to able adults. Hobhouse seemed to be struggling to balance these issues. As Barry (1990, p. 41) observed: "The theory of the modern welfare state derives very largely from an enquiry into the alleged inadequacies of the individualistic market order rather than from a fully-fledged socialist or Marxist theory."

The legacy of the English liberals (united in their pro-market and pro-individualism stands but divided in their positions about whether the state should provide welfare) influenced many later scholars in England and the United States, who experienced the same conflict. This conflict seems to center on whether there should be any welfare and, if so, whether it should be provided with strings attached. On one side of this conflict were Smith, Mandeville, and Chadwick, joined by Herbert Spencer and, more recently, by Milton Friedman, Robert Nozick, and Charles Murray. On the other side were L.T. Hobhouse, Vilfredo Pareto (who was Italian), John Maynard Keynes,

William H. Beveridge, John Kenneth Galbraith, and Frederick Hayek. Spencer, for example, was concerned about how welfare, if it was introduced, would be used by middle-class people for their own political interests (see Barry, 1990, p. 44). (The "self-appointed advocates" for transfer recipients, shown in Figure 6-5, are, for the most part, of middle-class origin, as Gans, 1972, has claimed.) Nozick (1974) argued that the state should be instrumental in protecting persons and property but should not become an agent of transfer or distribution. Murray (1984) contended that the state, when attempting to be an agent of transfer, does an extremely poor job. In fact, he stated that increased transfer by the state as a transfer agent leads to greater poverty.

The believers in state intervention within the English liberal tradition continued to grow. On this side was Pareto, arguing that the state can be an "optimizing" agent by making the condition of at least one individual better without making that of any other worse (see Schumpeter, 1989, comments on the Pareto principle). Pareto was joined by Hayek, who suggested that some people are clearly not capable of market exchange and argued for an optimization of scarcity, human vulnerability, and limited altruism (Barry, 1990, p. 91). M. Friedman made similar points (Barry, 1990, p. 59). Keynes (see Mishra, 1984) developed the deficit-spending theory of the welfare state by which the state can make continued transfer possible, and Beveridge in England and Galbraith in the United States worked to legitimate a fiscal policy based on this theory.

In many ways, what Adam Smith is to the market economy and individualism, Karl Marx is to planned economy and collectivism. By the late 19th century, various types of collectivism emerged in Europe and other parts of the world. Of these various types, Fabian socialists and State socialists had some substantial presence in England in the early 20th century (George & Wilding, 1976). The Fabian socialists believed in collectivism, planned economy, and incremental nonviolent change toward a classless society, whereas the State socialists believed in collectivism, a planned economy, and radical change (either violent and revolutionary or nonviolent but still revolutionary). Among the believers in State socialism, Ralph Miliband and Harold Laski were prominent. These two men also influenced many nationalist leaders of the then-colonial countries who had studied in English universities in the early 19th century. The aspirations of several newly freed countries in Asia and Africa (like India and Ghana) later reflected this trend.

The Fabian socialists, however, had their social origins in the English middle and upper classes. Booth's work on poverty (1889/1967) and the efforts of Sidney and Beatrice Webb (in partnership with George Bernard Shaw) on social reform set the state for early Fabian socialism in England. The Fabian trend continued in the works of Tawney (1931, 1964), Townsend (1979), Abel-Smith and Townsend (1954), and Titmuss (1958, 1968, 1974). Few other authors have had as much influence on social welfare policy and the welfare state as had Titmuss. More recently, these efforts have been supplemented by those of Plant (1988), who stated that one of the important functions of the state is to respond to crises generated by market failure, and by LeGrand (1982), who argued that equality can be better achieved not by breaking up existing privilege (as State socialists advocate) but by supplementing those who are not privileged through the state's transfer functions (see Barry, 1990; George & Wilding, 1976).

The debates about market versus state, individualism versus collectivism, and welfare as a right or a gratuity continued during the expansion of the economies and technological bases of England and the United States. In Anglo-American thought, there seem to be four types of justifications for welfare—freedom, or liberty; justice; equality; and protection—and that welfare is the *means* to attain one or more of these *ends*. Furthermore, some scholars have tried to seek not one but several of these four ends. Consequently, the idea of the welfare state seems to have been built on contradictory ideas or different bases of legitimation (K.V. Friedman, 1981; Offe, 1984). Arrow (1971) referred to such contradictions as problems of the social ordering of values and behavior. More recently, Esping-Andersen (1990) and Orloff (1993) joined this discussion on the side of state intervention and collectivism with the concept of *decommodification* (an idea essentially borrowed from Marx) as a basis for the welfare state.

I suggest that these debates legitimated the ways of thinking about social welfare policy and the welfare state. These debates still continue, and I discuss them in greater detail in chapters 4 and 5. In the next chapter, I trace the distribution of the welfare state from a worldwide perspective.

REFERENCES

Abel-Smith, B., & Townsend, P. (1954). *New pensions for the old.* London: Fabian Publications.

Aries, P. (1962). *Centuries of childhood.* New York: Alfred A. Knopf.

Arrow, K. (1971). *Social choice and individual values.* New York: John Wiley & Sons.

Banfield, E. (1971). *The unheavenly city.* Boston: Little, Brown.

Barry, N. (1990). *Welfare.* Minneapolis: University of Minnesota Press.

Beeghley, L. (1988). *The structure of social stratification in the United States.* Boston: Allyn & Bacon.

Booth, C. (1967). *Life and labour of the people in London.* New York: Pantheon. (Original work published 1889)

Bronfenbrenner, U. (1972). *Influences on human development.* Hinsdale, IL: Dryden Press.

Coulton, C. J., Rosenberg, M. L., & Yankey, J. (1981). Scarcity and the rationing of services. *Public Welfare, 39*(3), 15–21.

Eliade, M. (1975). *Patanjali and yoga.* New York: Schocken Books.

Esping-Andersen, G. (1990). *The three worlds of welfare capitalism.* Princeton, NJ: Princeton University Press.

Friedman, K. V. (1981). *Legitimation of social rights and the Western welfare state.* Chapel Hill: University of North Carolina Press.

Friedman, M. (1962). *Capitalism and freedom.* Chicago: University of Chicago Press.

Gans, H. (1972). The positive functions of poverty. *American Journal of Sociology, 78,* 275–289.

George, V., & Wilding, P. (1976). *Ideology and the welfare state.* Boston: Routledge & Kegan Paul.

Gilbert, N., & Specht, H. (1974). *Dimensions of social welfare policy.* Englewood Cliffs, NJ: Prentice Hall.

Hobhouse, L. T. (1922). *The elements of social justice.* London: George Allen & Unwin.

Hobhouse, L. T. (1964). *Liberalism.* Oxford, England: Oxford University Press.

Karger, H. J., & Stoesz, D. (1994). *American social welfare policy.* New York: Longman.

Larson, M. S. (1977). *The rise of professionalism.* Berkeley: University of California Press.

LeGrand, J. (1982). *The strategy of equality.* London: George Allen & Unwin.

Lipsky, M. (1980). *Street-level bureaucracy: Dilemmas of the individual in public services.* New York: Russell Sage Foundation.

Mishra, R. (1984). *The welfare state in crisis.* New York: St. Martin's Press.

Murray, C. (1984). *Losing ground: American social policy, 1950–1980.* New York: Basic Books.

Nozick, R. (1974). *Anarchy, state and utopia.* Oxford, England: Basil Blackwell.

O'Connell, B. (1993). *The board member's book.* New York: Foundation Center.

Offe, C. (1984). *Contradictions of the welfare state.* Cambridge, MA: MIT Press.

Orloff, A. S. (1993). Gender and the social rights of citizenship. *American Sociological Review, 58,* 303–328.

Plant, R. (1988). Needs, agency, and welfare rights. In J. D. Moon (Ed.), *Responsibility, rights, and welfare* (pp. 55–74). Boulder, Co: Westview Press.

Schumpeter, J. (1989). *Business cycles*. Philadelphia: Porcupine Press.

Shah, I. (1977). *The way of Sufi*. London: Penguin Books.

Smith, A. (1963). *An inquiry into the nature and causes of the wealth of nations*. New York: Modern Library. (Original work published 1776)

Sommerville, J. (1982). *The rise and fall of childhood*. Beverly Hills, CA: Sage Publications.

Tawney, R. H. (1931). *Equality*. London: George Allen & Unwin.

Tawney, R. H. (1964). *The radical tradition*. London: Penguin Books.

Titmuss, R. M. (1958). *Essays on the welfare state*. London: George Allen & Unwin.

Titmuss, R. M. (1968). *Commitment to welfare*. London: George Allen & Unwin.

Titmuss, R. M. (1974). *Social policy*. London: George Allen & Unwin.

Townsend, P. (1979). *Poverty in the United Kingdom*. Harmondsworth, England: Penguin Books.

Weber, M. (1946). *From Max Weber: Essays in sociology* (H. H. Gerth & C. W. Mills, Trans.). New York: Oxford University Press.

3

THE WELFARE STATE IN A WORLD SYSTEM

He saw all these forms and faces in a thousand relationships to each other, all helping each other, loving, hating,
and destroying each other and become newly born. Each
one was mortal, a passionate, painful example of all that is
transitory. Yet none of them died, they only changed, were
always reborn, continually had a new face: only time stood
between one face and another.

Hesse, *Siddhartha*

In this chapter, I map the distribution of welfare states in the world
system. Toward that end, I explore how the world system can be identified in geocultural terms and trace how the welfare states are distributed in that system.

THE WORLD SYSTEM

There seem to be two prominent models for understanding the present
world system. The first model, which was developed right after World War
II, can be called the model of three discrete worlds: the capitalist, the (former)
communist, and the Third World (Wright, 1956). The second model was
conceptualized by a number of writers, including Bell (1973), Bollen and
Appold (1993), Shils (1975), Snyder and Kick (1979), and Wallerstein (1976).
It is referred to as the model of three concentric worlds: the core, the
semiperiphery, and the periphery.

THREE DISCRETE WORLDS

This way of viewing the world was formally ordained at the 1955
Bandung Conference of 29 African and Asian nations after two large Asian
countries gained freedom from colonial rule (India from British rule in 1947
and Indonesia from Dutch rule in 1949) and shortly before Ghana gained
freedom from British rule in 1956. The leaders of these three countries—
Jawaharlal Nehru of India, Kwame Nkrumah of Ghana, and Sukarno
Sosrodihardjo of Indonesia—formed a core political alliance. The goal of

the conference was to draw more newly independent nations into the alliance. These nations, primarily nonwhite, poor, and preindustrial, were emerging from centuries of colonization by white European industrialized nations (Belgium, France, Great Britain, the Netherlands, and Portugal). They were called the Third World.

The term *Third World* was used to contrast these nations with the First World (also called the Free World), which included the rich, capitalist, and (mostly) white nations of North America and western Europe (plus Japan), and the Second World, which included the Communist Block countries. At that time, the First World capitalist countries with market economies were forming a political, economic, and military alliance against the communist Second World countries with planned economies. Most of the Third World countries were sympathetic to socialism, against racism and colonialism, and for the worldwide redistribution of wealth and income.

It should be noted that by the 1960s, the term Third World came to mean two things: countries not in a formal alliance with the First World or the Second World (except the former Yugoslavia led by Josip Tito) and the developing countries of the world, which were poor, preindustrial, and mostly nonwhite (see Map 3-1). The first definition is, for the most part, a subset of the second.

Nehru, prime minister of India and an important architect of the Third World alliance, had been educated in England, where he adopted Harold Laski, an English intellectual and socialist, as his mentor. Nehru's fondness for Laski, coupled with his dislike of colonialism, imperialism, and mercantile capitalism and his solidarity with the leaders of the poor and nonwhite nations, caused him to promote nationalism and socialism as key ideologies of the Third World. Thus, the Third World originated as an anticapitalist, anticolonial, anti-imperialist, and antiracist political block with a mixed economic base.

The leaders of the Third World in general, and Nehru in particular, wanted to pursue equality and justice (Bowles, 1954). They envisioned a "just state" (a term used by Mohandas Gandhi to refer to the rebirth of the Hindu utopia under the mythical King Rama), or welfare state, which was to be attained by a mixed economy—a nationalist, partly planned economy, antithetical to Anglo-American–style capitalism.

The Asian countries that did not join the Third World nonaligned nations were Taiwan, South Korea, Hong Kong, and Singapore. These countries remained in the Anglo-American (or First World) orbit and, by the mid-1980s, had sufficiently distanced themselves from the Third World alliance. These four countries were somewhat marginal members of the Third World during the 1950s and 1960s because of their geographic proximity to other Third World nations. In the 1990s, they are thought of as Pacific Rim countries, which puts them neither in the Third World nor in the First World. In this book, I have included them as part of the Third World. Berger (1986)

Map 3-1.
The Third World (Nonaligned Nations) in 1964 (shaded areas)

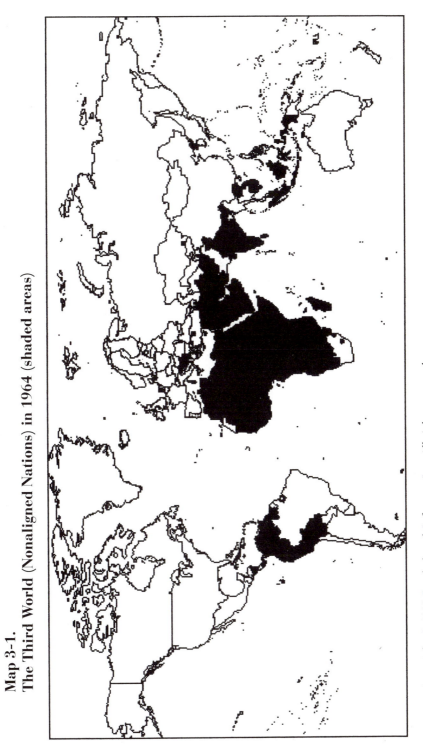

referred to their phenomenal growth as "the capitalist revolution," and many social welfare policies, like old age pensions and basic health care, are being introduced in them (Kim, 1994). Their growth as welfare states is discussed in chapters 8 and 9.

THREE CONCENTRIC WORLDS

Bell (1973) categorized three types of societies, depending on their level of technology: preindustrial, industrial, and postindustrial. In preindustrial societies, the economy is extractive (it includes farming, fishing, and mining), and the basic technology is dependent on raw materials. In industrial societies, the economy is goods producing (like factory-made products from raw materials), and the basic technology is dependent on energy. In postindustrial societies, the economy is a service economy, and the basic technology is dependent on information (for a more detailed discussion of Bell's model, see chapter 8).

Shils (1975) thought that the world could be identified as having a *core* with *peripheries* around it. Wallerstein (1976, 1980, 1989) agreed that since the 16th century, the entire world has been organized into an economic system (and an exploitive system at that). The core of this system was formed in western Europe and later in North America, the semiperiphery emerged around the core, and the periphery emerged outside the semiperiphery. Using the metaphor of concentric circles, the core is at the center, the semiperiphery forms its immediate outer circle, and the outermost circle forms the periphery (see chapter 6 for further discussion of Wallerstein's model).

These views of the world as a system seem to overlap substantially. Wallerstein's core is, for the most part, the information-processing service economy, with a substantial, established industrial base; geoculturally, it is North America and western Europe. The semipheriphery is most of the former Communist Bloc countries, some of the former colonies of the European powers in Asia, and selected parts of Latin America. The periphery is the remaining parts of Africa, Asia, and Latin America.

Snyder and Kick (1979) noted that the concepts of core, semiperiphery, and periphery suggest a hierarchy of the world system. In this hierarchy, the core seems to be at the top and the periphery at the bottom, as indicated by the countries, per capita gross national products (GNPs), and other factors. They further suggested (in an elaborate empirical study) that the *position* of a country in this hierarchy seems to have an influence on the country's capacity to build key institutions, one of which is the welfare infrastructure. This view leads to an important hypothesis: The higher the position of a state in the world system, the more likely it is that the state will have a welfare infrastructure.

Bollen and Appold (1993) found that Snyder and Kick's (1979) observations were still tenable in 1992. Maps 3-2, 3-3, and 3-4 represent the world system as they saw it in 1992, with the shaded areas representing the First, Second, and Third Worlds, respectively.

CONVERGENCE OF THE TWO WORLDVIEWS

By the early 1990s, the two views of the world system seem to have come together. Thus, today the world system consist of the following:

1. the First World, also known as the core, which includes North America, western Europe, Australia, and Japan, and is wealthy, capitalist, industrial, and based on the traditions of a market economy and individualism
2. the Second World, somewhat outside the core, which consists of eastern Europe, central and northern Asia, and Cuba, and is neither wealthy nor poor, socialist, selectively industrial, based on the traditions of a planned economy and collectivism, and a substantial part of which has been attempting to convert to a market economy since 1991
3. the Third World, a combination of the semiperiphery and the periphery, which is located mostly in Africa, southern and Southeast Asia, and South America, and is mostly poor, often nationalist, selectively industrial to preindustrial, and based on a mixed economy and regional loyalties.

The following sections and Figures 3-1 to 3-6 present within- and between-group comparisons of the three worlds. They review the populations, per capital GNPs, growth of the GNPs, female life expectancy, population per hospital bed, and GNPs for education. (More information on the three worlds appears in chapters 8 and 9.)

TRENDS IN THE THREE WORLDS

Figures 3-1 through 3-6 present information on 11 selected countries from each of the three worlds. From the First World, they are Australia, Canada, Denmark, France, Germany, Italy, Japan, Sweden, Switzerland, the United Kingdom, and the United States. From the Second World, they are Albania, Bulgaria, China, Cuba, Czechoslovakia, the former East Germany, Hungary, North Korea, Romania, Russia, and the former Yugoslavia. From the Third World, they are India, Indonesia, Iran, Malaysia, Pakistan, the Philippines, Singapore, South Korea, Taiwan, Tanzania, and Venezuela. Although certain trends vividly contrast the three worlds, several trends within each world are also obvious.

Map 3-2.
The First World in 1992 (shaded areas)

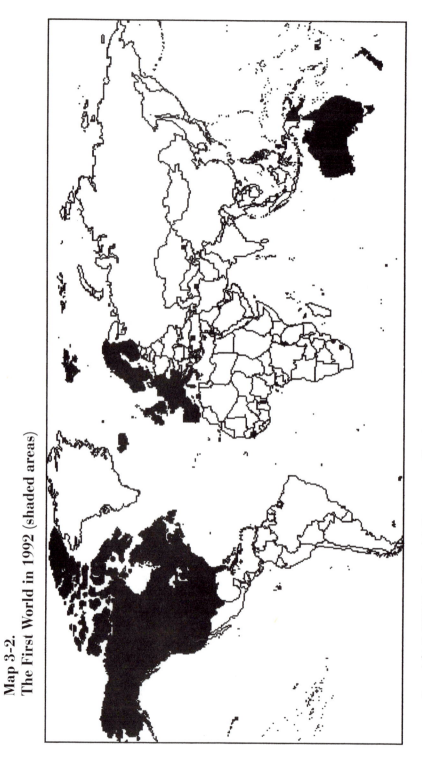

Map 3-3.
The Second World in 1992 (shaded areas)

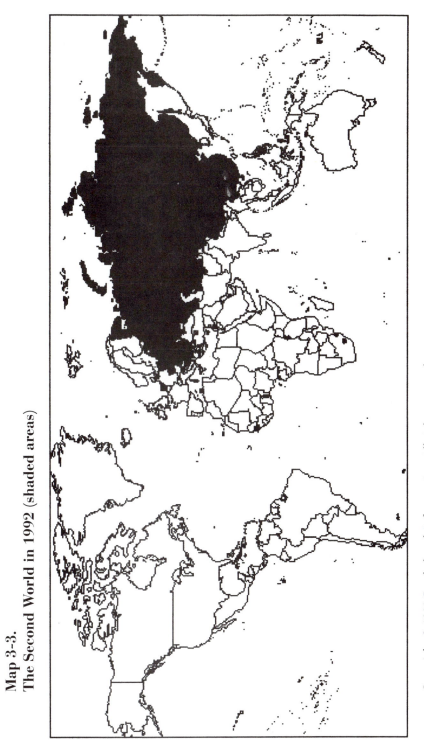

Map 3-4.
The Third World in 1992 (shaded areas)

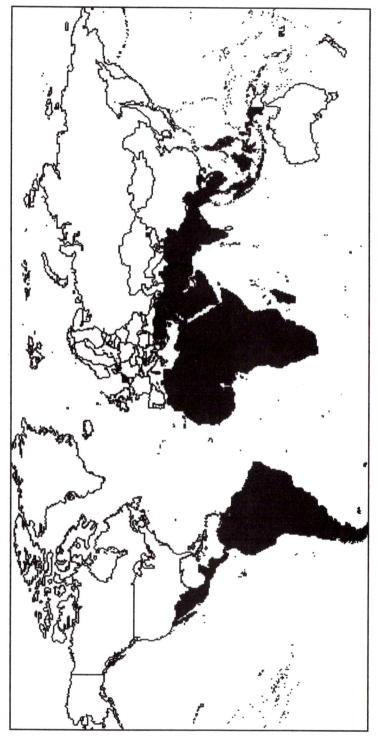

POPULATION

Figure 3-1 shows the populations of the three worlds in 1991. In that year, the First World had a substantially lower population (in thousands) (692,554) than did the Second World (1,569,131) and the Third World (1,374,750). The population of the United States was about 36 percent of the First World's, whereas China's population was about 73 percent of the Second World's and India's population was about 63 percent of the Third World's. The Second World had almost 2.26 times the population of the First World, and the Third World had about 1.99 times the population of the First World.

PER CAPITA GNP

Figure 3-2 presents data on the per capita GNPs of the three worlds for 1991. In the First World, Switzerland was at the top, with a per capita GNP of U.S. $30,304, and Australia was at the bottom, with a per capita GNP of U.S. $14,888. In the Second World, the former East Germany was at the top, with a per capita GNP of U.S. $9,779, and China at the bottom, with a per capita GNP of U.S. $417. However, it should be noted that since the reunification of Germany, the former East Germany has joined the former West Germany as part of the First World. In addition, the former Yugoslavia, which, under the leadership of Tito, left the Second World in 1948 and aligned itself with Nehru's nonaligned bloc (see Map 3-1), was, before its breakup in 1991–92, a Third World country by the choice of its leader but a First World country in its economic development. According to Bollen and Appold (1993), it belongs in the core, rather than in the peripheral or semiperipheral category. In the Third World, Singapore is at the top, with a per capita GNP of U.S. $11,656, and Tanzania is at the bottom, with a per capita GNP of U.S. $120.

Singapore, Taiwan, and South Korea, which followed the path of a market economy and capitalism (rather than a mixed economy and socialism) and were not part of the nonaligned Third World movement, had the three highest per capita GNPs in the Third World in 1991 (see Figure 3-2). In fact, their GNPs compared favorably with those at the top of the Second World, with Singapore's being higher than the top of the Second World.

Thus, it seems that three natural experiments have taken place: in North and South Korea; in the former East and West Germany; and in two groups in the Third World, one with market-based capitalist economies (Singapore, Taiwan, and South Korea) and one with socialist-based mixed economies (almost all the other countries in the Third World). In these natural experiments, one can see the differences in economic development between East and West Germany, between North and South Korea, and between the two groups of countries in the Third World.

Figure 3-1.
Population of Selected Countries in the Three Worlds: 1991 (in thousands)

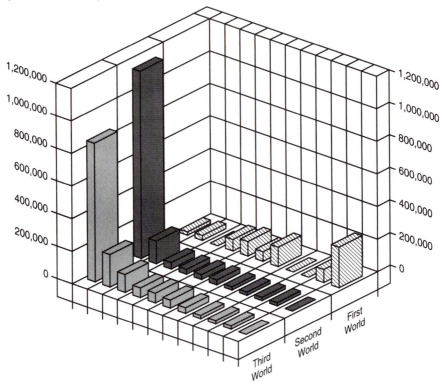

Legend (from left to right, in thousands)	First World (in rear) Australia Canada Denmark France Former West Germany Italy Japan Sweden Switzerland United Kingdom United States	Second World (in middle) China Russia Poland Former Yugoslavia Romania N Korea Former East Czechoslovakia Cuba Hungary Albania	Third World (in front) India Indonesia Pakistan Philippines Iran S Korea Tanzania Taiwan Venezuela Malaysia Singapore

Figure 3-2.
Per Capita GNPs of Selected Countries in the Three Worlds: 1991 (in U.S. dollars)

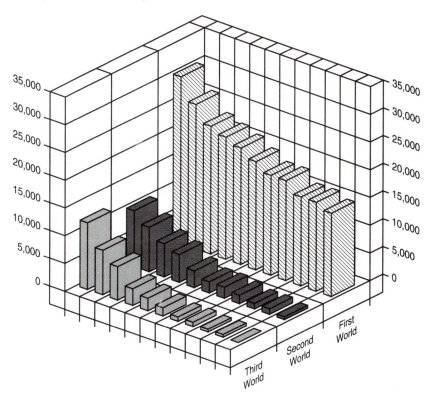

Legend (from left to right, in $ U.S.)	First World (in rear)	Second World (in middle)	Third World (in front)
	Switzerland	Former East Germany	Singapore
	Japan	Czechoslovakia	Taiwan
	Sweden	Russia	S Korea
	United States	Former Yugoslavia	Venezuela
	Denmark	Romania	Malaysia
	Canada	Hungary	Iran
	Former West Germany	Cuba	Philippines
	France	Poland	Indonesia
	Italy	ALbania	Pakistan
	United Kingdom	N Korea	India
	Australia	China	Tanzania

GROWTH IN *GNPS*

Figure 3-3 depicts the annual percentage of the GNPs of the countries in the three worlds from 1990 to 1991. In the First World, Japan was at the top, and West Germany was at the bottom. In the Second World, China was at the top (10.5 percent), and Cuba was at the bottom (–1.0 percent). In the Third World, South Korea (9.2 percent) was at the top (closely followed by Taiwan and Singapore), and the Philippines (with 0 percent) was at the bottom. The results of the natural experiments are also visible here: the former West Germany had a higher growth rate than did the former East Germany, South Korea had a higher growth rate than did North Korea, and the three capitalist countries of the Third World (Singapore, Taiwan, and South Korea) had far higher growth rates than did the remaining countries in the Third World. In the Second World, China had a high growth rate (10.5 percent), but its growth was offset by its large population (see Figures 3-1 and 3-2).

FEMALE LIFE EXPECTANCY

Figure 3-4 shows the female life-expectancy rates in the three worlds in 1991. The life expectancy of females is often an important social indicator (Bell, 1967) because it reflects the quality of health care available to them and perhaps the impact of many other gender-based inequalities. In the First World, Switzerland had the highest female life expectancy (83 years), and the United States had the lowest (79 years) because of the much lower life expectancy of its minorities, a situation that I examine later. In the Second World, Albania had the highest female life expectancy (79 years), and North Korea had the lowest (72 years). In the Third World, Taiwan and Venezuela had the highest female life-expectancy rates (both 78 years), and Tanzania had the lowest (55 years). Again, the rates of three capitalist countries of the Third World were among the top four of the Third World hierarchy, and South Korea was ahead of North Korea.

POPULATION PER HOSPITAL BED

Figure 3-5 presents the population distribution per hospital bed in 1991. It clearly shows that the Third World ranked far below the other two worlds in this regard. It is interesting to note that the Second World, except China, ranked somewhat higher than the First World, perhaps because of the commitment of these planned economies to make health care accessible and evenly distributed to their populations. In fact, most planned economies consider health care a social right (as conceptualized by Marshall, 1964). Furthermore, in the Third World, the three capitalist countries—South Korea, Singapore, and Taiwan—rated substantially higher than did the other countries.

Figure 3-3.
Growth in the GNPs of Selected Countries in the Three Worlds: 1990–91 (percentage)

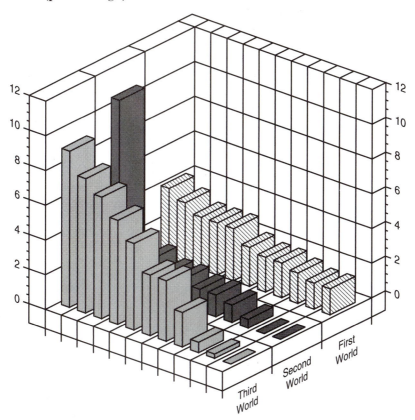

Legend (from left to right, in percentages)	First World (in rear)	Second World (in middle)	Third World (in front)
	Japan	China	S Korea
	Canada	N Korea	Taiwan
	Australia	Poland	Singapore
	United States	Hungary	Pakistan
	United Kingdom	Czechoslovakia	India
	Denmark	Russia	Malayasia
	Italy	Former East Germany	Indonesia
	Sweden	Romania	Tanzania
	Switzerland	Former Yugoslavia	Iran
	France	Albania	Venezuela
	Former West Germany	Cuba	Philippines

Figure 3-4.
Female Life Expectancy in Selected Countries in the Three Worlds: 1991 (in years)

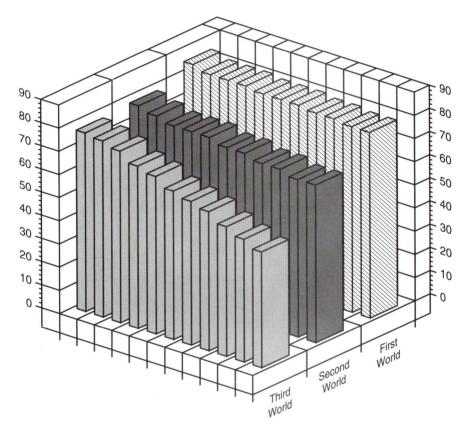

Legend (from left to right, in years)	First World (in rear)	Second World (in middle)	Third World (in front)
	Switzerland	Albania	Taiwan
	France	Cuba	Venezuela
	Italy	Czechoslovakia	Singapore
	Japan	Former East Germany	S Korea
	Canada	Poland	Malaysia
	Sweden	Hungary	Philippines
	Australia	Former Yugoslavia	Iran
	Denmark	Romania	Indonesia
	Former West Germany	Russia	India
	United Kingdom	China	Pakistan
	United States	N Korea	Tanzania

Figure 3-5.
Population per Hospital Bed in Selected Countries in the Three Worlds: 1991 (in absolute numbers)

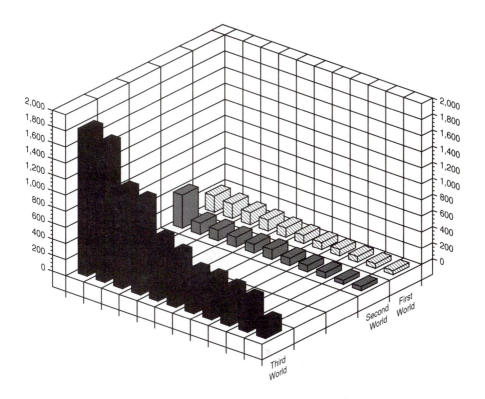

Legend (from left to right, in absolute numbers)	First World (in rear)	Second World (in middle)	Third World (in front)
	Australia	China	Pakistan
	United States	Albania	Indonesia
	Denmark	Cuba	India
	Canada	Poland	Tanzania
	Sweden	Former Yugoslavia	Iran
	United Kingdom	Romania	Philippines
	Italy	Hungary	Malayasia
	Switzerland	Czechoslovakia	S Korea
	Former West Germany	Former East Germany	Venezuela
	France	N Korea	Singapore
	Japan	Russia	Taiwan

GNP FOR EDUCATION

Figure 3-6 presents the percentage of the GNP spent on education in the three worlds in 1991. On this indicator, the top four countries of the First World compare somewhat favorably with the top three countries of the Second World and the top country (Malaysia) of the Third World (all over 6.5 percent). In general, the First World seems to spend more on education than do the other two. The bottoms of the Second and Third Worlds look similar, with percentages of the GNP for education of 3.5 or lower. China and Romania from the Second World are in this category, as are India, Pakistan, Indonesia, and the Philippines (highly populated countries) in the Third World.

IMPACT OF THE 1980s ON THE WORLD SYSTEM

The 1980s should be viewed as a crucial decade for two major reasons: there were major changes in the world system and these changes had a strong impact on the various welfare systems that had developed worldwide (see Kaldor, 1990; MacKinnon, 1989; Piccone, 1990). Some of the major trends are documented next (see Table 3-1).

THE FIRST WORLD

The 1980s began with the election of Ronald Reagan as president of the United States and, soon after, the selection of Margaret Thatcher as the prime minister of England. The United States, in particular, and most countries of the First World, in general, were emerging from the "hostage crisis" in Iran (when Islamic nationalist groups held American embassy personnel prisoners). The First World had failed to maintain the shah of Iran in power and was dealing with a nationalist backlash from that country.

The Reagan administration attempted to dismantle many social programs in the United States that had been in place since the War on Poverty of the administration of President Lyndon B. Johnson in the 1960s and reduced the tax burdens of the rich. The same trend was followed by the Thatcher administration in England. The key administrative concept in the United States and England was *deregulation,* meaning reduced state intervention in the activities of the big corporations. A related administrative concept was *privatization,* meaning the shift of many production and transfer activities from the state to private entrepreneurs.

In Europe, the impact of Anglo-American political behavior was seen in a series of antiwelfare actions. France, Germany, and Sweden faced taxpayer revolts and increased political activity against the provision of welfare benefits to working-class people. Also apparent was the hostility to

Figure 3-6.
Percentage of the GNP for Education in Selected Countries in the Three Worlds: 1991

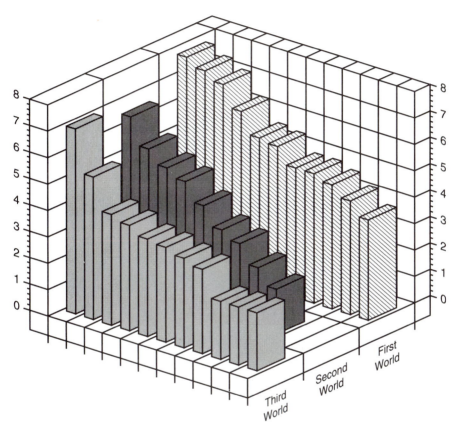

Legend (from left to right, in percentages)	First World (in rear)	Second World (in middle)	Third World (in front)
	Denmark	Cuba	Malaysia
	Sweden	Hungary	Venezuela
	Canada	Czechoslovakia	S Korea
	United States	Former East Germany	Tanzania
	Australia	Poland	Iran
	France	Former Yugoslavia	Singapore
	Japan	N Korea	Taiwan
	United Kingdom	China	India
	Switzerland	Romania	Pakistan
	Former West Germany	Albania (N/A)	Indonesia
	Italy	Russia (N/A)	Philippines

Table 3-1. Welfare Trends in the Three Worlds

ITEMS	FIRST WORLD	SECOND WORLD	THIRD WORLD
Economy	Market economy	Planned economy being converted to market economy	Mixed economy (except for Singapore, South Korea, Taiwan, and Hong Kong)
Level of industrial-ization	Postindustrial, or advanced industrial	Selectively industrial	Mostly pre-industrial (except for Singapore, South Korea, Taiwan, and Hong Kong)
Dominant ideologies	Individualism and capitalism	Collectivism and socialism	Collectivism and nationalism (except for Singapore, South Korea, Taiwan, and Hong Kong)
Welfare	Welfare states, to protect the market economy and selected citizens Welfare commu-nity and welfare church	Welfare states, to protect citizens	Welfare family, welfare commu-nity, and welfare church
Income mainte-nance	Almost all countries	Almost all countries (inflation creates problems)	Almost none (except in Singapore, South Korea, Taiwan, and Hong Kong)
Health care	Almost all countries (except the United States)—spiraling cost	Almost all countries (getting supplies and equipment are serious prob-lems)	Charitable clinics or hospitals give some crisis-based care to the poor

(Continued)

Table 3-1. *Continued*

ITEMS	FIRST WORLD	SECOND WORLD	THIRD WORLD
Housing	Public housing for the poor peole in the United States, some rent control or rent subsidy	Rationed housing for all	No such concept—bustees and barrios for poor people
Education	State supported (extremely uneven in the United States)	State supported	State efforts do not reach all
	A highly educated poulation except poor people	Educated population	Educted elites and uneducated poor masses (except in Singapore, South Korea, Taiwan, and Hong Kong)
Social construction of women	Women's labor devalued—glass ceiling	Women's labor more respected	Subservience of women to severe oppression of women
Social construction of children	Child labor restricted but children of color are poorly protected	Child labor restricted	No such concept—child labor and child prostitution are prevalent

immigrants of color in France, Germany, Italy, and Great Britain, who were seen as competitors of the white working-class citizens of these countries. Similar problems arose in the United States in the 1990s, when the governors of Florida and California called for the denial of the benefits of the welfare state to illegal immigrants, most of whom are people of color.

In addition, a tremendous amount of wealth had been transferred from the rest of the world to Japan. Japanese workers became accustomed to guaranteed lifetime jobs, and there was interest in importing Japanese management technologies to other parts of the First World and to selected countries (Singapore and South Korea) in the Third World.

The social construction of women as a vulnerable group had been changing in the First World for several decades. The 1970s had seen changes in divorce and alimony laws and an increase in women's participation in the labor force. By the 1980s, however, it was apparent that almost all over the First World, both women's labor and occupations and professions in which women were in the majority were still devalued, and the metaphoric "glass ceiling" was being used to indicate the impossibility of women's upward mobility to well-paying senior-level jobs. At the bottom levels of social stratification, there were more women, a condition which some scholars (see, for example, Ehrenreich & Piven, 1984; Weitzman, 1985) called the "feminization of poverty."

In the United States, the number of transgenerational poor people with a high fertility rate was growing (Wilson, 1979, 1987), and some scholars (see, for instance, Auletta, 1982; Wilson, 1987) referred to this group as the "underclass." For the most part, this group was poor and black, with little attachment to the labor force and without the skills to participate in the labor force of a First World society. In contrast, Japan and most European countries did not have a transgenerational poor population that was comparable to that of the United States.

In the 1980s, the economic condition of aged people improved in the First World (Cottingham & Ellwood, 1989). However, a longer life expectancy had contributed to the increased cost of providing health care in the welfare states.

American social work as an occupational group and a profession had become the model for welfare state personnel, and the model of social work education was being emulated in Great Britain and several European countries (see Bose, 1992; Jones, 1992; Lee, 1992). In the United States, the market for clinical social workers who focus on the inability of individuals to function in society had expanded, and the market for social workers trained in community work or social advocacy had diminished substantially.

In this period, changes in intellectual efforts to understand the world system were also obvious. Before the 1980s, structural functionalism, conflict theories, the demand-and-supply matrix, and theories of monopoly capital had been prominent. By the mid-1980s, postmodernism, feminist theory, rational choice theory, neofunctionalism, game theory, and theories of the dual labor market were being used to understand the changing world system. These theories and the impact of the changes in them in the 1980s are discussed in chapters 8 and 9.

By the beginning of the 1990s, the increased cost and bureaucratization of health and social welfare in Europe surfaced as problems in the First World. In the United States, two problems emerged: the lack of health care coverage for a large number of Americans and the need to extend a "safety net" to them in a cost-effective manner.

THE SECOND WORLD

By the early 1980s, Yugoslavia had become a "core" country (Snyder & Kick, 1979) with newly formed wealth. China had followed a separate path in the communist world, with North Korea in its orbit. Cuba, however, remained heavily subsidized by the Soviet Union, and its president, Fidel Castro (1983), had openly proclaimed it a Third World country.

By the early 1990s, the Second World (termed the "Evil Empire" by Ronald Reagan) had disintegrated. The Soviet Union and Yugoslavia had broken up along ethnic and geocultural lines, and East Germany had re-united with West Germany. With the exception of China, North Korea, and Cuba, all other Second World countries had begun the arduous task of changing from planned economies to market economies. The pursuit of market economies in the Second World created substantial interest in the capitalist First World. Many groups in the First World are engaging in entrepreneurial activities in various parts of the Second World or are planning to do so.

Almost all the countries in the Second World had been welfare states, with elaborate provisions for income protection and health coverage. The lack of economic productivity, coupled with inflation, had substantially reduced the value of income supplied by the planned economies and had lowered the quality of health care, guaranteed to all citizens, to the point where health care settings lacked basic medications, supplies, and equipment (Castro, 1983).

Goodin (1988) suggested that in the First World, the welfare state was designed to respond to market failure (both unexpected and known and preventable crises). In the Second World, however, the crisis in the welfare state was due to the failure of planning or, put differently, to the inability of the economic system to produce and maintain the infrastructure for income protection and health coverage.

THE THIRD WORLD

The 1980s began with the failure of "modernization" efforts in Iran and with the "Islamization" of the country. Somewhat paralleling the attempt of the Second World to export communism decades earlier, Iran became an important center of "Islamizing" the world.

Ideologically, the Third World saw the tension between four competing ideologies: Islamization, ethnolingual or ethnotribal nationalism, capitalism, and liberation theology. The Islamic Conference countries represented the efforts of Islamization, though its impact was felt in almost all Third World countries. India, Bangladesh, and most countries of Africa also experienced ethnolingual or ethnotribal nationalism. Singapore, Taiwan, South Korea, and Hong Kong, however, followed the route of traditional capitalism. Most of Latin America, on the other hand, saw the influence of liberation theology, a worldview based mainly in the Catholic Church about basic inequalities in any national culture (Fox, 1991; Freire, 1970; Schutte, 1993).

While capitalism was being exported from the Anglo-American alliance to parts of the Third World, Islamization had a powerful impact on the people of color in the United States. Malcolm X had been a Black Muslim and gave credibility to Islam. By the 1980s, Nehru's Third World solidarity was all but forgotten, and Islam was an important ideological base, calling for family preservation, revulsion against substance abuse, and empowering men among the black minority of the United States.

In India, the assassination of Indira Gandhi (Nehru's daughter) and of Rajiv Gandhi (Nehru's grandson) ended the Nehru dynasty. The new leaders of India were reluctantly interested in changing from a mixed economy to a market economy, but this was not an easy undertaking. Various ethnolingual loyalties were making India unstable for the pursuit of free-market capitalism (Taylor, 1987; Wolpert, 1991).

In most parts of the Third World, there was wide variation in the social construction of women and children as vulnerable groups. The use of child labor in agriculture and key industries (especially in carpet weaving) was common and without any welfare state protection. Child prostitution turned into a major industry in Bangkok, Manila, Dacca, and other cities. The severe exploitation and abuse of women at home and in the labor force were also reported (Chatterjee, 1995; Sen, 1993).

In the First World, the chronic health problems of an aging population were an issue, whereas in the Third World the ability to reach old age was the issue. Contrary to popular stereotypes, in the Third World, only aged people with property are respected and have political clout, because they represent wealth (Kertzer & Keith, 1984; Kimmel, 1990; Phillips, 1992).

In the First World, hostility against immigrants from the Third World became a problem, whereas in the Third World, the problem was hostility against migrants from the rural hinterlands to the highly populated cities. In most Third World cities, there was a substantial growth in the street populations, most of whom were migrants from rural areas who came to the cities in search of work (Castles, 1993; Mueller, 1982) In Brazil, as well as many other countries, street children were posing safety problems for all (Viswanathan & Arje, 1995).

In the 1980s, the newly emergent welfare states in the Third World appeared to be Singapore, South Korea, Taiwan, and Hong Kong (Berger, 1986), the four countries that had pursued capitalism and a market economy for several decades.

Two experiments in the Third World, however, were outstanding successes. The first was in Chile, with the adoption of a two-tier income maintenance plan. The second, in Bangladesh, was the introduction of the concept of microlending. Chile replaced its earlier social security program, which was based on the concept of income transfer from those in the labor force to those who are not, with a two-tier system. In the first-tier program, poor aged people (who have no assets or other means) are paid a flat amount on a means-tested basis from the state's general revenues, and this program forms one tier. In the second-tier program, all people in the labor force are required to put 12 percent of their annual wages into one of 24 investment funds that are vigilantly supervised. The second-tier program has boosted Chile's savings rate to 29 percent of the overall wages (compared to 3 percent in the United States) and the overall growth rate of its national GNP to 8 percent. The first tier is a *transfer* program, whereas the second tier forms an *asset-accumulation* program. By the beginning of the 1990s, the Chilean model was being adopted in Argentina, Australia, and Sweden (Dixon & Scheurell, 1990, 1995; Klein, 1994; Ratan, 1995).

In Bangladesh, the concept of microlending was introduced by Grameen Bank (meaning the village bank), founded by Muhammad Yunus. Microlending is a program in which tiny amounts of money (as low as U.S. $5.00 to U.S. $10.00) are lent to poor women or poor laborers. Traditionally, the banks or even cooperative societies had not entered this small-loan market because it was not thought of as profitable. By the mid-1990s, however, Grameen Bank was the immensely successful innovator of microlending—a model that is being emulated in the United States in two areas: as a major intervention tool for antipoverty programs and as a device for private profit making (Johnston, 1995).

WELFARE INFRASTRUCTURE IN THE WORLD SYSTEM

At this point, I return to the model of the welfare infrastructure introduced in Chapter 2 (see Figures 2-2 through 2-7) and use it to explain the distribution of welfare states in the world system.

THE FIRST WORLD

Payers

In the First World, there seems to be a substantial within-group variation in payers. In the Anglo-American part of the First World (Australia, Canada, the United Kingdom, and the United States, which Esping-Andersen, 1990, called the "liberal" group of welfare states), the voluntary payers range from working-class to upper-class individuals. In addition, corporations and foundations contribute heavily, and much of this voluntary effort is in the private, nonprofit sector (Weisbrod, 1988). In this area of voluntary giving and transfer, an entire subculture of "corporate social responsibility" has emerged. It can be argued that such responsibility is likely to promote a good "business climate" and buys goodwill for the corporations. In contrast, private and voluntary transfer is not as common in the rest of the First World (Esping-Andersen, 1990).

In addition to voluntary and private payers, a substantial number of involuntary payers in the First World share a tax burden to support welfare programs. In this area, most European countries have a higher tax structure and, in turn, higher per capita involuntary payers than do the Anglo-American countries.

Types of Transfer

With regard to types of transfer, again, the Anglo-American countries seem to have a wider variation than do the other First World countries. Both centric transfer (owing to government activities in operating the welfare state) and noncentric transfer (owing to the many voluntary and private contributions to the various types of recipients) are more prevalent in the liberal Anglo-American countries than in the other First World countries. Furthermore, the Anglo-American countries are accused of having more regressive transfer policies than are the European countries and Japan because in the Anglo-American countries, income transfer from the middle and working classes to the lower and upper classes accounts for a high volume of transfers (Pohlmann, 1990).

Transfer Agents

In addition, the First World has a large number of transfer agents: the family, the community, the church, the unions and professional associations (collective-bargaining bodies), the corporations, and the state (see Table 3-1). It seems, however, that the state's role in transfer has been increasing over time. Furthermore, the state in the European countries and the corporation in Japan seem to be more involved in transfer activity than they are in the Anglo-American countries.

Recipients

Perhaps the largest within-group variation in the First World is in recipients. In the Anglo-American countries, especially the United States, protected entrepreneurs and upper- and middle-class individuals and groups are the recipients of many types of transfer, but such transfers are more covert than they are in the European countries (Beeghley, 1988). On the other hand, many types of transfers to poor people in the United States are done with substantial stigma attached unlike in the Nordic countries (Esping-Andersen, 1990).

Whereas poor people are stigmatized for receiving transfers, noncitizens, or "outsiders," are denied any income transfers of health coverage (not supported by market exchange) in the United States. This situation is not uniform throughout the First World. In most European welfare states, health coverage is extended to all, although there is some form of rationing.

Former colonial powers, like Great Britain, France, the Netherlands, and Italy, have been experiencing an influx of immigrants of color from their former colonies (such as India, Pakistan, Bangladesh, Algeria, Indonesia, and Ethiopia); this influx has created two types of problems. On the one hand, the outmigration of highly skilled people creates a brain drain in the Third World. On the other hand, the outmigration of relatively unskilled people further reduces the demand for unskilled labor in the First World and contributes to the hostility of white working-class people toward these immigrants.

The welfare systems in these First World countries are not well equipped to deal with these problems. In addition, during the 1970s and 1980s, Germany (as well as other First World countries) imported a large number of people from outside (called "guest laborers" or "contract laborers") who were expected to do the jobs that German workers did not want to do. During the 1990s, these guest workers became the targets of hostile attacks by white working-class Germans. It has been argued that the First World countries owe a social debt to persons from the Third World because of their centuries of exploitation of the latter, and one way to repay that debt is to allow them to receive welfare benefits (Pierson, 1991; Wallerstein, 1976, 1989).

Social hierarchy, or stratification, is prevalent in all countries. However, only the United States, of all the First World countries, has an entrenched and transgenerational poor population at the bottom of the social hierarchy. This group has more people of color and has fewer skills to participate in a postindustrial economy (Wilson, 1979, 1987). Murray (1984) argued that continued social welfare benefits to this group had led to an *increase* in this population. Immigrants of color in Britain, France, Italy, and other parts of Europe are occupying a similar place in the social ladders of Europe, though they are not as sizable as they are in the United States.

Not all the recipients of welfare activities in the First World countries are located within that world's geopolitical boundaries. In addition, numerous private and voluntary efforts are provided by a large network of churches and other interest groups that perform various types of transfers in different parts of the Second and Third Worlds. Such transfers include support to providers of educational, health care, and child welfare services, as well as some income transfer.

Providers

Another source of variation among the welfare states of the First World is the providers. For example, in some countries (like the United States), health care is provided by a complex mixture of public hospitals or clinics and private practitioners. If a person is covered by some form of private health insurance or by a public transfer payment scheme, then he or she can obtain health care. However, a large number of people are not covered by either scheme and hence receive no health coverage. In contrast, Canada and almost all European countries *employ* a large number of health care providers. In such cases, the state *is* the provider (as opposed to the state paying or contracting with private providers).

When the state is the provider of professional services, one consequence is some form of rationing. Other consequences are a cumbersome services delivery structure or accountability structure. One source of conflict is between the norms of bureaucracy and the norms of professional services delivery. These conflicts surface throughout the First World in some form.

Perhaps the most problematic scenario is when the state attempts to provide personal social services. In its effort to deliver these services, the state may become a surrogate parent or an extended family member. This is the case when the state covers child welfare services, family counseling, protection of children or elderly persons from abuse or neglect, adoption, foster care or institutionalization of persons, and juvenile justice. Major policy issues have emerged in the First World countries about whether and how well the state can take on these surrogate family roles. Furthermore, since the state acquires such surrogate family roles in relation to poor people, immigrants, and racial and ethnic groups more often than in relation to privileged people, the question arises, Does it violate its efforts to pursue equality, justice, or protection?

The professionalization of social workers ("self-appointed advocates for recipients" in Figure 2-6), who provide services to children, families, elderly people, and other vulnerable populations, is an emerging trend in most First World countries. In the United States, many social workers do not work with transfer recipients at all and are recompensed by market exchange.

All welfare states in the First World face issues of rationing, whether in the area of income support, health care, or other goods and services. Figure 2-7 outlined the various forms of rationing that occur. Given that rationing is inevitable, the major policy question in social welfare is, What kind (not whether) of rationing devices are to be implemented?

Several works have documented specific social welfare programs of the First World countries (see Eisenstadt & Ahimeir, 1985; Gould, 1993; Hokenstad, Khinduka, & Midgley, 1992). Table 3-2 outlines the programs of four selected First World countries.

THE SECOND WORLD

Payers

In the Second World, there seems to be less variation in the groups of payers than in the First World. Before the breakup of the Communist

Table 3-2. Social Welfare Provisions in Four First World Countries

PROVISION	BRITAIN	JAPAN	SWEDEN	UNITED STATES
Income maintenance	National Insurance Act of 1946 provided flat-rate pensions Means-tested Social Security Act of 1966 Means-tested Family Income Supplement Act of 1971 Index-linked benefits	Various pension insurances cover all Means-tested social assistance called Livelihood Protection Index-linked benefits Unemployment insurance covered by employer so Unemployment Insurance by the government does not cover all	Means-tested old age pension begun in 1913 Today most benefits are added to a base, which is index linked to price change Unified national system under a Social Insurance Board Allowance for every child Means-tested social assistance Earnings-related flexible pension Unemployment covered by unions	Earnings-related pension (social security) begun in the 1930s Several non-earnings-related social assistance with national and local transfers Benefits partly index linked Means-tested social assistance

(Continued)

Table 3-2. *Continued*

PROVISION	BRITAIN	JAPAN	SWEDEN	UNITED STATES
Health care	National health insurance covers all, plus there are private plans	Various health plans cover all, plus there are private plans— elderly people are often over- hospitalized	National health insurance covers all, plus there are private plans; sick people can claim substantial sick pay	Various private insurance plans through market exchange and crisis care in public settings leave a large number uncovered
Social services	Since 1974 social services have consumed 1.0 percent of the gross domestic product; increasing professional- ization of social work	Low number of social workers— community- based volunteers	Social Services Law covers services to children, handicapped people, substance abusers, and so forth	Highly professional- ized social workers trained to work with families, children, and others; direct service more popular than community work

SOURCES: Gould, A. (1993). *Capitalist welfare system*. London: Longman; Pierson, C. (1991). *Beyond the welfare state?* University Park: Pennsylvania State University Press.

Bloc, labor was considered to be the only legitimate source of income (Dixon & Macarov, 1992), and income transfer from the working population to the recipients through the state (as the transfer agent) was the major source of social welfare efforts. Compared to the First World, there were far fewer voluntary services by private agencies, although in some cases, the Catholic Church supplemented some social welfare programs. Furthermore, although the payers of cash transfers were primarily the working population, many in-kind transfers were (and are) provided by the family and the community (Dixon & Macarov, 1992).

Thus, in the Second World (more than in the First World), the payers have been primarily involuntary, of the middle and working classes (the

Second World has not developed any substantial upper or lower class), and from the public sector.

Types of Transfer

With regard to types of transfer, it seems that there was a great deal of variation. In the eastern European countries, both income transfer and other social services were carried out by the state (Les, 1992; Ruzica, 1992). In contrast, in China, there has been some income transfer through the state, and many social support services have been provided by the extended family and the local community (Dixon, 1992). It seems that for the most part, transfer policy was progressive rather than regressive (see Figures 1-3, 1-4, and 2-3), and in all there were both centric and noncentric transfers.

Transfer Agents

In the Second World countries, the main transfer agent was the state (Dixon & Macarov, 1992), although its efforts were supplemented by the family, the community, the church, and the labor unions. Except in the former Yugoslavia (Ruzica, 1992), the corporation was not a transfer agent. In this regard, the Second World was different from the First World, where corporations have been involved in many transfer activities.

Recipients

In terms of recipients, there seems to have been less variation in the category of recipients in the Second World than in the First World (Dixon & Macarov, 1992; Esping-Andersen, 1990). Because both the payers and the recipients were from the middle and working classes, there was a substantial overlap between the two groups. There were, however, clear definitions of vulnerable populations (Dixon & Kim, 1992), and the "victim" category, for the most part, meant victims of work-related injuries or accidents. In comparison with the First World, there were no protected entrepreneurs. However, Communist Party "insiders" had been favored in the Soviet Union since Stalin's regime (Dixon & Kim, 1992).

Providers

In relation to providers, the largest variation seems to have been between the First and the Second Worlds. More providers (of health care and social services) were in the employ of the state in the Second World than is usually true in the First World. The dominant model was the nationalization of providers, and the purchase-of-services (from independent contractors) model was less common. Furthermore, social work in the Second World did not emerge as a semiprofession (see Etzioni, 1969), and social workers did not operate as individual entrepreneurs and were often government employees who provided services to vulnerable and victimized groups (see Dixon & Macarov, 1992). Privatization was not an important concept in the Second World, although it has been selectively introduced by certain interest groups since the start of the push to convert planned economies into market economies.

There is not much literature on the limits on transfer or rationing in the Second World (or for that matter, in the First World). From the reports on service delivery structures, it appears that the following rationing devices were in effect: queuing, hiding benefits, creaming, creating preferred categories of recipients, using triage, and requiring recipients to provide some services (see Dixon & Macarov, 1992).

The antecedent factors that contributed to the initial construction of the welfare states in the Second World are relatively clear. These factors were a focus on collectivism; the needs of an individual as a basis for allocation (ideological loyalties were added by Stalin); and the state as an agent of transfer, clearly delineating what were entitlements and what were gratuities. Race, ethnicity, gender, and class stratification were not to be a basis for any allocations, although gender-based allocation did become a basis for social welfare policy in most Second World countries (Dixon & Macarov, 1992). There were promises of protection from poverty, illness, disability, and isolation in old age and equality of opportunity in the former Soviet Union and in most eastern European Second World countries (Dixon & Kim, 1992; Madison, 1968). In actuality, the steadily broadening income assistance to several categories of recipients could be called protection. Such protection was an entitlement, but it was kept under or close to the minimum wage (Dixon & Kim, 1992; Madison, 1968). Furthermore, the pursuit of "equality," though one of the anticipated factors, was never seriously pursued (Dixon & Kim, 1992).The dream of "community" gave way to the pursuit of hierarchy.

By the late 1960s, income maintenance and health programs existed in Cuba and the European parts of the Second World. However, they were deemed inadequate and insufficient by First World standards (Castro, 1983; Madison, 1968).

In sum, the Second World succeeded in providing some floor of income, basic health care, housing, and education. Almost all these provisions were inadequate by First World standards, but at least they existed.

Detailed reports by governmental officials, documenting specific social welfare programs in the Second World countries, are suspect with regard to their accuracy and whether they were devised as instruments of propaganda. However, some scholars outside the Second World attempted to document these programs (see Dixon & Macarov, 1992; Madison, 1968; Rimlinger, 1971; Sidel, 1974; Sidel & Sidel, 1982). Table 3-3 outlines the programs of four selected Second World countries based on various reports.

Table 3-3. Social Welfare Provisions in Four Second World Countries

PROVISION	CHINA	CUBA	POLAND	RUSSIA
Income maintenance	Locally administered earnings-related old age pension (does not cover all) Means-tested disability allowance	Earnings-related old age pension covers all Means-tested wage supplement	Earnings-related old age pension covers all Family allowance Sickness allowance Disability allowance	Earnings-related old age pension covers all Family allowance Minimum income as entitlement Disability allowance
Health care	Free health care only for employees Subsidized health care facilities	Free health care from the state for all	Free health care from the state for all	Free health care from the state for all
Social services	Strong focus on family and community as caregivers	Community-based care and care from unions	State-based care for substance abuse and family issues	Focus on *Dvor* (joint family) and *Mir* (community) as caregivers, state supports for community-based personal social services

Sources: Castro, F. (1983). *The world economic and social crisis: Its impact on the underdeveloped countries, its somber prospects and the need to struggle if we are to survive*. Havana: Council of State; Dixon, J. E. (1981). *The Chinese welfare system, 1949–1979*. New York: Praeger; Dixon, J. E., & Macarov, D. (Eds.). (1992). *Social welfare in socialist countries*. London: Routledge & Kegan Paul; Madison, B. (1968). *Social welfare in the Soviet Union*. Stanford, CA: Stanford University Press; and Sidel, R. (1974). *Revolutionary China*. New York: Delacorte Press.

Since the breakup of the Soviet Union, many Second World countries have been trying to shift from planned economies to market economies. It seems that the changes will have to be slow because they will involve changes not only in the production style (from planned to market responsive) but in the taxation, banking, and transfer systems.

THE THIRD WORLD

Payers

In the Third World, the variation in groups of payers is also less, especially than in the First World. For the most part, payers are private donors to recipients of their choice. Two ancient religions, Islam and Hinduism, set up the traditions of giving in most parts of the Third World (India, Pakistan, Bangladesh, Malaysia, Indonesia, the Middle East, and most of Africa). In these traditions, *zakat* in Islam and *danadharma* in Hinduism are prescriptions for the successful and the affluent to give generously (Mauss, 1967). In both traditions, giving is an obligation to the community, but the community is often interpreted as the ethnoreligious community. In most of Latin America, the ethnoreligious community is identified through the Catholic Church (Dixon & Scheurell, 1990, 1995).

In most parts of the Third World, the commitment to ethnoreligious and ethnolingual communities appears to be far greater than the commitment to the state. Thus, giving leads, for the most part, to a welfare community or a welfare church. The payers give according to their ability and, using the concepts of the First World, are individuals who are voluntary and private donors.

Types of Transfer and Transfer Agents

Except for South Korea, Singapore, and Taiwan, there is no system of centric transfer, and hence there is almost no concept of a welfare state. Given that most transfers are private and voluntary, most of the transfer systems that do exist are noncentric. In terms of transfer agents, the extended family, the community, and the church (or temple) are the major ones.

A wide variety of people would qualify as transfer recipients. Since there is no formal old age pension with centric transfer, aged people without means look to the extended family and the community for support. Those who are disabled or chronically ill and are unable to receive support from their families or communities become part of the street population or live near affluent estates or places of worship (where they have a better chance of getting voluntary donations). A visible and large population of orphaned or abandoned children also live in the streets (Viswanathan & Arje, 1995). Although middle-class educated women occupy roles in the occupations and professions, women who are uneducated and abandoned by their families live in the slums, perform menial jobs, or take to prostitution. Cities like

Bangkok, Djakarta, Dacca, Calcutta, Bombay, and Karachi have large neighborhoods of prostitution, in which there are shelters that find, house, and prepare uneducated and abandoned women for prostitution (Chatterjee, 1995; "Prostitutes and Their Children," 1994).

New ideas about women's rights, however, are emerging. In Bangladesh, a poor country with a Muslim majority, the publication of the works of feminist author Taslima Nasrin made Muslim clerics so angry that they demanded her immediate execution ("Justice for Taslima," 1994). These clerics called Nasrin's work a violation of Islamic religious law. Further publications of her works were banned, but they kept on reappearing from underground sources. Nasrin was secretly flown to Sweden, where she was granted asylum.

Providers

Charity hospitals and sometimes government-supported hospitals provide health care to indigenous populations. There is no national health care system comparable to those in the First or Second World countries (with the exception of Singapore, South Korea, and Taiwan).

Professional social work, patterned after the American model (requiring graduate-level work at a university), has emerged in most of the Asian countries of the Third World (see Ankrah, 1992; Bose, 1992; Lee, 1992). Government-sponsored community development efforts employ a large number of social workers, and the objective of these efforts is to provide multiple services (like public health services, consultation with agricultural technology, and family services) to large rural populations.

Limits on Transfer and Antecedent Factors

In relation to limits on transfer, the most common type of rationing device is queuing. Whenever voluntary donations of food, health care, or other in-kind distributions are made, they are done on a first-come, first-served basis. In some countries, there are categories of preferred recipients as well (Chatterjee, 1995; Dixon, 1987a, 1987b; Dixon & Kim, 1985).

The long-standing traditions of welfare community and welfare church are traditions of communal (ethnoreligious and ethnolingual) collectivism and gratuitous noncentric transfers. There is no tradition of entitlements for vulnerable populations, although there are traditionally sanctioned entitlements for privileged groups like the Brahmans of India (Mauss, 1967). The newly developed state is seen as a source and a leader of collective action, and the concept of citizenship is new.

In sum, there is no floor for income, basic health care, housing, and education in most Third World countries, with the exception of South Korea, Singapore, and Taiwan (Berger, 1986; Lee, 1992).

Table 3-4 lists the social welfare provisions in four selected Third World countries.

QUESTIONS ABOUT WELFARE INFRASTRUCTURES

When the features of programs in the three worlds are summarized, the following questions emerge. These questions put the three worlds in a comparative perspective. The answers to these questions are presented in Table 3-5.

1. Once a person has been socially defined (by tradition and then by social policy) as not employable (because of illness, disability, lack of skills, age, or whatever), can he or she ask the state for support?
2. Once a person has been socially defined as employable but is unemployed (owing to illness, disability, changes in the labor market, and so on), can he or she ask the state for support?
3. Once a person has been socially defined as employable but is marginally employed (employment does not produce sufficient income), can he or she ask the state for support?
4. If the state is providing support (transfer), is it means tested?
5. If the state is providing support, is it related to past or potential future earnings?
6. If the state is providing support, is it at a flat rate or with a minimum and a maximum, or is it linked to an index of fluctuating living costs?
7. Is the state committed to seeing that each citizen receives a basic (rationed) package of health care services? If so, then has it set up a formal structure to provide such care, or has it engaged other qualified parties to provide the care?
8. Is the state committed to seeing that each citizen receives a basic education? If so, has it set up a formal structure to provide such education itself, or has it engaged other qualified parties to do so?
9. Is the state committed to the idea of definable basic housing for all citizens? If so, has it set up a formal structure to provide such housing or engaged other parties to do so?
10. Is the state committed to providing protection to various vulnerable groups (children, elderly, developmentally disabled, mentally ill)? If so, has it set up a formal structure to provide such protection, or has it engaged other qualified parties to do so?
11. Have one or more occupational groups emerged within the state, who are self-appointed advocates for vulnerable groups and are seeking increased professionalization?

Table 3-4. Social Welfare Provisions in Four Third World Countries

PROVISIONS	INDIA	PAKISTAN	S. KOREA	TAIWAN
Income maintenance	No state old age pension No disability allowance	No state old age pension No disability allowance	Earnings-related old age pension being implemented Means-tested disability alllowance being implemented	Earnings-related old age pension being implemented Means-tested disability allowance being implemented
Health care	Provided by public and private charities	Provided by public and private charities	Health care insurance for employees, a state-covered supplement being discussed	Public–private mix of care being discussed
Social services	Strong focus on family and community	Strong focus on family and community	Provided by the family and community; state-sponsored personal social services being discussed	Provided by the family and community; state-sponsored personal social services being discussed

Sources: Berger, P. (1986). *The capitalist revolution.* New York: Basic Books; Bulsara, J. F. (1984). *Perspectives on social welfare in India.* New Delhi: S. Chand; Castro, F. (1983). *The World economic and social crisis: Its impact on the underdeveloped countries, its somber prospects and the need to struggle if we are to survive.* Havana: Council of State; Dixon, J. E. (Ed.). (1987a). *Social welfare in Africa.* London: Croom Helm; Dixon, J. E. (Ed.). (1987b). *Social welfare in the Middle East.* London: Croom Helm; Dixon, J. E., & Kim, H. S. (Eds.). (1985). *Social welfare in Asia.* London: Croom Helm; Dixon, J. E., & Scheurell, R. (Eds.). (1990). *Social welfare in Latin America.* London: Routledge & Kegan Paul; Ogle, G. E. (1990). *South Korea: Dissent within the economic miracle.* London: Zed Books; Pae, S. M. (1992). *Korea leading developing nations.* Lanham, MD: University Press of America; and Robinson, T. W. (Ed.). (1991). *Democracy and development in east Asia.* Washington, DC: AEI Press.

Table 3-5. Comparison of 11 Variables in the Welfare States

QUESTION	FIRST WORLD	SECOND WORLD	THIRD WORLD
1	Yes	Mostly yes	Mostly no
2	Yes	Mostly yes	No
3	Mostly yes	Mostly yes	No
4	Mostly yes	Mostly yes	Question does not apply
5	Mostly yes	Mostly yes	Question does not apply
6	Mostly yes	Mostly yes	Question does not apply
7	Yes (except in the United States)	Yes	No
8	Mostly yes	Mostly yes	No
9	Mostly yes	Yes	No
10	Yes	Mostly yes	No
11	Yes	Partially yes	Partially yes

REFERENCES

Ankrah, E. M. (1992). Social work in Uganda: Survival in the midst of turbulence. In M. C. Hokenstad, S. K. Khinduka, & J. Midgley (Eds.), *Profiles in international social work* (pp. 145–162). Washington, DC: NASW Press.

Auletta, K. (1982). *The underclass*. New York: Random House.

Beeghley, L. (1988). *The structure of social stratification in the United States*. Boston: Allyn & Bacon.

Bell, D. (1967). The year 2000—The trajectory of an idea. *Daedalus 93,* 639–655.

Bell, D. (1973). *The coming of post-industrial society*. New York: Basic Books.

Berger, P. (1986). *The capitalist revolution*. New York: Basic Books.

Bollen, K., & Appold, S. J. (1993). National industrial structure and the global system. *American Sociological Review, 45,* 370–390.

Bose, A. B. (1992). Social work in India: Developmental roles for a helping profession. In M. C. Hokenstad, S. K. Khinduka, & J. Midgley (Eds.), *Profiles in international social work* (pp. 71–83). Washington, DC: NASW Press.

Bowles, C. (1954). *Ambassador's report.* New York: Harper & Row.

Bulsara, J. F. (1984). *Perspectives on social welfare in India.* New Delhi: S. Chand.

Castles, S. (1993). *The age of migration: International populations movement in the modern world.* New York: Guilford Press.

Castro, F. (1983). *The world economic and social crisis: Its impact on the underdeveloped countries, its somber prospects and the need to struggle if we are to survive.* Havana: Council of State.

Chatterjee, P. (1995, July 31). *The commodification of women in south and Southeast Asia.* Paper presented at the conference on International Social Welfare in a Changing World, Calgary, Canada.

Cottingham, P., & Ellwood, D. T. (1989). *Welfare policy for the 1990s.* Cambridge, MA: Harvard University Press.

Dixon, J. E. (1981). *The Chinese welfare system, 1949–1979.* New York: Praeger.

Dixon, J. E. (Ed.). (1987a). *Social welfare in Africa.* London: Croom Helm.

Dixon, J. E. (Ed.). (1987b). *Social welfare in the Middle East.* London: Croom Helm.

Dixon, J. E. (1992). China. In J. E. Dixon & D. Macarov (Eds.), *Social welfare in socialist countries* (pp. 10–46). London: Routledge & Kegan Paul.

Dixon, J. E., & Kim, H. S. (Eds.). (1985). *Social welfare in Asia.* London: Croom Helm.

Dixon, J. E., & Kim, H. S. (1992). Social welfare under socialism. In J. E. Dixon & D. Macarov (Eds.), *Social welfare in socialist countries* (pp. 1–9). London: Routledge & Kegan Paul.

Dixon, J. E., & Macarov, D. (Eds.). (1992). *Social welfare in socialist countries.* London: Routledge & Kegan Paul.

Dixon, J. E., & Scheurell, R. (Eds.). (1990). *Social welfare in Latin America.* London: Routledge & Kegan Paul.

Dixon, J. E., & Scheurell, R. (Eds.). (1995). *Social security programs: A cross-cultural comparative perspective.* Westport, CT: Greenwood Press.

Ehrenreich, B., & Piven, F. F. (1984). The feminization of poverty. *Dissent, 31,* 162–170.

Eisenstadt, S. N., & Ahimeir, O. (1985). *The welfare state and its aftermath.* Totowa, NJ: Barnes & Noble.

Esping-Andersen, G. (1990). *The three worlds of welfare capitalism.* Princeton, NJ: Princeton University Press.

Etzioni, A. (1969). *The semi-professionals and their organization: Teachers, nurses, and social workers.* New York: Free Press.

Fox, M. (1991). *Creation spirituality: Liberating gifts for the peoples of the earth.* San Francisco: Harper & Row.

Freire, P. (1970). *The pedagogy of the oppressed.* New York: Seabury Press.

Goodin, R. E. (1988). Reasons for welfare: Economic, sociological, and political—but ultimately moral. In J. D. Moon (Ed.), *Responsibility, rights, and welfare: The theory of the welfare state* (pp. 19–54). Boulder, CO: Westview Press.

Gould, A. (1993). *Capitalist welfare system.* London: Longman.

Hesse, H. (1951). *Siddhartha* (H. Rosner, Trans.). New York: New Directions.

Hokenstad, M. C., Khinduka, S. K., & Midgley, J. (Eds.). (1992). *Profiles in international social work.* Washington, DC: NASW Press.

Johnston, J. (1995). To boldly loan where no banker has loaned before. *Business Ethics, 9,* 45–46.

Jones, C. (1992). Social work in Great Britain: Surviving the challenge of conservative ideology. In M. C. Hokenstad, S. K. Khinduka, & J. Midgley (Eds.), *Profiles in international social work* (pp. 43–57). Washington, DC: NASW Press.

Justice for Taslima. (1994, November 26). *Prabashi Anandabazar Patrika, 6,* p. 1.

Kaldor, M. (1990). After the cold war. *New Left Review, 180,* 25–40.

Kertzer, D. I., & Keith, J. (1984). *Age and anthropological theory.* Ithaca, NY: Cornell University Press.

Kim, J. (1994). *Ideological orientations for Korean public opinion on income assistance to poor families.* Unpublished Ph.D. dissertation, Case Western Reserve University, Cleveland.

Kimmel, D. C. (1990). *Adulthood and aging: An interdisciplinary developmental view.* New York: John Wiley & Sons.

Klein, J. (1994, December 12). If Chile can do it . . . . *Newsweek, 124,* 50.

Lee, P. C. (1992). Social work in Hong Kong, Singapore, South Korea, and Taiwan: Asia's four little dragons. In M. C. Hokenstad, S. K. Khinduka, & J. Midgley (Eds.), *Profiles in international social work* (pp. 99–114). Washington, DC: NASW Press.

Les, E. (1992). Poland. In J. E. Dixon & D. Macarov (Eds.), *Social welfare in socialist countries* (pp. 156–183). London: Routledge & Kegan Paul.

MacKinnon, C. (1989). *Towards a feminist theory of the state.* Cambridge, MA: Harvard University Press.

Madison, B. (1968). *Social welfare in the Soviet Union.* Stanford, CA: Stanford University Press.

Marshall, T. H. (1964). *Class, citizenship, and social development.* Garden City, NY: Doubleday.

Mauss, M. (1967). *The gift.* New York: W. W. Norton.

Mueller, C. F. (1982). *The economist of labor migration.* New York: Academic Press.

Murray, C. (1984). *Losing ground: American social policy: 1950–1980.* New York: Basic Books.

Ogle, G. E. (1990). *South Korea: Dissent within the economic miracle.* London: Zed Books.

Pae, S. M. (1992). *Korea leading developing nations.* Lanham, MD: University Press of America.

Phillips, D. R. (Ed.). (1992). *Ageing in east and Southeast Asia.* London: E. Arnold.

Piccone, P. (1990). Paradoxes of perestroika. *Telos, 84,* 3–32.

Pierson, C. (1991). *Beyond the welfare state?* University Park: Pennsylvania State University Press.

Pohlmann, M. (1990). *Black politics in conservative America.* New York: Longman.

Prostitutes and their children. (1994, April 16). *Prabashi Anandabazar Patrika, 5,* p. 7.

Ratan, S. (1995, March 20). How Chile got it right. *Time, 145,* 30.

Rimlinger, G. (1971). *The welfare state and industrialization in Europe, America, and Russia.* New York: John Wiley & Sons.

Robinson, T. W. (Ed.). (1991). *Democracy and development in east Asia.* Washington, DC: AEI Press.

Ruzica, M. (1992). Yugoslavia. In J. E. Dixon & D. Macarov (Eds.), *Social welfare in socialist countries* (pp. 208–233). London: Routledge & Kegan Paul.

Schutte, O. (1993). *Cultural identity and social liberation in Latin American thought.* Albany: State University of New York Press.

Sen, A. K. (1993). *On economic equality.* New York: Oxford University Press.

Shils, E. (1975). *Center and periphery: Essays in macrosociology.* Chicago: University of Chicago Press.

Sidel, R. (1974). *Revolutionary China*. New York: Delacorte Press.

Sidel, R., & Sidel, V. W. (1982). *The health of China*. Boston: Beacon Press.

Snyder, D., & Kick, E. (1979). Structural position in the world-system and economic growth, 1965–1970: A multiple network analysis of transnational interactions. *American Journal of Sociology, 84,* 1096–1126.

Taylor, J. (1987). *The dragon and the wild goose: China and India*. Westport, CT: Greenwood Press.

Viswanathan, N., & Arje, M. (1995, August 1). *Street children: An international perspective*. Paper presented at the conference on International Social Welfare in a Changing World, Calgary, Canada.

Wallerstein, I. (1976). *The modern world-system*. New York: Academic Press.

Wallerstein, I. (1980). *The modern world system II: Mercantilism and the consolidation of the European world economy, 1600–1750*. New York: Academic Press.

Wallerstein, I. (1989). *The modern world system III: The second era of great expansion of the capitalist world economy, 1730–1840*. New York: Academic Press.

Weisbrod, B. A. (1988). *The nonprofit economy*. Cambridge, MA: Harvard University Press.

Weitzman, L. (1985). *The divorce revolution*. New York: Free Press.

Wilson, W. J. (1979). *The declining significance of race*. Chicago: University of Chicago Press.

Wilson, W. J. (1987). *The truly disadvantaged*. Chicago: University of Chicago Press.

Wolpert, S. A. (1991). *India*. Berkeley: University of California Press.

Wright, R. (1956). *The color curtain*. Cleveland: World.

Part 2

THREE COMPETING THESES ABOUT THE WELFARE STATE

P art 2 consists of six chapters that are devoted to examining the three different theses about how the welfare state originates and is sustained. Chapters 4 and 5 examine the thesis that the welfare state originates from the ideological positions of important interest groups or elite groups and that the continued presence of these ideologies in the national culture sustains the welfare state. In chapters 6 and 7 I explore the thesis that the welfare state emerges in capitalist economies to disguise class, gender, and interest-group conflicts. In planned economies, the welfare state originates from certain ideologies of redistribution, but planned economies are usually not in a position to sustain it. Chapters 8 and 9 discuss the thesis that the welfare state is a by-product of industrialization. Industrialization creates conditions that require either full or partial state intervention to support vulnerable populations. It also creates "relative deprivation" or a "revolution of rising expectations" in the geopolitical areas that come in contact with industrialized areas. Thus, the welfare state emerges in areas that have been industrialized, and demands for modernization begin in areas that come into contact with industrialized areas.

4

WELFARE IS AN IDEOLOGICAL COMPROMISE: 1

> "It is to ideology," barked Napolean in 1812, "this gloomy
> metaphysics which subtly looks for first causes upon which
> to base the legislation of people—that all the misfortune of
> our beautiful France must be attributed."
>
> L. Coser, in de Huszer, *The Intellectuals*

I n social work, a thesis proposing a relationship between ideology and
social welfare is popular among some scholars who are interested in
studying the comparative historical evolution of the welfare state and
among those who study social policy. In sociology, such a thesis is popular
among some Marxist scholars and those who are interested in the sociology
of knowledge.

To comprehend the thesis that welfare is an ideological compromise, it is important to know (1) the definition of *ideology* (the term seems
to have many meanings), (2) which groups hold specific ideological views,
and (3) how the disciplines in question propose a relationship between
ideology and social welfare. In this chapter, I discuss how different disciplines have understood the concept of ideology. In chapter 5, I review how
the concept has been used to explain the development of the welfare state.

WHAT IS IDEOLOGY?

The term *ideology* has many meanings and many usages. However, the
simplest but most comprehensive definition of it was by Berger and Luckman
(1967), who proposed that the term refers to *the legitimation of relationships.* The relationship can be between genders; between generations; between employees and employers; between co-workers; between humans
and the land, artifacts (objects produced by humans), or ideas: between
humans and their group membership; between a salesperson and a customer; between a professional and a client; or between the governor and
the governed. Furthermore, the relationship can be egalitarian or hierarchical and a means to an end or an end in itself.

DIFFERENT IDEOLOGIES

The ideology of *patriarchy* (see Walby, 1990), for example, requires a hierarchical relationship between the genders (men are dominant and women are not), leading to a preferred way of identifying generational relationships (patrilineal descent). It may dictate the ideology of *ownership,* which calls for a preferred way by which the genders and generations can own land, artifacts, and ideas. Related to the ideology of ownership may be an ideology of *inheritance,* meaning how the genders and generations may be entitled to land, artifacts, and ideas owned by previous generations. The ideology of *deism,* for example, sanctions patriarchy as a way of organizing the family, religious institutions, and relationships between the governor and the governed when authority follows from a male god to a male governor of state and then to a male head of household (Marnell, 1968). Modern *feminism* is, for the most part, an ideology that opposes deism.

Capitalism as an ideology is based on the assumption that human needs (from the basic needs for food, shelter, and safety to the need for self-actualization proposed by Maslow, 1962) can be understood only as individual needs, not as the needs of the members of a community (see Dolbeare & Dolbeare, 1971). According to this ideology, competition (rather than collaboration) leads to efficiency in production, and the operation of a free market based on demand and supply ensures maximal happiness for most people. The free market also is a good mechanism for distributing scarce goods and services. "Consumer sovereignty" is extremely "sacred" in capitalism (Dolbeare & Dolbeare, 1971). Given this emphasis, capitalism stresses *individualism,* the pursuit of self-interest, materialism, and the sanctity of private property. As an ideology, it can and often does legitimate relationships between employers and employees; between humans and the land, artifacts, or ideas (by viewing them as private property); between a salesperson and a customer; and between a professional and a client. All these relationships are basically market-driven. The role of the state is to ensure the operation of the free market and the protection of private property.

In contrast, the ideology of the several varieties of *socialism* (see Crick, 1987) assumes that human needs can be understood as being on a continuum from the needs of individuals to the needs of members of the community. In a conflict between individual liberty and the interests of the community, the community has primacy. According to this ideology, collaboration and cooperation lead to efficiency and effectiveness in production, and central planning is the best way to organize the operation of production and distribution. Furthermore, there should be limits on defining which land, artifacts, and ideas can be private property and on reducing human labor and human health to commodities (to be bought and sold in a marketplace). Given this emphasis, socialism stresses the importance of *collectivism* and the commitment to collective interests.

Like capitalism, socialism also influences relationships between employees and employers; between humans and the land, artifacts, or ideas; between humans and their various group memberships; and between humans engaged in commercial transactions. The role of the state is to represent and protect the interests that are considered to be collective interests.

Patriarchy, or *deism,* can be viewed as ideologies of the family. Both capitalism and socialism can be seen as ideologies of production and distribution, or ideologies of economic behavior. In comparison, democracy and its variants are ideologies of governance. However, each of these ideologies has an impact on areas beyond its usual realms; each has implications for the family, the economy, and the polity (or the organization of governance).

Rejai (1991, p. 156) noted that the concept of democracy originated in classical Greece as a counterthought to the autocracy of the elites, or elitism, and was not popular until the "English, American, and French revolutions of the seventeenth and eighteenth centuries . . . popularized and legitimized democratic government throughout the Western world." He also stated that democracy involves self-rule by popular participation in decision making—a principle that has come to be known as the one-person, one-voice, one-vote rule. Inherent in democracy is the assumption that this type of governance is the best for the common good, that individuals in it are equals, that the freedom of these individuals is "natural" and "inalienable," and that these individuals are inherently good and rational.

As democracy was adapted to rule large societies, it took on pluralistic or representative forms. For such forms to work, the existence of many interest groups and many practices (of "checks and balances") are required. An almost insolvable problem in the operation of a representative democracy is the required commitment to opposing values—liberty and equality—which are basically incompatible with each other. During the French Revolution, intellectuals added the value of fraternity. The result was not two, but three contradictory values.

The ideology of democracy "can be fused with either a socialist or a capitalist economy" (Rejai, 1991, p. 167), leading to democratic socialism or democratic capitalism. At times, a blend of the two is also possible. The contradictions among liberty, equality, and community remain in some form or other in both types of governance. Table 4-1 summarizes the key components of the ideologies discussed so far.

It should be noted that the concept of social welfare, meaning nonmarket distribution, or transfer from the payer to the recipient (Figures 2-2 through 2-7) by a transfer agent, is basically incompatible with capitalism and democratic capitalism (which require distribution by market forces, not by the state or another transfer agent) and compatible with socialism (which requires distribution on a planned basis) or democratic socialism (which combines governance by a one-person, one-vote mechanism and

Table 4-1. Components of Four Ideologies

IDEOLOGY	FOCUS	DESIGN OF HUMAN RELATIONSHIPS	ENDS SOUGHT	ROLE OF THE STATE
Patriarchy	Family	Dominance of men over women, hierarchical gender relationships	Stability of power relationships over time	Support the patriarchal family and model itself by patriarchy
Capitalism	Economy	Dominance of the free market, called "the Invisible Hand" (Smith, 1776/1963);[a] free choice for the consumer; almost all relationships can be understood by this design; human needs are personal	Liberty	Support the free market and private property
Socialism	Economy	Dominance of central planning; human needs are the needs of a community member	Community and equality	Support the planning process and enforce loyalty to the collectivity
Democracy	Polity	Dominance of the concept of self-rule; human needs are both personal and communal	Liberty and equality	Support the electoral process and pluralist institutions

[a] Smith, A. (1963). *An inquiry into the nature and causes of the wealth of nations.* New York: Modern Library. (Original work published 1776)

distribution by both market forces and by catering to victims of market failure on a planned basis). Scholars in social work, from Coyle (1948) to Balgopal and Vassil (1983), Tropman (1989), Brown (1991), Karger and Stoesz (1994), and Groskind (1994), have emphasized this fact.

Ideology defines the relationship between humans and between humans and their culturally produced artifacts or services. The next section discusses how different ideologies interpret health care, housing, and education.

IDEOLOGY AND INCOME

Because income is a culturally produced artifact, what is or should be the legitimate source of acquiring it: capital or labor? If capital is a legitimate source of income, can it be inherited? If it can be inherited from a biological ancestor, then why is *this* biological relationship valued more than other biological relationships?

Under capitalism, both capital and labor (of individuals) are legitimate sources of income, and owners of capital often define what one's labor is worth. Collective bargaining by providers of labor is an attempt to increase the worth of labor. In patriarchy, capital can be inherited from men of previous generations. Labor cannot be inherited; its worth must be defined within one life span. Thus in patriarchal capitalism, those with capital are at an advantage over those who use labor as a source of income, and they can *commodify* labor, or convert it into a commodity. Furthermore, in patriarchal capitalism, the labor of men is usually more highly commodified than is the labor of women and hence is worth more (Crick, 1987; Friedman, 1962; MacFarlane, 1987).

In an ideology that combines patriarchy, capitalism, and social Darwinism, those with a low commodification of labor should be allowed to perish. In one that combines patriarchy, capitalism, and pragmatism, or rationalism, those with a low commodification of labor can be allowed a nominal transfer to survive. In one that combines patriarchy, capitalism, and democracy, there is a conflict between the commodification of labor and rights emanating from citizenship, since citizenship leads to the concept of entitlement in one form or another.

Under socialism, only labor (of individuals) is a legitimate source of income, and owners of capital are suspect (Crick, 1987). Collective bargaining by providers of labor is legitimate, but must take second place to the interests of the state (in state socialism). In patriarchal socialism, men are still at an advantage over women because the labor of men is either explicitly or unwittingly given a higher value than the labor of women. In an ideology that combines patriarchy, socialism, and democracy, there is less conflict between the value of labor and rights emanating from citizenship. In this case, labor is not placed on a continuum from high to low commodification, but is considered dichotomous (the ability versus the inability to provide it) and is supposedly unrelated to any entitlement guaranteed by citizenship.

IDEOLOGY AND HEALTH CARE

Health care is a combination of culturally produced services and artifacts. Perhaps the first question about health care is, Should health be allowed to become a *commodity* to be bought and sold under market forces?

Or, should it be seen as a *commitment* defined and maintained by collective effort, much like national defense? If health is allowed to become a commodity, then how should it be delivered to those who are not part of the market-exchange system? If it is national or collective commitment, then what should be the mechanism for delivering health care to all individuals?

Under capitalism, both knowledge (health related) and labor provided from the knowledge are commodities and can be exchanged in the marketplace for income (often high income). Artifacts that are needed to deliver health care (like machines, medications, equipment, and furniture) are also commodities and so can be exchanged (Friedman, 1962; MacFarlane, 1987). Insuring patients, insuring liability, financing the knowledge industry, and financing the manufacture of necessary artifacts are all subjected to market exchange. The health care industry in many capitalist countries is a growth industry. In addition, liability collections supported by the legal profession may create high windfall profits for some. Different types of patients can be seen as different segments of markets.

In an ideology that combines patriarchy and capitalism, the people in dominant positions in the health care system are men from the upper levels of the stratification system, and those in less dominant positions are women of more humble origins. In an ideology that combines patriarchy, capitalism, and social Darwinism, patients who do not have insurance or who cannot pay for health care may be allowed to perish or be given perfunctory care on a crisis-to-crisis basis (Navarro, 1992). In one that combines patriarchy, capitalism, and pragmatism, health care is provided to transfer recipients through one or more transfer systems.

Another ideological development in health care under capitalism and patriarchy is *medicalization*. In medicalization, there is a tendency to define somatic problems, aesthetic problems, psychological problems, interpersonal problems, and social problems as problems in the individual that can be dealt with with the medical metaphors of diagnosis and treatment. With medicalization, all problems (from individual to social) can be marketed—a situation that Chatterjee (1979) called the "marketing of human vulnerability"—and can be subjected to profit-seeking behavior.

Under socialism, health care is often another right emanating from the rights of a citizen (who may be a patient). There is either a limited market or no market for the private sale of health care knowledge under market provisions, in that such knowledge is privately sold only to the wealthier members of society. The artifacts needed for delivering health care are produced by the state or under a planned economy and are often in short supply or not available when needed (Navarro, 1992). In an ideology that combines socialism and patriarchy, health policy is made by men, who are also the dominant providers of care.

IDEOLOGY AND EDUCATION

Given that knowledge is culturally produced, who should be allowed to acquire it and to what degree become crucial questions. And different ideologies promote different answers to them.

Under capitalism, knowledge or information is another commodity and can be subjected to market transaction (MacFarlane, 1987). In the United States, which has a long history of commodifying education and efforts to provide elementary and secondary education to all citizens, a dual system of education has emerged: a superior educational system for middle- and upper-class children and young adults and an inferior educational system for those from working-class and poor families.

In the United States, working-class and poor students usually cannot attend the expensive private universities, many of which are vehicles for retaining class status over generations by students from the upper classes (Jencks, 1972). The public universities make commodified higher education available to middle-class students at a subsidized price while working-class and poor students rarely attend them (Wilensky, 1975). Thus, under capitalism, the commodification of education, even when coupled with efforts to achieve universal distribution, leads to a dual system: one for the privileged classes, which gives them more opportunities in the market, and another for the less privileged classes, which does not allow them to develop sufficient skills for the market.

The impact of ideology on education may take several forms. In the foregoing examples from the United States, *market rationing* is used to prevent education from truly being universally available, whereas in most western European countries *triage rationing* (the selection of students by the state on the basis of who can gain the most from education) is used for the same purpose. Triage rationing of education was and still is the basic practice in the Second World countries. The problem is that education (meaning "good" education, which fosters labor force entry and subsequent labor force attachment) is rationed in one way or another in every society. And ideology is used to justify such rationing practices.

In an ideology that combines patriarchy with either capitalism or socialism, more teachers at the lower end of the educational continuum are women whose labor is devalued. In addition, labor in occupations and professions where women predominate is also devalued.

IDEOLOGY AND HOUSING

Housing is another artifact that is culturally produced. Under capitalism, it is subjected to intense commodification. In the United States, a dual system of housing has emerged: one for those who are attached to the labor market and one for those who are not. For those who obtain housing from the transfer sector, the housing is usually of poor quality and located in impoverished neighborhoods with inferior schools. In western Europe, there is a similar dual housing system in France, Great Britain, Italy, and Spain.

Under capitalism, the quality of housing is subjected to market rationing. Under socialism, housing is a social right, whose availability may depend on the culture's capacity to produce sufficient items, and may be subjected to different forms of nonmarket rationing. In the Third World, the quality of housing is almost linearly related to the quality of people's attachment to the labor force.

IDEOLOGY AND PERSONAL SOCIAL SERVICE

Perhaps nowhere else in the welfare state is the presence of ideology as openly visible as it is in the realm of personal social services. Often the term means that the agents (often social workers) of the welfare state are asking given people or populations *not* to do something (like child abuse, elder abuse, or domestic violence) or are providing something to a given population (like Meals on Wheels, home visiting, or advice and counseling) or are assuming custody of given persons or groups (like children of mentally ill or other people who are unable to maintain self-sustaining social roles). In all these capacities, what the agents do or provide is guided by such ideological issues as who is a child (or a mentally ill person), what is abuse, what should be done about a given problem, and what is appropriate behavior in a given context.

Even setting objectives of personal social services can be an ideological issue. For example, should finding an appropriate spouse for a person receiving social services be an objective? In the North American and western European countries of the First World, such a venture is not likely to be an objective of social services, but on the Malay Peninsula, it would indeed be seen as appropriate. Should a pregnant adolescent be advised to carry her pregnancy to term, or should she be advised to have an abortion at the state's expense? Again, such a matter would be seen as a source of ideological conflict in many First World countries but not in many Third World countries.

According to classic patriarchy, such matters as child abuse or domestic violence are not social services issues but matters to be solved within the family. However, in a liberal democracy, the state begins to mediate many family conflicts and may even enforce a solution that is antipatriarchal (like legally disciplining male abusers). Under capitalism, an individual's personal or domestic problems are not the concern of the state, since the state's function is to ensure the operation of a trouble-free market. However, if state intervention in people's personal problems can be seen to produce a better workforce (or labor force), then such an effort may be justified. The state's intervention efforts may even be more justifiable if people's personal problems can be commodified, that is, turned into a new form of market-place (Chatterjee, 1979).

HISTORY OF SOCIOLOGICAL PERSPECTIVES

In the sociological literature, there are three schools of thought or traditions with regard to ideology. The first is the Marxist tradition (Israel, 1971; McLellan, 1986). The second may be called the Frankfurt school tradition, which was partly influenced by the Marxist tradition. The third is a combination of perspectives that have been grouped together and called the non-Marxist tradition (McLellan, 1986). In addition, there is the social work tradition.

THE MARXIST TRADITION

Bottomore (1983, p. 219) stated that "from its inception ideology has a clear-cut negative and critical connotation." It is negative because "it conceals the contradictory character of the hidden essential pattern by focusing upon the way in which the economic relations appear on the surface," and it is critical because it is "the totality of forms of social consciousness" (Bottomore, 1983, pp. 220–221). Both connotations appear in Marx's formulations of three sources of the alienation of human beings (Israel, 1971). The first two sources are religion and the state, where external projections of the best in human nature, which, when objectified, demand total devotion from human beings. The third source, and perhaps the most famous Marxist contention, is human labor under capitalism, which is sold as a commodity without any meaningful attachment to the products generated by it. According to the Marxist vision, freeing the human spirit from the ideologies (religious, political, and economic) of the dominant capitalist groups is a major objective.

Marxist thought had a major impact on many reformers and humanists in England, France, Russia, China, and other countries. At the turn of the 20th century, a group of humanist reformers in England, called *Fabian socialists* (named after the Roman general Fabius Maximus, who had become famous for his incremental tactics), agreed with Marx's diagnosis of the sources of human suffering and oppression. However, they were against the use of violent revolution to bring about radical change, and devoted themselves instead to incremental reform by introducing various transfer systems.

In France, Sorel (1906/1963) argued that incremental and selective violence against dominant groups would bring about a better and just society, in which the ownership and control of industries would rest in the hands of workers' unions (rather than the state), an approach that came to be known as *syndicalism.* Another group in France and in other parts of continental Europe in the early 1900s, known as *anarchists,* were socialists who were opposed to both violent revolution and the necessity of the state as a way of organizing society and were devoted to the formation of natural communities (comparable to tribal societies) as a way of achieving a just society. Two famous anarchists were Pierre-Joseph Proudhon and Peter Kropotkin, who wrote on ways of dealing with poverty (Proudhon, 1846/ 1969) and developing a network of mutual aid at the community level, rather than at the state level (Kropotkin, 1902/1969). Some of the visions of the anarchists are still popular among selected social welfare theoreticians (see Macarov, 1978).

In Russia, the revolutionary Vladimir Lenin (cited in Rejai, 1991) favored the organized state as the means of attaining a just society (in direct contrast to the anarchists). The Russian revolutionary Leon Trotsky (1938/ 1963, p. 36), commenting on the ideological justifications of the means and ends of human endeavors, wrote:

> A means can be justified only by its end. But the end in its turn needs to be justified. From the Marxist point of view, which expresses the historical interests of the proletariat, the end is justified if it leads to increasing the power of man over nature and to the abolition of the power of man over man.

Trotsky's comments about ends and means were to influence the American community organizer Alinsky (1970, p. 208), a conflict strategist, when he wrote:

> Means and ends are so qualitatively interrelated that the question of the ends justifying the means is unreal non- sense. The true question has never been the proverbial one, "Does the end justify the means?" but always has been and is "Does *this particular* end justify *this particular* means?"

Guild socialism arose in England as a variant of syndicalism in the early 1900s. Like the French variety, it also argued for workers' control of industry, rather than state control. However, it was against direct action or selective violence. In this regard, both Fabian socialism and guild socialism acknowledged the issue of means and ends, since both ideologies were opposed to violence as a means of reaching the ends of a just society. Guild socialism died out in England by the late 1920s but had an impact on the concept of trade-union-based social welfare or social services. In this con- cept, the collective bargaining unit or organization, rather than the state, becomes the transfer agent.

Maoism, a Chinese interpretation and adaptation of Marxism by Mao Tse-tung, emerged in China in the early part of the 20th century (Rejai,

1991). Mao argued that whereas the European variation of socialism expects its major audience to be urban populations and industrial workers, a semicolonial and semifeudal country like China (China had colonial status to several imperial nations like Japan, England, and the United States) should focus on rural populations and farmworkers. Mao contended that the ideological conversion of the rural hinterland was necessary (and, in fact, it ultimately produced the Chinese revolution). The idea of community-based social welfare, rather than state-based social welfare, in China (discussed in chapter 3) originated with this perspective.

In the European tradition of Marxism, the works of later writers were also influential. Lukacs (1971) continued the Marxist position that relationships between human beings are transformed into commodity relations and into class relations, especially under capitalism, and that the concept of the market has been deified and is used to justify existing power relationships. Gramsci (1971) argued that an alliance between the ruling classes and a large number of intellectuals has contributed to the creation of an ideological hegemony (like the concept of rationality and efficiency in modern business management) to continue the capitalist design of human relationships. Althusser (1971) stated that ideology is a potent instrument that defines what and how people think. Thus, people look at their relationships not as they are but as they are prompted to do by a given ideology. In societies dominated by capitalism, "it cements a system of class domination" (McLellan, 1986, p. 33).

In Brazil, Freire (1970) contended that although certain ideologies function as instruments of oppression, it is possible to transform human beings, however much they are trained to accept the existing ideological hegemonies, into questioning the contradictions (like differential reward systems in the labor market or differential transfer systems in social welfare) in any culture. In many parts of Latin America, many Catholic priests have been supporting this idea, which is now called liberation theology.

In sum, the Marxist legacy on ideology seems to have contributed the following key ideas:

- Ideology is a prescription for thinking and perceiving.
- Such thinking and perceiving include class relations, relations between a citizen and the church, between a citizen and the state, between the church and the state, and between the worker and the manager.
- There is lack of agreement about the legitimacy of violence as a means.
- There is lack of agreement about ends justifying the means, in general.
- There is lack of agreement about what is the proper unit to make socialism feasible: the community or the state.

- There is lack of agreement about who is the proper transfer agent: the community, the trade union, or the state.
- There is almost uniform agreement about the value of labor.

THE FRANKFURT SCHOOL

The Frankfurt school represents a vast intellectual tradition in the social sciences that has been influenced by Karl Marx, Sigmund Freud, and Max Weber. In this tradition, one of the earlier works on ideology was by Mannheim (1936). Influenced by the Marxist ambivalence to the concept of ideology because of its negative and critical meanings, Mannheim converted the negative meaning into a clearly defined concept of *ideology* and the critical meaning into a clearly defined concept of *utopia*. The prescriptions for thinking and perceiving, devised and used by the ruling or dominant classes, are ideology, whereas the aspirations and perceptions of the oppressed or subjected classes are utopia. The function of ideology is to preserve the status quo, whereas the function of utopia is to guide radical social change. Members of oppressed groups who subscribe to ideology (rather than to utopia) are said to have *false consciousness,* a concept comparable with *identification with the aggressor* in psychodynamic or Freudian theory (A. Freud, 1967; see also Fanon, 1968).

Herbert Marcuse became interested in psychoanalytic theory later in life. Trained in Hegelian and Marxist thought, he sought a synthesis between Marxism and Freudian psychoanalysis. For Marcuse, the Freudian concept of the unconscious was important because his concern with human consciousness predated his interest in psychoanalysis. The unconscious, he believed, could be used to view the fundamental conflicts in society.

Marcuse (1966) also extended the Freudian intrapsychic processes of repression and the reality principle in his creation of two new concepts: surplus repression and performance principle. *Surplus repression* is an extension of Marx's concept of surplus value, which refers to profits made through the exploitation of a person's labor. It is an intrapsychic process whereby repression is used to justify the domination of one group (class) over another. In this regard, Marcuse discussed the quantification of human relationships, which facilitates a certain social order (capitalism). The *performance principle,* Marcuse's term for Freud's reality principle, is a process by which "body and mind are made into instruments of alienated labor" (Marcuse, 1966, p. 46). In his discussion of the performance principle, Robinson (1969, pp. 205–206) observed that the "desexualization of the body resulted in a radical reduction of man's potential for pleasure. . . . Libido became concentrated in one part of the body, namely the genitals, in order to have the rest of the body free for use as an instrument of labor."

In *Eros and Civilization,* Marcuse (1955) argued that the stories of Oedipus and Prometheus became popular in the Western world because they supported the patriarchal family and the performance principle, respectively.

The stories of Narcissus (used by Freud to describe neurotic self-love, called narcissism) and Orpheus, "the voice that does not command but sings," were unpopular because they were too far from the "reality principle" that supports the work ethic (Marcuse, 1966, p. 161). Most theorists in the Freudian mainstream, it should be noted, consider the pleasure principle undesirable and believe it must be held in check by the reality principle. For Marcuse, the pleasure principle is held in check by the performance principle, which is compatible with the ideology of capitalism.

For Erich Fromm, the ideology of the external environment becomes "anchored" in the character structure (personality) and is internalized by the individual. He held that the family is produced by a certain economic environment and political ideology, which, in turn, helps nurture certain ideologies in the character structure of infants who will later be supportive of that economic order and ideology. Fromm (1941) suggested that when human beings find themselves incapable of handling freedom, they "escape" to ideologies like fascism. His concern about the individual was, in most of his writings, centered on the concept of identity and need. According to Fromm (1955), *identity* is the process by which one's personality is forged not by *being* someone but by *belonging* to someone. Furthermore, human beings have *extra-biological needs:* the need for creative outlets, for natural roots, to define one's identity, and for a frame of reference. Fromm is responsible for the formulation of a new idea. It is not the individual who is sick but a certain kind of society that makes people sick. He argued that mental or emotional "sickness" in individuals is brought about by a sick society.

Fromm believed that an individual cultivates social character during childhood through the ideologies of child rearing. He argued that social character is formed during the developmental phases and is structured by the interaction among the psychological, cultural, macroeconomic, and technical bases of society. When social character makes demands on the individual that do not fulfill his or her extra-biological needs, the person becomes "sick."

Berger and Luckman (1967) stated that ideologies are the source of legitimation of what is socially construed to be "truth." Such truth usually develops at four levels: the linguistic, the aphoristic, the institutional, and the ideological. The linguistic level involves the use of a word (for example, the word *sick*); the aphoristic level prescribes appropriate behavior associated with the word (for instance, sick people "need treatment"); the institutional level, where the words and the aphorisms lead to social roles appropriate for the situation (such as the role of "treatment agent or healer" who is about to take care of the sick "patient"); and the ideological level, where the infrastructure of roles is given legitimation and normative dignity (for example, the illness, not the patient, should be blamed for the situation, the patient should submit to an examination and treatment by the healer, the healer should be recompensated either by the patient or by a third party, and the healer should be given a relatively high status in the status hierarchy of his or her culture).

Habermas (1970) noted that awareness of the presence of ideology is rather new and is to be found in modern (meaning, for the most part, industrial) rather than traditional (meaning, for the most part, preindustrial) societies. He stated that traditional societies relied on a restricted and hierarchically oriented source of authority. Story lines or myths (like the Prophet said, "Do this" or "Don't do that") legitimated the exercise of authority, and there was no competition between such story lines (except when there was clear collision between two religious systems, like Christianity and Islam or Islam and Hinduism). One was not confused by two story lines, but was expected to be loyal to only one. In contrast, modern societies do not demand such loyalty to one myth or story line but have multiple, competing ideologies. Consequently, intellectuals become aware of the presence of competing ideologies on the lives of people. Put differently, traditional societies depend on one ideology, which is a religious ideology that prescribes all behavior—in the family, in the economic arena, and in the political arena—whereas in modern societies the multiple competing ideologies are geared toward legitimating behavior in different arenas.

Alvin Gouldner, originally an American empiricist in the tradition of structural functionalism (see chapter 8), became fascinated with the ideas of the Frankfurt school later in his career. In *The Coming Crisis of Western Sociology* (1970), he argued that value-free scientific ventures in the social sciences are impossible and that most sociological (and, by implication, other social science) theories are ideologically biased in one direction or another. In *The Dialectic of Ideology and Technology* (1976), he suggested that since the French Revolution, the capitalist societies had rejected any traditional authority and had anchored their belief systems on science, technology, and rationality. Such belief systems have led to a social construction of the meaning of science, technology, and rationality and have become the ideology of modern societies. The presence of such ideologies is to be seen in the development of the professions and in the professionalization of business, in general, or nonprofit management, in particular. What is called "scientific management" or "scientific professional practice" is facilitating "the pursuit of some but not all courses of *action,* and thus [encouraging] us to change or to accept the world as it is, to say yea or nay to it" (Gouldner, 1970, p. 47).

THE NON–MARXIST TRADITION

The non-Marxist tradition represents a number of German, British, and American scholars who have written about ideology. In this tradition, it is important first to list Weber's classic thesis, *The Protestant Ethic and the Spirit of Capitalism* (1922/1958). In this book, Weber argued that certain key values, such as thrift; equality; a focus on work; a focus on life in this world, rather than on the world after death; and an emphasis on rationality, emerged in England, the United States, and parts of western Europe from Protestantism, especially the reformation efforts of Calvinism. These key values led to the development of capitalism as an ideology, which, in turn, is responsible for the wealth of the nations in western Europe and North America. In another work, Weber (1946) noted that an important development in modern societies is the growth of *rational authority* (which is the basis of bureaucracy or most modern organizational behavior).

Responding to Weber's thesis about the Protestant ethic and capitalism, both Tawney (1926) and Samuelsson (1961) contended that historically neither capitalism nor wealth building was a consequence of the Protestant ethic and that the two can emerge in various non-Protestant settings. More, recently, Berger (1986) observed that wealth building in the Pacific Rim has taken place (see chapter 5 for a discussion of Berger's thesis), primarily because of the growth of capitalism, but that this region is mostly Buddhist, rather than Protestant.

Continuing in the non-Marxist tradition, Freud (1939; see also A. Freud, 1967) observed that ideology has important functions in legitimating authority. According to him, ideology creates a positive relationship between the governor and the governed, and often this relationship manifests libidinal ties (cf. McLellan, 1986).

After World War II, Adorno, Frankel-Brunswik, Levinson, and Sanford (1950), of the Frankfurt school, found that authoritarianism could be an ideology somewhat close to fascism and that it develops in childhood. Lipset (1963) observed that the American working class, instead of embracing a utopia, as Mannheim (1936) had proposed, had become committed to an ideology of authoritarianism, primarily because of its collective bargaining successes (at that time). Arendt (1958), who also dealt with the development of authoritarian ideologies, suggested that ideology finds "truth," orders history, defines reality, and organizes logic and that it can be either manifest or latent, overt or covert.

Two American scholars, Bendix (1956) and Marnell (1968), working independently, developed classification schemes of ideologies that were prominent in England and the United States. Bendix was interested in the ideologies of work, or the legitimation of authority in economic behavior. He proposed that four ideologies of work had been prominent in both countries: the theory of dependence, laissez-faire, social Darwinism, and human relations theory.

The *theory of dependence,* devised by John Stuart Mill during the early days of industrialization, stated that the laboring poor need to be treated like children and to be protected from themselves.

According to *laissez-faire* (French for "leave them alone"), the state should leave the poor alone and should not bother the rich with taxes or transfer schemes.

In *social Darwinism,* social groups were compared to biological species in Darwinian biology. In Darwin's biological theory, only the "fit" or the "able" species, which are capable of adaptation, survive. When the motto of this ideology, "the survival of the fittest," was applied to social groups, it meant that only social groups who were fit or able should be allowed to survive and that those who are not (such as the poor) should not be helped to continue by giving them charity or transfer payments.

Human relations theory was adapted from the human relations school of managerial orientation that evolved after the Great Depression of the 1930s. According to this theory, laboring groups should be treated with dignity and equality.

Marnell (1968) translated the four ideologies of work into four ideologies that influenced the two societies in general: deism, utilitarianism, social Darwinism, and pragmatism. The basic premise of *deism,* which today seems to be the opposite of feminism, was that patriarchy is justified by natural law. The assumption of deism was that authority flows from a male God (referred to as "He"), to a male head of state (called the king), and then to a male head of household (known as the patriarch).

Utilitarianism fostered the "maximal happiness of the maximal number," an axiom adapted from Jeremy Bentham. The origins and development of *social Darwinism,* discussed under Bendix's classification, were chronicled by the historian Hofstadter (1955). *Pragmatism,* summarized by the axiom "truth is successful experience," was uniquely American and was built on the educational philosophy of John Dewey.

A parallel ideology to the uniquely American pragmatism was *rationalism,* which developed in British politics. Michael Oakshott (quoted in McLellan, 1986, p. 53) stated that rationalism reflected "the politics of felt need," which was "interpreted by reason."

In the 1960s, Bell (1973) in the United States and Aron (1962) in France suggested that ideology had lost its relevance in the First and Second Worlds because their basic belief systems were firmly established. However, in the Third World, ideological debates were becoming more important because the legitimation of governing systems had not yet been firmly established. Some scholars (see, for example, Choi, Martin, Chatterjee, & Holland, 1978) reacted to this claim by arguing that the emergence of black nationalism, feminism, and religious fundamentalism in the United States in the 1960s and in the 1970s did not support the idea that ideology was no longer relevant. They noted that what was important, perhaps, was the difference between the ideologies of the rich and the managerial classes (the persons occupying top positions on the stratification ladders) and of the poor, the divided laboring classes (the persons occupying the lower positions on the stratification ladders). Feuer (1975) observed that ideology, in whatever disguise, was built on the following premises: (1) that there is a myth or a story line for people to follow as a self-evident truth; (2) that there is a group of chosen people (who are blessed by the myth of the story line and who will inherit the Earth); and (3) that there are a set of doctrines prescribing the behavior of the chosen people, both among themselves and with outsiders.

In an effort to understand ideology as a variable in empirical research, Hofstede (1980a, 1980b, 1983, 1991) proposed that four component dimensions, which often constitute an ideological core, vary from national culture to national culture. They are (1) the permissible degree of individualism; (2) the acknowledgment of power inequality; (3) the degree of uncertainty avoidance; and (4) assertive acquisition (attributed to masculine roles) versus submissive, conflict-avoidance sharing and care providing (attributed to feminine roles). On such a scale, Scandinavian cultures would rank low on 1, 2, and 4 and high on 3, and the United States would rate high on 1 and 4 and low on 2 and 3. In the Second World, Russia and China would rank low on 1, high on 2 and 3, and somewhat conflicted on 4. In the Third World, India and Pakistan would rate low on 1 (though this may be changing) and 4 and high on 2 and 3.

IDEOLOGY AND SOCIAL WELFARE

CONTRIBUTIONS BY SOCIAL WORK SCHOLARS

While sociologists have been engaged in defining and understanding the concept of ideology, many social work scholars have given ad hoc definitions of the term and have envisioned certain types of social welfare (and, by implication, certain designs of human relationships) as desirable. Such efforts began in the United States in the 1890s and were led mostly by a group of women who were both scholars and activists.

The ideologies of the Protestant ethic and of capitalism, which Weber (1922/1958) stated was responsible for the wealth of nations, influenced early social workers like Jane Addams, Mary Richmond, Sophonisba Breckinridge, Katherine B. Davis, Frances A. Kellor, and Edith Abbott, who became "scientists of society" (Fitzpatrick, 1990) and drew attention to the pockets of poverty, vulnerability, and victimization in the wealthiest nation (the United States). These American women were all Protestants with Calvinistic backgrounds from the upper or upper middle class, and all had been socialized by the capitalist system. And some of them were suspected of being socialist sympathizers (Fitzpatrick, 1990).

All but Addams and Richmond were at the University of Chicago, and Addams started her model of social work (the settlement movement) in the city of Chicago. For the most part, they designed social welfare policy and the social work profession within a capitalistic framework. They argued not for a radical redistribution of income or wealth but for respect for the ability of individuals to climb from lower to higher positions on the class ladder.

All were immensely dignified women, at a time when women were second-class citizens and could only teach school, practice nursing, or prosletyze unbelievers. From these roles that the capitalistic society allowed them, they developed a model of quiet and dignified struggle for individual mobility and growth (comparable to individual salvation). In essence, they were committed to the ideologies of individualism, personal liberty, equality, and justice.

The alleged "socialist sympathies" of these pioneering women came to be identified as the American "liberal tradition," which refers to community and state intervention to support marginal and vulnerable groups. The community intervention efforts that these women developed defined what nongovernmental efforts in social problem solving can be like and became a model of the "privatization" of social welfare. The rationale for state intervention was developed later (in the 1930s and 1940s) by many, including Charlotte Towle (discussed later). This American liberal tradition (of community and state intervention for solving social problems), unlike the English liberal tradition described earlier, formed almost as a polar opposite of social Darwinism and rested on the belief that the state or the community can or should intervene to support marginal and vulnerable groups. It was at the core of the newly emergent social work profession. The belief system of this tradition asserts the importance of community and state intervention and sets a model for community-level intervention and for private (rather than public) social welfare. Scholars of social welfare policy still use this tradition (and its opposite, conservatism, referring to the belief system that the community and the state cannot and should not try to solve social problems) as a benchmark for policy analysis (see Karger & Stoesz, 1994; Tropman, 1989).

A comparable model of private and community-based social intervention for community problem solving developed in Britain (at Toynbee Hall) is the late 19th century and in India during the early 1900s. In 1922, India's Nobel laureate Rabindranath Tagore started a pioneering private community development effort, called Rural Reconstruction, in Sriniketan, about 100 miles north of Calcutta. This effort was emulated by Mahatma Gandhi on the west coast of India, and became the prototype of the regional community development model that many Third World countries were using by the mid-1950s (United Nations, 1955).

Thus, private and community-based social interventions evolved in parts of the First and Third Worlds, but not in the Second World, perhaps because of the emphasis on the state as the only intervention agent. As was indicated in chapter 3, state-sponsored, community-based efforts are common in the Second World, and private efforts are being attempted only since the breakup of the Soviet Union in the early 1990s.

IDEOLOGY, HUMAN NEEDS, AND HUMAN VALUES

Types of Needs

Charlotte Towle, a social worker by background and profession, taught at the University of Chicago for many years. Her seminal work, *Common Human Needs,* is a landmark monograph on the theories of human need. First published in 1945 by the Bureau of Public Assistance, U.S. Federal Security Administration, it was suppressed by the federal government in 1951 (the same year that the American Medical Association called it a socialist position paper), then distributed by the American Association of Social Workers, and reissued by the National Association of Social Workers in 1987 (see Towle, 1945/1987).

Towle's work remains a pioneering humanist work on the vulnerability of human beings. It is indeed a position paper in favor of income transfer to poor and vulnerable people, but its thesis is the universality of human needs, from infancy to old age. These needs are physical well-being, psychological (emotional) well-being, intellectual well-being, people's relationships with each other, and spiritual well-being. These forms of well-being are the core of common human needs. Any "ill-being," so to speak, in any of these needs, leads to human problems that require assistance because it creates anxiety, conflict, and disharmony. People frequently return to earlier satisfactory behavior when faced with any ill-being and have a "strong impulse to live beyond a mere survival level" (Towle, 1945/1987, p. 34). In short, people have needs ranging from basic, physical well-being to higher, spiritual well-being.

Maslow (1962) suggested that human needs are hierarchical in nature. Some needs, like need for food, water, and warmth, are basic and must be met before a person can worry about meeting his or her needs for justice, beauty, or order. If basic needs are not met, then a person is likely to become ill. Basic needs are deficiency needs. Another set of needs are growth needs or meta-needs, like the need for intellectual fulfillment, order, and an aesthetic environment. When meta-needs are not met, a person becomes apathetic and alienated.

Prescriptions for Meeting Needs

Returning to the matter of ideology and human needs, it seems that every ideology is a prescription for meeting human needs. Thus, patriarchy is an ideology that requires the basic needs of males to be met before the needs of females (Brownmiller, 1975) and seems to be less concerned about the meta-needs of women than of men. Capitalism, although it acknowledged that human needs are personal (see Table 4-1), was built with the support of the patriarchal family and deism (Orloff, 1993; Schumpeter, 1950) and consequently institutionalized the need-meeting prescriptions with gender inequality. It also created another hierarchy, on the basis of social class (and often race). People at the top of the class or stratification ladder met their basic needs easily, so meeting their meta-needs was their prime concern, whereas meeting just basic needs was a problem for persons at the lower end of the class hierarchy and social Darwinism gave further legitimacy to this unequal prescription for meeting needs. On the other hand, rationalism in England

and pragmatism in the United States provided the ideological premise for caring for victims of gender, class, and racial inequality.

In the United States, democracy started with and, for the most part, remained dependent on patriarchy and capitalism (de Tocqueville, 1835/1969; Trattner, 1979). American immigration patterns, coupled with ideology of capitalist democracy, produced uniform geographic communities of ethnicity and class. Seeking community was never as important in the United States as seeking liberty and equality. Therefore, community organization frequently meant a concern with city services and the retention of property values. Seeking solidarity was not a major American theme, except in immigrant communities (see Wirth, 1939), in communities of color (Chatterjee, 1967) that were facing a hostile environment, and in communities and organizations involved in the labor movement (Dickman, 1987; see also Lipset, 1963). The Democratic Party has gained most of its support in these three constituencies, so it is not surprising that most social welfare efforts have come from that party.

In contrast, in western Europe (especially in the First World countries) democracy developed as a function of the tension between three dominant ideologies: patriarchy, capitalism, and socialism (Schumpeter, 1950). Patriarchy, in the form of deism and imperialism, gave legitimacy to the monarchies, aristocracies, and upper classes of Europe, as well as to the colonialism of many European powers. Capitalism gave legitimacy to wealth building. Socialism, ranging from the Fabian kind in England to syndicalism and anarchist socialism on the Continent, was always prominent in calling for equality in distribution, both in industry and in the affairs of the state (Dumont, 1977; Gould, 1993).

Thus, the English-speaking and non-English-speaking parts of the First World, although both capitalist, have seen two different ideological configurations of responses to meeting human needs. The English-speaking countries, primarily England, Australia, Canada, and the United States, have experienced the impact of patriarchy, capitalism, and democracy, and England experienced the impact of Fabian socialism, which is a gentle and incremental form of socialism. In contrast, the non-English-speaking part of the First World has undergone strong crosscurrents of patriarchy (deism), capitalism, and several types of militant socialism. These two different ideological heritages perhaps contributed to two different visions of meeting human needs and, in turn, two different ways of building the welfare state. I will return to this theme several times in this book.

For the most part, the ideology common to the Second World was Lenin's (and Stalin's) interpretation of socialism. Democracy, with the appropriate political institutions to support it, is rather new in most Second World countries. Besides socialism, patriarchy inherent in Catholicism, various forms of Orthodox Christianity, and Islam were the ideological legacies. But it was socialism that enforced the idea of meeting human needs at the state level.

Without socialism, meeting human needs might have been left to the family and the community.

The Third World has seen a vast mixture of ideological prescriptions for meeting human needs. Most of the Third World countries subscribe to the religious legacies of patriarchy in the form of classic Islam, Catholicism, Buddhism, or Hinduism. The caregiving systems inherent in these religious ideologies are in the family and the community, and the concept of the state is new. Other than India, which has succeeded in building democratic institutions, democracy has not yet developed in other parts of the Third World. India has not yet built a welfare state, and the caregiving functions in that country rest at the family and the community levels. Furthermore, India has a legacy of Gandhianism, which is essentially a patriarchal ideology that justifies poverty and justice in an agrarian society. In most other parts of the Third World, human needs are met by patriarchal religious institutions at the family and the community (rather than the state) levels.

Ideology and Methodology

It seems that almost any study that has attributed a given behavior to a given ideology has used a qualitative historical method (see, for example, Berger, 1986; Choi et al., 1978; George & Wilding, 1977; Schumpeter, 1950). The reasons for using these methods are twofold: (1) the belief that ideology is a cause for something (such as the welfare state) originated in Marxist thought and in Marxist methodology, which use historical analysis as a framework, and (2) the fact that *ideology* has never been clearly defined, except in general terms to mean prescriptions for the behavior of large groups like communities, elite groups, and nations. One can argue that what human values are to the individual, ideology is to the large group. Studies of human values are common, both those that use positivistic and phenomenological methods, but studies of ideologies, with the methodological rigors of design, sample, and measurement, have never been plentiful in the social sciences.

Ideology: A Summary

All the traditions discussed in this chapter seem to agree with the premise that ideology is a prescription or design for human relationships. Some ideologies prescribe egalitarianism in human relations, whereas others prescribe hierarchy. Ideology also directs humans' relationship with nature, artifacts, and time. It is applicable to human activities in the family, in work, in governance, and in the realm of spirituality. Built into it are certain perceptions about human needs and human values. In a way, each ideological system is an effort to balance human needs and attempts to respond to them.

WHOSE IDEOLOGY?

It is perhaps easy to understand that human values are motivators of or reasons for behavior at the individual level. If ideology is a prescription for group behavior, then it is fair to ask: Whose behavior? Put another way, the question is, the ideology of which group?

In the well-known works on the relationship between ideology and social welfare discussed in this section, it seems that most of the authors (though not all) are interested in the ideology of elites or elite groups. Who are the elite groups? Mills (1956) referred to three types of elites in the United States (economic, political, and military) and, by implication, in all industrialized countries. The economic elite originated from a country's upper class, and, for the most part, the political elite originated from the upper and upper middle classes. Thus, the term *elites* means groups at the top of the social class ladder of an industrial society, and it follows that understanding class rankings and class structures may be an important factor in understanding the welfare state. One may rephrase the concept of the elites and their ideologies to the upper classes and their ideologies.

The ideas of class and class ideologies are found in sociology, political sociology, and political science. Earlier, I discussed the authoritarianism of the American working class (Lipset, 1963), which is a class ideology. Gans (1972) showed that there is an identifiable working-class ideology, and Wilensky (1975) argued extensively that middle- and working-class attitudes and values are an important factor in welfare state spending. (Wilensky's work is discussed in chapter 9.) However, it seems that not many writers have followed this route (of exploring the relationship between class ideologies and social welfare), except with regard to the ideologies of the elites.

The ideas of ethnic, ethnolingual, and ethnoreligious ideologies have also been examined in the social sciences. In fact Weber's (1922/1958) famous thesis about the Protestant ethic and the spirit of capitalism (mentioned earlier) is, put another way, a thesis about a given ethnoreligious group (Anglo-Saxon Protestants) and their ideology (capitalism). However, recent writings on the relationship between ideology and social welfare have not explored that route either.

In reviewing the infrastructure of social welfare (see chapter 2), one finds that the *collective legacy* about transfer—the ideologies of payers, of officials who oversee transfers, of transfer agents, of different categories of recipients, and of various providers—is important. However, as chapter 5 shows, most of the literature on ideology and social welfare has focused only on the collective legacy of the payers. In chapters 6 and 7, I return to the notion of conflict among the ideologies of transfer agents, providers, and recipients and of conflicts within nonelites. In sum, the answer to the question "Whose ideology?" often is the ideology of the elites and, by implication, the ideology of the upper and upper middle classes. By implication, it also is conflict within and between the social classes (as Mannheim, 1936, proposed).

IDEOLOGY: CAUSE OR JUSTIFICATION?

There are two approaches to the idea that certain ideologies are responsible for certain welfare systems: (1) the social welfare system represents a compromise among ideologies and that compromise is the cause of welfare systems and (2) welfare systems evolve for several reasons but are either justified or challenged by the ideological preferences of key groups, and hence ideology is the justification for welfare systems. Furthermore, ideology as cause or justification can be applied to an entire national system or to different pieces of a national system. When it is applied to different pieces of a national system, it is possible that in a given national system the ideology of income or health care is not compatible with the ideology of education or housing. For example, the ideology of health care in the United States calls for commodified, capitalistic production and distribution of health care, but that same country has also had a partially decommodified, universal educational system. In other words, the ideology of production and distribution in one sector (health care) of that society is not the same in another (public education). Figure 4-1 is a model for conceptualizing the complex relationship between ideology and social welfare.

Figure 4-1.
Four Ways of Viewing Ideology and Social Welfare

	Social Welfare among National Systems	Social Welfare within National Systems
Ideology as Cause	Thesis 1: The variations among national systems are due to ideology.	Thesis 2: The variations within national systems are due to ideology.
Ideology as Justification	Thesis 3: The variations among national systems are justified by ideology.	Thesis 4: The variations within national systems are justified by ideology.

REFERENCES

Adorno, T., Frankel-Brunswik, E., Levinson, D. J., & Sanford, R. N. (1950). *The authoritarian personality*. New York: Harper & Row.

Alinsky, S. (1970). Of ends and means. In F. M. Cox, J. L. Ehrlich, J. Rothman, & J. E. Tropman (Eds.), *Strategies for community organization* (pp. 199–208). Itasca, IL: F. E. Peacock.

Althusser, A. (1971). *Lenin and philosophy*. London: New Left Books.

Arendt, H. (1958). *The origins of totalitarianism*. New York: Harcourt, Brace, & World.

Aron, R. (1962). *The opium of the intellectuals*. Garden City, NY: Doubleday.

Balgopal, P., & Vassil, T. (1983). *Groups in social work: An ecological perspective*. New York: Macmillan.

Bell, D. (1973). *The coming of post-industrial society*. New York: Basic Books.

Bendix, R. (1956). *Work and authority in industry*. New York: Harper & Row.

Berger, P. (1986). *The capitalist revolution*. New York: Basic Books.

Berger, P., & Luckman, T. (1967). *The social construction of reality*. Garden City, NY: Doubleday Anchor Books.

Bottomore, T. (Ed.). (1983). *A dictionary of Marxist thought*. Cambridge, MA: Harvard University Press.

Brown, L. N. (1991). *Groups for growth and change*. New York: Longman.

Brownmiller, S. (1975). *Against our will*. New York: Simon & Schuster.

Chatterjee, P. (1967). Neighborhoods by choice or compulsion: A focus for settlement policy. *Social Work, 12,* 95–101.

Chatterjee, P. (1979). A market of human vulnerability. *Social Development Issues, 3,* 1–12.

Choi, I., Martin, E., Chatterjee, P., & Holland, T. (1978). Ideology and social welfare. *Indian Journal of Social Work, 39*(2), 139–160.

Coser, L. (1960). Intellectuals and men of power. In G. B. de Huszer (Ed.), *The intellectuals: A controversial portrait* (p. 80). New York: Free Press.

Coyle, G. L. (1948). *Group work with American youth: A guide to the practice of leadership*. New York: Harper & Row.

Crick, B. (1987). *Socialism*. Minneapolis: University of Minnesota Press.

de Tocqueville, A. (1969). *Democracy in America* (Vols. 1 & 2). Garden City, NY: Doubleday. (Original work published 1835)

Dickman, H. (1987). *Industrial democracy in America: Ideological origins of national labor relations policy*. La Salle, IL: Open Court.

Dolbeare, K. M., & Dolbeare, P. (1971). *American ideologies.* Chicago: Markham.

Dumont, L. (1977). *From Mandeville to Marx.* Chicago: University of Chicago Press.

Fanon, F. (1968). *The wretched of the earth.* New York: Grove Press.

Feuer, L. (1975). *Ideology and ideologists.* New York: Harper & Row.

Fitzpatrick, E. (1990). *Endless crusade.* New York: Oxford University Press.

Freire, P. (1970). *The pedagogy of the oppressed.* New York: Seabury Press.

Freud, A. (1967). *Group psychology and the analysis of the ego.* London: Hogarth Press.

Freud, S. (1939). *Totem and taboo.* Harmondsworth, England: Penguin Books.

Friedman, M. (1962). *Capitalism and freedom.* Chicago: University of Chicago Press.

Fromm, E. (1941). *Escape from freedom.* New York: Holt, Rinehart & Winston.

Fromm, E. (1955). *The sane society.* New York: Holt, Rinehart & Winston.

Gans, H. (1972). The positive functions of poverty. *American Journal of Sociology, 78,* 275–289.

George, V., & Wilding, P. (1977). *Ideology and social welfare.* Boston: Routledge & Kegan Paul.

Gould, A. (1993). *Capitalist welfare systems.* London: Longman.

Gouldner, A. (1970). *The coming crisis in Western Sociology.* New York: Basic Books.

Gouldner, A. (1976). *The dialectic of ideology and technology.* New York: Seabury Press.

Gramsci, A. (1971). *Selections from prison notebooks.* London: Lawrence & Wishart.

Groskind, F. (1994). Ideological influences on public support for assistance to poor families. *Social Work, 39,* 81–89.

Habermas, J. (1970). *Towards a rational society.* London: Heinemann.

Hofstadter, R. (1955). *Social Darwinism in American life.* Boston: Beacon Press.

Hofstede, G. (1980a). *Cultural consequences: International differences in work-related values.* Beverly Hills, CA: Sage Publications.

Hofstede, G. (1980b, Summer). Motivation, leadership, and organization: Do American theories apply abroad? *Organizational Dynamics,* pp. 42–63.

Hofstede, G. (1983, Fall). The cultural relativity of organizational practice and theories. *Journal of International Business Studies,* pp. 75–89.

Hofstede, G. (1991). *Cultures and organizations: Software of the mind*. London: McGraw-Hill.

Israel, J. (1971). *Alienation: From Marx to modern sociology*. Boston: Allyn & Bacon.

Jencks, C. (1972). *Inequality*. New York: Basic Books.

Karger, H. J., & Stoesz, D. (1994). *American social welfare policy*. New York: Longman.

Kropotkin P. (1969). *Mutual aid*. Boston: Porter Sargent. (Original work published 1902)

Lipset, S. M. (1963). Working class authoritarianism. In S. M. Lipset (Ed.), *Political man* (pp. 87–126). Garden City, NY: Doubleday.

Lukacs, G. (1971). *History and class consciousness*. Cambridge, MA: MIT Press.

Macarov, D. (1978). *The design of social welfare*. New York: Holt, Rinehart & Winston.

MacFarlane, A. (1987). *The culture of capitalism*. Oxford, England: Basil Blackwell.

Mannheim, K. (1936). *Ideology and utopia*. New York: Harcourt, Brace & World.

Marcuse, H. (1955). *Eros and civilization*. Boston: Beacon Press.

Marcuse, H. (1966). *Reason and revolution*. Boston: Beacon Press.

Marnell, W. (1968). *Man-made morals: Four ideologies which shaped England and America*. Garden City, NY: Doubleday.

Maslow, A. H. (1962). *Toward a psychology of being*. Princeton, NJ: Van Nostrand.

McLellan, D. (1986). *Ideology*. Minneapolis: University of Minnesota Press.

Mills, C. W. (1956). *The power elite*. New York: Oxford University Press.

Navarro, V. (Ed.). (1992). *Why the United States does not have a national health program*. Amityville, NY: Baywood.

Orloff, A. S. (1993). Gender and the social rights of citizenship. *American Sociological Review, 58,* 303–328.

Proudhon, P. (1969). *Selected writings of P. J. Proudhon*. Garden City, NY: Doubleday. (Original work published 1846)

Rejai, M. (1991). *Political ideologies*. Armonk, NY: M. E. Sharpe.

Robinson, P. A. (1969). *The Freudian left: Wilhelm Reich, Geza Roheim, Herbert Marcuse*. New York: Harper & Row.

Samuelsson, K. (1961). *Religion and economic action*. New York: Basic Books.

Schumpeter, J. (1950). *Capitalism, socialism, and democracy*. New York:

Harper & Row.

Smith, A. (1963). *An inquiry into the nature and causes of the wealth of nations.* New York: Modern Library. (Original work published 1776)

Sorel, G. (1963). The ethics of violence. In H. Ruitenbeek (Ed.), *Varieties of classic social theory* (pp. 365–384). New York: E. P. Dutton. (Original work published 1906)

Tawney, R. H. (1926). *Religion and the rise of capitalism.* New York: Harcourt, Brace.

Towle, C. (1987). *Common human needs.* Sliver Spring, MD: National Association of Social Workers. (Original work published 1945)

Trattner, W. I. (1979). *From Poor Law to welfare state.* New York: Free Press.

Tropman, J. E. (1989). *American values and social welfare.* Englewood Cliffs, NJ: Prentice Hall.

Trotsky, L. (1963). Their morals and ours. In L. Trotsky, J. Dewey, & G. Novack (Eds.), *Their morals and ours* (pp. 9–39). New York: Merit Publishers. (Original work published 1938)

United Nations. (1955). *Urban and rural community development.* Petropolis: Brazilian Committee of the International Conference of Social Work.

Walby, S. (1990). *Theorizing patriarchy.* London: Basil Blackwell.

Weber, M. (1946). *From Max Weber: Essays in sociology* (H. H. Gerth and C. W. Mills, Trans.). New York: Oxford University Press.

Weber, M. (1958). *The Protestant ethic and the spirit of capitalism.* New York: Charles Scribner's Sons. (Original work published 1922)

Wilensky, H. (1975). *The welfare state and equality.* Berkeley: University of California Press.

Wirth, L. (1939). *The ghetto.* Chicago: University of Chicago Press.

5

WELFARE IS AN IDEOLOGICAL COMPROMISE: 2

The essence of revolution is not struggle for bread; it is struggle for dignity.

Adolfo Gilly, in Fanon, *A Dying Colonialism*

In chapters 2 and 4, I noted that the relationship between ideology and social welfare can be viewed in four ways. Figure 4-1 summarized four theses and illustrated that each represents a variant of the basic hypothesis that social welfare is a function of ideology. The first two theses divide ideology into either the reason for or the justification of social welfare, and the second two depict ideology as influencing either the entire social welfare system of a national culture or only a part of that system (like income maintenance or health care programs). In this chapter, I elaborate on these four theses.

ON REASONS AND JUSTIFICATIONS

Ideology as reason and ideology as justification differ on several points. Ideology as reason assumes that a basic commitment to certain provisions for all citizens has led to the development of the social welfare system, whereas ideology as justification assumes that the system evolved because of a series of complex econopolitical factors and that ideology is being used to justify the system's continued existence. Thus, ideology as reason refers to the use of ideology before the fact (before a social welfare system has been established), whereas ideology as justification means that the ideology is used as a rationale after the fact (after a social welfare system has been established). In the first case, the idea of social provisions was embedded in the ideology, and the social welfare system merely established compliance with the ideology. In the second case, the idea of social provisions either never arose or was ignored earlier. After the social welfare system was established for reasons other than an ideological heritage, then ideology was used to justify the presence of social provisions. Furthermore, the proposition of ideology as reason seems to be value directed, with basic commitments to equality or justice, whereas that of ideology as justification seems to be goal directed, with commitments to established interest groups. Figures 5-1 and 5-2 graphically illustrate this point.

On Entire Systems and Subsystems

Some scholars prefer to study an entire national social welfare system and explore its possible relationship to ideology. In contrast, others prefer to review a part of the national welfare system, like the income maintenance devices, health care organizations, or other subsystems, and then trace the specific relationship of that part to ideology.

Thesis 1: Variations between National Systems Are Due to Ideology

This thesis is perhaps the most popular among scholars who view welfare as a function of ideology. The basic argument begins with the positions of Adam Smith and Karl Marx, with Smith's (the ideology of capitalism)

Figure 5-1.
Ideology as the Reason for Social Welfare

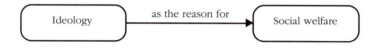

Figure 5-2.
Ideology as Justification for Social Welfare

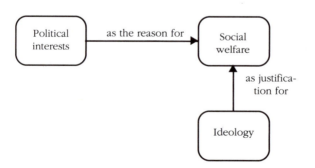

belief that the state *should not* promise entitlement to its citizens and Marx's axiom (the ideology of socialism) that the state *should* both promise and provide it. In both positions, patriarchy, or deism, is present (despite the efforts of Marx and Friedrich Engles to promote gender egalitarianism) and is the reason for granting higher entitlement to males than to females.

The classic positions of capitalism and socialism toward social welfare are illustrated in M. Friedman's (1962) *Capitalism and Freedom* and in Kropotkins's (1902/1969) *Mutual Aid*. At the end of his book, Friedman seemed to agree with the proposition that the state should not attempt to help poor or needy people because it does such a poor job whenever it attempts to do so. Kropotkin (an anarchist socialist, discussed in chapter 4), however, argued not only that the state should engage in helping needy or poor people but that this helping process is a law of nature and has occurred in almost all societies from ancient times to the present. Kropotkin was not trained in anthropological methods, but the evidence he presented is anthropological in nature. Although Kropotkin's arguments may have been influenced more by his ideology (that the state should provide social welfare) than by his body of evidence, the same can be said about Friedman's commitment to the ideology of free-market capitalism.

The position of Proudhon (1846/1969, p. 57), another anarchist, is close to Kropotkin's. Proudhon believed that socialism, applied at the community level, would bring about "a society that is not based on convention, but on reality; a society that converts the division of labor into a scientific instrument; a society that stops men from being the slaves of machines and foresees the crisis that these will cause." The crises that he referred to are the creation of vulnerabilities in human beings, which call for state aid and intervention. Such vulnerabilities, he believed, are the fault not of individuals but of the social system's impact on individuals. They may surface as unemployment, disability, industrial accidents, or a poor match between the qualifications of individuals and the requirements of a technological system. Proudhon, like many other socialists, both anarchists and Fabians, was interested in predictable crises and how to build solutions, or safety nets, into social institutions to deal with or prevent these crises.

Influence of Industrializing Elites

Kerr, Dunlop, Harbison, and Myers (1965) presented a detailed argument in support of Proudhon's thesis. In their version of the thesis, industrialization of a society is started by an industrializing elite, of which there are five varieties: (1) the middle class, (2) dynastic leaders, (3) colonial administrators, (4) revolutionary intellectuals, and (5) nationalist leaders. Furthermore, the types of management, forms of protest, labor organizations, and nature of social welfare in a given national culture can be understood in relation to which of the five varieties ushers in industrialization. The ideology of the usher, then, influences the "rule-making process" in that society, which, in turn, influences the rules of the transfer process.

According to Kerr et al. (1965), exemplars of the countries in which industrialization was done by the five "ushers" are as follows: the middle class, Great Britain and the United States; dynastic leaders, Kuwait and Saudi Arabia; colonial administrators, India, Indonesia, and other colonial countries before independence; revolutionary intellectuals, Russia (from 1917 to 1989) and China (after 1948); and nationalist leaders, India, Indonesia, and other countries after independence. When the middle class industrializes a country, their ideology—capitalism and faith in a free-market system—determines the rules of the game. The state is a reluctant and sometimes recalcitrant provider of welfare, and individualistic direct services are often more popular than are collectivistic community organization or community development efforts.

When a dynastic elite industrializes a country, their ideology— paternalism–deism and a hierarchical design of human relationships—influences the rules of the game. The state is a paternalistic provider of welfare because it is the obligation of the nobility to take care of those who are socially beneath them. In addition to the Middle Eastern kingdoms and sheikhdoms of the late 20th century, 19th-century Germany under Bismarck is an example. When colonial administrators industrialize a country, their ideology (which is either racist or patronizing or both) will influence the *liaison elite* (appointed rulers from the mother country and their agents, a local elite from the colonized country) of the colony. In such cases, the relationship between ideology and social welfare may be different in the colonies than it is in the mother country.

When a revolutionary elite industrializes a country, their ideology is a predictor of the nature of social welfare. Thus, in the case of Bolshevik Russia or Castro's Cuba, the socialist ideologies of the revolutionaries influenced the nature of the social welfare systems in those countries. When nationalist leaders industrialize a country, the ideology of the leaders, who often fought for the country's independence, comes to influence the nature of social policy. This ideology is frequently a collectivistic ideology, sometimes with strong socialist overtones. In such cases, community organization and community development efforts, rather than individualistic direct services, are prevalent.

Titmuss and the London School

Richard M. Titmuss (1907–73), an English scholar and ideologue in favor of the welfare state, developed several arguments that linked ideology and the welfare state. As an ideologue, he was a Fabian socialist (see chapter 4). As a scholar, he was often dependent on historical and qualitative data. Almost all his works, some very famous in the literature on social welfare, reflect these qualities.

Between 1945 and 1973, Titmuss wrote essays and books on the welfare state. In all his works, including *Problems of Social Policy* (1950), *Essays on the Welfare State* (1958), *Social Policy* (1974), and *Commitment to Welfare* (1968), prescriptions for the state ("the state should") are interwoven into the arguments. Furthermore, his basic thesis can be reduced to Proudhon's idea of predictable crises: Because industrial societies generate many crises that are predictable, a safety net should be built into social institutions. The absence of a safety net, Titmuss contended, means that the society is committed to a "residual" form of social welfare, in which people in need or in crisis are dealt with on an ad hoc or after-the-crisis basis. In contrast, the presence of a safety net means that the society is committed to an "institutional" form of social welfare, in which social institutions are in place to deal with vulnerable human beings or those in predictable crises.

As Figure 2-1 indicated, the building of institutions to meet predictable crises should be ideologically supported by interweaving such ideologies into the *antecedent factors* or foundations of any transfer structure. For Titmuss, social welfare should be an *entitlement,* not a gratuity, and available regardless of race, class, or gender, as a *nonmarket distribution* and geared to meeting the needs of vulnerable people. The entire orientation is collectivistic (Fabian), rather than individualistic (pro–Adam Smith or capitalism). To Titmuss, a commitment to social welfare is moral, and the lack of commitment is immoral. What is moral is right, and what is immoral is wrong.

The moral orientation to social policy led Titmuss to another provocative argument in *The Gift Relationship* (1969). The central thesis of this book is that almost all societies establish some rules by which ill patients receive blood transfusions. In some societies (like Britain), donors are expected to give blood voluntarily to those who are needy, whereas in others (like the United States) donors are often recompensed for giving blood. (It should be noted that this work was published a decade before AIDS was identified as a disease.) Titmuss believed that giving blood freely is moral, right, and altruistic, whereas giving blood in a commercialized exchange is immoral, wrong, and self-serving. In the altruistic system (as in Britain), blood is easily available when needed, the cost per unit and the percentage wasted are low, and the transmission of communicable diseases (from donor to recipient) is rare. In the mercantile system (as in the United States), blood is not as easily available, the cost per unit and the percentage wasted are high, and the transmission of communicable diseases is frequent. Thus, in Titmuss's view it is the moral and right orientation that makes the British blood policy superior to the American blood policy.

Titmuss (and T. H. Marshall) educated one or more generations of English scholars of the welfare state. The publication of *Ideology and Social Welfare* (1977) by George and Wilding reflected their influence. This work presented an elaborate and carefully compiled thesis about ideology and social welfare. Outside England, the authors' position is sometimes thought of as the London school approach.

George and Wilding claimed that there have been four ideological orientations to the welfare state in Britain and that the evolution of the British welfare state was due to a compromise among these ideologies. The four orientations (or schools of thought) are (1) anticollectivism, (2) reluctant collectivism, (3) Fabian socialism, and (4) Marxism (see Table 5-1 for a summary of their discussion). The typology appears to be ordinal in that redistribution was extremely unwelcome among the anticollectivists, selectively tolerated by the reluctant collectivists, welcomed incrementally by the Fabian socialists, and welcomed immediately by the Marxists.

The anticollectivists see capitalism as self-regulating; the reluctant collectivists see it as not self-regulating but still the best foundation of society; the Fabians see it as an ideology that generates and perpetuates most inequalities; and the Marxists see it as an undesirable and alien ideology that corrupts all people. Furthermore, the anticollectivists are for a market economy, the reluctant collectivists and the Fabians are for a mixed economy, and the Marxists are for a planned economy.

To the idea of the welfare state, the anticollectivists are openly hostile, because they believe it undermines the free market. The reluctant collectivists are often for the privatization of social welfare, sometimes with state support (see Figure 2-6). The Fabians are for state-supported and state-administered social services that should move the state incrementally toward a total welfare state. The Marxists believe that a welfare state under regulated capitalism is a means of social control by the elites, that it is a way of hiding the basic weaknesses of capitalism, and that it should not coexist with a free or regulated market. The Marxist view of the welfare state is the socialist state. A welfare state in a nonsocialist state, Marxists believe, is a disguised means of placating the poor and the working classes. (I return to the Marxist views in chapters 6 and 7.)

Relating ideas to their proponents, George and Wilding suggested that the most notable anticollectivists were Friedrich A. von Hayek and Milton Friedman; that among the reluctant collectivists were John Maynard Keynes, William H. Beveridge, and John Kenneth Galbraith; that prominent Fabians included Richard Tawney, Richard Titmuss, and Charles A. Crosland; and that among the Marxists were Karl Marx, Friedrich Engels, Harold Laski, Lytton Strachey, and Ralph Miliband. The ideas of these people were discussed in chapter 2, and the impact of Laski in the Third World was covered in chapter 3.

The London school approach (of Titmuss and George and Wilding) bases its conclusions about the British situation on British historical data. However, because of the prominent intellectual location of the London school and its influence on scholars of social welfare and social policy in Australia, Canada, India, South Africa, and the United States, the London school thesis, that differences in social welfare within and among nations are due to ideology (a compromise of the four just discussed), is often taken as the only explanation for variations in the welfare state. Other explanations (outlined in chapters 6 through 9) are not as popular.

THESIS 2: VARIATIONS WITHIN NATIONAL SYSTEMS ARE DUE TO IDEOLOGY

Both liberals and conservatives (in the American sense) seem to agree with this thesis. However, the liberals' action plan that flows from this thesis is that such variations mean a poor form of social welfare and that a better form (which will be guided by more state intervention) is needed. In contrast, the conservatives' action plan also calls for a better form of social welfare but one guided by market principles (and reduced state intervention).

In chapter 4 I identified the contributions of Jane Addams and a group of pioneering women in introducing social welfare programs in the United States. Much of their efforts went into establishing the base of American private social welfare programs (see Figure 2-6) and legitimating state-supported social welfare (see Fitzpatrick, 1990). They were far from being Marxists (according to George & Wilding's, 1977, typology), but their ideologies could be placed somewhere between reluctant collectivism and Fabian socialism (although there was no organized Fabian tradition in the United States, Fabian ideas have always been popular with American social workers), which are the foundation of the American liberal tradition. In contrast, the social Darwinists' position (discussed in chapter 4) is similar to the anticollectivists'. In the 1980s President Ronald Reagan of the United States and Prime Minister Margaret Thatcher of England attempted to apply conservative (in the American sense) or anticollectivist (using George and Wilding's terminology) ideology to social policy.

The American liberal tradition was reflected in the positions of Charlotte Towle (discussed in chapter 4); the American social work profession; the Democratic Party; and the labor movement (Rayback, 1959). In contrast, the conservative tradition influenced American business and business school curricula (and as well as the business curricula of many other countries) and the Republican Party.

The thesis that the American welfare state was formed as a compromise between liberal and conservative ideologies and that this compromise is reflected in its diversified ideologies of income maintenance, health care, and the like has been supported by many writers. Handler and Hasenfeld (1991), Karger and Stoesz (1994), Murray (1984), Murray and Herrnstein (1994), Specht and Courtney (1993), Stoesz (1989), and Tropman (1989) showed how ideology has influenced the variations in the American welfare system in general, whereas Groskind (1994), Mechanic (1986), Navarro (1992), Rose (1992), Salamon (1992), and Waitzkin and Waterman (1974) studied

Table 5-1. Four Ideologies Discussed by George and Wilding

COMPONENTS	ANTICOLLECTIVISM	RELUCTANT COLLECTIVISM	FABIAN SOCIALISM	MARXISM
Values	Liberty Individualism Inevitability of inequality	Liberty Individualism Some efforts to change inequality	Liberty Fellowship Equality Deploring inequality	Liberty Collectivism Equality Active pursuit of equality
Basic assumptions	Perfect competition	Regulated competition	Planned and incremental state intervention	Central planning by the state
Visions of society	Inequality is the price of liberty	Make efforts to remove blatent inequalities	Promote equality	Remove class conflict
Role of the state	As little as possible—maintain competition	Some role in removing of inequalities	Substantial role in promoting equality	Exclusive role in maintaining equality
Role of the market	The ultimate regulator—not to be interfered with	Regulator of society with some help from other sources	Should be brought under state control incrementally	To be strictly kept under state control
Economy	Market economy	Mixed economy	Mixed economy	Planned economy
Taxation	Not for redistribution—uniform taxation	Redistribution to help the needy—progressive taxation	Stronger forms of redistribution (private wealth repulsive)—progressive taxation	Total redistribution (private wealth disallowed)—uniform taxation possible
Attitudes toward the welfare state	Welfare state undesirable	Welfare state tolerable	Welfare state desirable	Welfare state necessary

SOURCE: George, V., & Wilding, P. (1977). *Ideology and social welfare*. Boston: Routledge & Kegan Paul.

different subsets of the system, such as personal social services, income maintenance, and health care. Other writers have suggested that the same basic thesis holds true for the Scandinavian countries (Hansen, Ringen, Uusitalo, & Erickson, 1993) and for Australia (Beilharz, Condidine, & Watts, 1992).

Murray (1984) argued against a transfer system, or for what he called a "zero-transfer system." He, supported by several other conservatives, contended that a transfer system to poor people does not alleviate the problems of poverty but, rather, encourages the perpetuation of poverty (for a summary of this thesis, see Karger & Stoesz, 1994). This view was further developed by Murray and Herrnstein (1994).

This thesis, which fits the template of American conservatives and British anticollectivists, is essentially a revisited form of social Darwinism. It contends that the state should not aid the poor or the needy because by so doing, it fosters continued dependence and undermines growth. Furthermore, it argues that by instituting a series of transfer programs during the 1960s and 1970s, the United States has become a good case exemplar of why the state should not engage in transfer programs.

Tropman (1989) suggested that "a clash of values" in that country resulted in ideologically inconsistent programs in health care, income maintenance, and so forth. After a detailed and documented description of the American welfare state, Karger and Stoesz (1994, p. 422) attributed the current American welfare state to a compromise between the neoconservatives and the neoliberals, and they concluded,

> If other industrial countries can manage to provide adequate social services to their people without severely retarding economic development, if they can contain the incidence of poverty, homelessness, and crime, and if they can improve the quality of life for the population as a whole, surely the United States, which has abundant human and natural resources, can do the same.

Thus, Karger and Stoesz came down on the liberal side of the argument: that the state should engage in some adequate amount of transfer.

Specht and Courtney (1993) faulted American social workers for abandoning the traditional mission of social work—community and communalism—espoused by the founding mothers of American social work. They stated that American social workers are moving from the voluntary sector to private practice and for-profit activity in the market-exchange sector.

The authors discussed so far seem to support the hypothesis that variations in the welfare state as a whole, as exemplified by Australia, the Scandinavian countries, and the United States, are due to compromises between one or more ideological dualities. In contrast, some authors have limited their observations to a subsystem of the welfare system, such as health care, income maintenance, personal social services, or case management in public social services.

With regard to health care, Waitzkin and Waterman (1974) noted that capitalist and socialist societies have different views of the "sick role" (a term that Parsons, 1951, introduced). In capitalist societies, people who are sick become customers of the medical industry, which has a stratification system that corresponds to the stratification system of the larger society. For those who are positioned at various levels in the medical stratification system, the illness of others becomes a mercantile opportunity. The organized effort to make opportunity out of illness, later called the "commodification" of illness (Esping-Andersen, 1990; Navarro, 1992) or "medicalization" (see chapter 4), leads to medical imperialism.

Mechanic (1986) argued that extending health care to all in the United States would mean dealing with the problems of demand (for services) and supply (sufficient resources to provide health care to all regardless of the ability to pay for them). Thus, some form of rationing (see Figure 2-7) of health care would be necessary.

The basic issue is how illness is socially constructed. Should it be a commodity that creates a market (as in capitalism), or should it be a condition that leads to an entitlement (as in socialism)? In other words, should or should not the state supply it? The same either/or issues have been raised with regard to income maintenance and personal social services (Groskind, 1994; Rose, 1992; Salamon, 1992).

THESIS 3: VARIATIONS AMONG NATIONAL SYSTEMS ARE JUSTIFIED BY IDEOLOGY

George and Wilding (1977) classified Beveridge (1945) as a reluctant collectivist but admitted that, to him, social welfare was not an end in itself, prompted by ideology, but a means to an end, prompted by political necessity. In Beveridge's view, social welfare is a necessity because it (1) can make the labor market a sellers' market, (2) preserves essential liberties (like freedom and equality or even justice), and (3) creates full employment. Since it is a political necessity, it can be justified by the ideology of reluctant collectivism or by joining those who argue that the state *should* engage in transfer programs.

Eulau (1962) made a similar case for the American welfare state. Its evolution, he stated, can be explained by the "mature politics" of Franklin D. Roosevelt's time because it was difficult for capitalism, with "the market" as a key concept, to coexist with the idea of the market failure of the Great Depression of the 1930s. Given that the welfare state is a political necessity, it can be justified by the ideology of democracy, rather than the ideology of socialism. To Eulau, mature politics is possible only when democratic institutions are at work, protecting the rights and well-being of all.

Choi, Martin, Chatterjee, and Holland (1978) agreed that ideology is not the reason for the development of social welfare. Instead, they claimed, ideology is used as an excuse for justifying the continued existence of social welfare once it has come into existence. The reason for the development of social welfare, they stated, is "the legitimation and preservation of the dominant classes" (p. 159).

Rimlinger (1971) also argued that ideology is used to justify social welfare programs launched by the state. The reasons for the development of social welfare, he contended, are inherent in the process of industrialization (the main thesis of chapters 8 and 9), and ideology is used by elites and other interest groups to justify or oppose welfare programs. I return to Rimlinger's thesis in chapter 9.

Pinker (1979), criticizing George and Wilding (1977), stated that the British welfare state is less a function of reluctant collectivism or Fabianism and more a function of "mercantile collectivism." Mercantile collectivism did not contribute to the development of the welfare state in Britain but was used as a justification of the welfare state after it came into being. Such justification was necessary to preserve mercantile (capitalistic) interests. Pinker's position, then, is not far removed from that of Choi et al. (1978).

Schoor (1986), reflecting on Reagan's and Thatcher's attempts to slow down the welfare state during the 1980s, came down in favor of the welfare state as a means of achieving full employment, egalitarian income distribution and transfer, and "mainstreaming" of minorities. His position was close to Beveridge's (1945).

K.V. Friedman (1981) argued that the modern welfare state (in Britain, the United States, and the European First World countries) evolved because of a complex set of relationships between the governor and the governed. Ideology is used (though she did not use the term) to "legitimate" the evolving and evolved relationship (between the state and the citizen). Legitimation is almost never possible without ideology (see the discussion of legitimation under the Frankfurt school in chapter 4). Friedman, then, also seems to concur with the thesis that ideology justifies the development of the welfare state.

THESIS 4: VARIATIONS WITHIN NATIONAL SYSTEMS ARE JUSTIFIED BY IDEOLOGY

Just as the activities of the state may need to be justified, so do those of specific interest groups within the state. Social workers are one such interest group, and, depending on which sector they work in, are likely to resort to different ideologies to justify their specific interests. Ephross and Reisch (1982) found partial support for this thesis in their study of the ideologies of social work textbooks.

Stoesz (1989) proposed that four different interest groups in the profession have different ideologies: the welfare bureaucrats, the repressed communalists (social workers in the voluntary sector), the "emerging" private practitioners, and the "challenging" for-profit corporate groups. Stoesz's basic argument was that the American welfare state is influenced by dominant and nondominant interest groups. The dominant group consists of the welfare bureaucrats, whose ideology is that governmental responses can solve public problems (a position somewhere between the Fabians and the Marxists).

The nondominant group, in Stoesz's topology, is divided among the repressed communalists and the emerging and challenging types. The repressed communalists are driven by the ideology of communal bonds and communalism (a position that is close to that of the Fabians and the founding mothers of American social work). The emerging private practitioners support the ideology of medicalized solutions to individual problems (a position that corresponds to that of the American conservatives and the English anticollectivists). The challenging types (the new for-profit corporate groups), who are attempting to find a lucrative "market of human vulnerability" (a term coined by Chatterjee, 1979), also concur with the ideology of the American conservatives ("What is good for business is good for America") and the English anticommunalists. All these positions are justifications of self-interests, legitimated by ideology.

Model of Help Giving

A more detailed picture of the justification of self-interests was painted by Chatterjee and Bailey (1993), who presented a model of nine ideologies of help giving, each of which includes a different view of how a "helping process" must be socially constructed. Table 5-2 summarizes this model.

The model assumes that the dyadic interaction between the provider and the recipient of help (see Figures 2-2 to 2-7) can be understood at the macro level only by specifying the institutionalized roles (column 3, Table 5-2) that the provider and recipient assume and the ideological infrastructures (column 4, Table 5-2) that are used to justify them. The entire paradigm is built on the template specified by Berger and Luckman (1967), discussed in chapter 4.

According to the model, the *linguistic level* describes the situation, the *aphoristic level* prescribes what is to be done about the situation, the *institutional level* assigns reciprocal roles to the provider and the recipient in dealing with the situation, and the *ideological level* legitimates the situation. For example, at the first ideological level, when a person from a transgenerational poverty class applies for what is called welfare from an American income maintenance bureaucracy, he or she is a suspect (linguistic level), who is thought of as needing handouts (aphoristic level), is considered

Table 5-2. Model of Nine Ideologies of Help

LINGUISTIC LEVEL	APHORISTIC LEVEL	INSTITU-TIONAL LEVEL	IDEOLOGI-CAL LEVEL	EXAMPLES OF INTER-EST GROUPS
"Suspect"	Needs handouts	Policing Chiseler	Blame the recipient	Traditional welfare bureaucrats
"Sick"	Needs treatment	Treatment agent Patient	Blame the disease	Medical-model social workers
"Problem"	Needs solutions	Technical consultant Client	Blame the malfunction	Problem-solving social workers
"Deviance"	Needs social control	Correctional agent Deviant	Blame the behavior	Human services welfare bureaucrats
"Crisis"	Needs crisis alleviation	Crisis manager Victim	Blame the perpetrator	Hotline services workers
"Growth"	Needs support for growth	Growth facilitator Responsible individual	Blame the roadblocks to growth	Private practice clinicians
"Social issues"	Needs justice	Advocate Victim	Blame society and injustice	Advocacy social workers
"Beneficiary"	Needs a transfer of resources	Clearing agent Receiving agent	Nobody to blame	New welfare bureaucrats
"Self-help"	Needs guidance from fellow sufferers	In-group organizer In-group member	Blame victimizers or any victimizing substance	Feminists, shelter workers, leaders of self-help groups (such as Alcoholics Anonymous)

a welfare chiseler who should be policed by the welfare worker (institutional level), and is blamed for being unworthy of support (ideological level).

In contrast, the same situation in, say, northern Europe would be handled at the eighth ideological level. The person would be thought of as a beneficiary (linguistic level), who needs an income transfer (aphoristic level), is a receiving agent from a state bureaucracy (institutional level), and is dealt with by a clearing agent. At this level, there is no one to blame (ideological level).

These two ideologies can also be used to compare how two people within one country may be treated. In the United States, a black single mother from a poverty-stricken area who asks for an income transfer is considered a "suspect," whereas a white retired blue-collar worker who asks for an income transfer is viewed as a "beneficiary." The first person will be construed as a welfare recipient, and the second will be thought of as a social security recipient. Often no mention is made of the facts that the social security recipient will receive far in excess of what he or she has paid into the social security program and has a life expectancy that is 20 years longer than the welfare recipient's.

A more comprehensive view of the workings of these ideologies may be had by comparing how one person in one country may be dealt with in different situations. In the case of a middle-class American woman who is a victim of ongoing domestic violence, the following scenarios may be played out in different settings:

- In a private, psychodynamically oriented agency, the woman would be viewed as a "sick" person (sadomasochistic), who needs treatment, and should be in a "treatment relationship" as a patient, and her illness would be blamed for her condition. The "sick" situation is guided by the ideology of medicalization (see chapter 4).

- In an eclectic family services agency, the woman would be defined as a person with a problem that has to be solved and who needs to be a client of a social worker (who is a technical consultant for finding a solution to the woman's problem); the recurrent malfunction of her marriage would be blamed for her situation.

- In a crisis-type agency, the woman would be thought of as someone who needs to get over the situation and who requires the help of a crisis manager to do so; the perpetrator of the abuse would be blamed for her problems.

- In a community organization or advocacy-oriented agency, the woman would be seen as a person who needs justice and who should have the help of a social worker to act as an advocate for her as a victim. In this case, the society that permits such an injustice to occur would be blamed.

- In a feminist shelter for battered women (self-help setting), she would be viewed as a fellow sufferer, who needs the help giving of her sisters, and the ideology supports political action against the actual and potential oppressors.
- If the abused woman is poor, she may be referred to a public social services agency, where she would be construed as being in a "deviance" situation, as someone who must be protected from the perpetrator (her husband or boyfriend), whose behavior needs to be controlled. In this scenario, the social worker would take on the role of correctional agent.

All the ideologies in the model either implicitly or explicitly include the role of the state and the role of the market. Table 5-3 outlines these roles. In addition, the model illustrates that ideology is or can be used by interest groups (as specified by Stoesz, 1989, for example) to justify their positions. Only the social issues and the self-help models reflect ideology as a reason for giving help. In all other instances, ideology is a justification rather than reason for supporting state-sponsored transfer.

Conclusions

Ideology and the Welfare Infrastructure

Most religious ideologies (the great religions), perhaps with the exception of Protestant Christianity, made prescriptions to successful people at the top of social hierarchies to become payers of transfer to needy people. Before the separation of church and state, religious ideologies also included political and economic ideologies. In most parts of the First and Second Worlds, these three ideologies are separated (Bell, 1960; Gouldner, 1976; Habermas, 1970). The modern literature on social welfare and the welfare state reflects a tension between the *political* ideologies of autocracy and democracy and *economic* ideologies of capitalism and socialism. Such tension creates different prescriptions to the payers of transfer, the transfer agent, the provider, and the recipient of transfer.

- Socialism (including Marxism and Fabianism) encourages and legitimates the obligation of payers to pay for social welfare, whereas capitalism does not. Under capitalism, the payers, instead of paying for social welfare, encourage the recipients to participate in the free market. However, even capitalism exempts children and chronically ill and disabled people from participating in the free market, but expects the family and the community to support these dependent populations.

Table 5-3. Ideologies of Help: Role of the State and the Market

LINGUISTIC LEVEL	ROLE OF THE STATE	ROLE OF THE MARKET
"Suspect"	To provide reluctant support to the recipient with policing through a "street-level bureaucracy" (Lipsky, 1980).	To reject the recipient because he or she is not a participant in the market-place.
"Sick"	1. To create reluctant support through a street-level bureaucracy to care for the recipient. 2. To allow the market to provide for recipients and license providers.	1. To obtain subsidies from the state to support recipient and then develop a new market for this type of care. 2. To develop a new market for recipients.
"Problem"	To allow the market to provide for recipients and license providers.	To develop a new market for the recipients.
"Deviance"	To develop street-level bureaucracies to offer social services.	To develop a new market that can offer purchase of social services.
"Crisis"	To develop street-level bureaucracies to offer help with crises.	To develop a new market that can offer purchase of crisis help.
"Growth"	To license or regulate a group of new service providers to middle-class recipients.	To develop a new market in this growth area providing services to those who are able to pay.
"Social issues"	To enact legislative or policy support only if there is sufficient interest-group support.	To develop new advocacy-oriented services only if there is a new market for them.
"Beneficiary"	To routinely transfer process through a service bureaucracy and to struggle to keep it from becoming a street-level bureaucracy.	To provide services to the recipient and bill the state according to procedures already in place.
"Self-help"	The state has no role here, but may develop one if it begins to move toward a "social issues" model.	No active role here, unless the group attains fame and can offer franchiselike marketable services.

- Socialism, having legitimated the obligation of the payers to support the welfare state, also legitimates the state as the principal transfer agent. The state, in this formula, should engage in centric transfer and the transfer scheme should be a progressive one. However, the family and the community seem to be acceptable supplementary transfer agents in socialism, as they are in capitalism.
- Although there is a wide variation of the categories of recipients both in socialism and in capitalism, socialism creates the idea of entitlement more often and among more recipients than does classic capitalism.
- The pro-market position in capitalism legitimates the development of many types of providers (including third-party providers) to the recipient, whereas in socialism the transfer agent itself is often the provider. For example, in capitalist systems, mental health services, health services, and even personal social services can be provided by a market participant (that is, not the state itself), and be reimbursed by the transfer agent (often the state). In contrast, in socialist systems, these in-kind services are often provided by the state itself. The trend seems to be toward more privatization of providers under capitalism but more nationalization under socialism.
- The rules of supply and demand seem to contribute to the limits of transfer, also known as rationing. The idea of rationing is indeed native to capitalism, since it follows the rules of supply and demand. On the other hand, rationing is alien to socialism because a fundamental premise of socialism is "to each according to his need."
- Although the economic ideologies of capitalism or socialism either contribute to or oppose social welfare, the political ideologies of autocracy or democracy do not seem to do so. Chapters 8 and 9 show that the wealth of a country is more often a contributor to the welfare state, while economic ideologies are used to justify the nature of transfer. Neither autocracy nor democracy seems to shape the development of the welfare state.

IDEOLOGY AND THE THREE WORLDS

So far the evidence for the thesis that the welfare state is an ideological compromise has depended on qualitative historical data. This situation is not uncommon, as I observed in chapter 4. However, when applied to the First World countries (as has been done in this chapter), the thesis warrants revision because there is more evidence and a stronger argument for the thesis that in the First World, ideology is used more often as a justification for social welfare. There is a reason to believe that the more one is influenced by the intellectual traditions of the London school, the more one argues that ideology is the reason for social welfare; whereas the more one is guided by traditions of the Frankfurt school, the more one argues that ideology is a justification for social welfare. British and American social workers, as a discipline and as one important interest group, often subscribe to the ideas of the London school.

On the other hand, social welfare in the Second World countries has been ideology driven (Bollen & Appold, 1993; Castro, 1983; Dixon & Macarov, 1992; Snyder & Kick, 1979). However, the economy has not been able to maintain an infrastructure to make the ideological promises viable in the long run. In the Third World countries, social welfare has been ideology aspired (Dixon, 1981, 1987a, 1987b, 1992; Dixon & Kim, 1985), but the state has often had no means to provide welfare programs. Consequently, the term welfare state does not even seem applicable to Third World countries except Hong Kong, Singapore, South Korea, and Taiwan (Berger, 1986).

In the First World, the dominant ideology has been various forms of capitalism and democracy, and various interest groups have been for or against the state having a role in the provision of welfare. However, the state role is justified by traditional Judeo-Christian ideologies of the distribution of resources (Fitzpatrick, 1990).

In the Second World, the dominant ideology until recently was various forms of socialism and Marxism. In their efforts to convert to a market economy, the Second World countries have been struggling to maintain their cherished welfare states (Dixon & Kim, 1992).

In the Third World, although nationalist leaders were attracted to socialism, this interest did not lead to the development of welfare states in these countries. Thus, social welfare remains under the auspices of the family, the community, or the equivalent of the church, and the driving ideologies have been the traditional religious ones (Dixon 1987a, 1987b, 1992; Dixon & Kim, 1985; Dixon & Scheurell, 1990).

REFERENCES

Beilharz, P., Condidine, M., & Watts, R. (1992). *Arguing about the welfare state: The Australian experience.* Sydney: George Allen & Unwin.

Bell, D. (1960). *The end of ideology.* New York: Free Press.

Berger, P. (1986). *The capitalist revolution.* New York: Basic Books.

Berger, P., & Luckman, T. (1967). *The social construction of reality.* Garden City, NY: Doubleday Anchor Books.

Beveridge, W. H. (1945). *Full employment in a free society.* New York: W. W. Norton.

Bollen, K., & Appold, S. J. (1993). National industrial structure and the global system. *American Sociological Review, 58,* 283–301.

Castro, F. (1983). *The world economic and social crisis: Its impact on the underdeveloped countries, its somber prospects and the need to struggle if we are to survive.* Havana: Council of State.

Chatterjee, P. (1979). A market of human vulnerability. *Social Development Issues, 3,* 1–12.

Chatterjee, P., & Bailey, D. (1993). Ideology and structure of nonprofit organizations. In P. Chatterjee & A. Abramovitz (Eds.), *Structure of nonprofit management* (pp. 3–26). Lanham, MD: University Press of America.

Choi, I., Martin, E., Chatterjee, P., & Holland, T. (1978). Ideology and social welfare. *Indian Journal of Social Work, 39*(2), 139–160.

Dixon, J. E. (1981). *The Chinese welfare system 1949–1979.* New York: Praeger.

Dixon, J. E. (Ed.). (1987a). *Social welfare in Africa.* London: Croom Helm.

Dixon, J. E. (Ed.). (1987b). *Social welfare in the Middle East.* London: Croom Helm.

Dixon, J. E. (1992). China. In J. E. Dixon & D. Macarov (Eds.), *Social welfare in socialist countries* (pp. 13–28). London: Routledge & Kegan Paul.

Dixon, J. E., & Kim, H. S. (Eds.). (1985). *Social welfare in Asia.* London: Croom Helm.

Dixon, J. E., & Kim, H. S. (1992). Social welfare under socialism. In J. E. Dixon & D. Macarov (Eds.), *Social welfare in socialist countries* (pp. 1–11). London: Routledge & Kegan Paul.

Dixon, J., & Macarov, D. (Eds.). (1992). *Social welfare in socialist countries.* London: Routledge & Kegan Paul.

Dixon, J. E., & Scheurell, R. (Eds.). (1990). *Social welfare in Latin America.* London: Routledge & Kegan Paul.

Ephross, P., & Reisch, M. (1982). The ideology of some social work texts. *Social Service Review, 56,* 273–283.

Esping-Andersen, G. (1990). *The three worlds of welfare capitalism.* Princeton, NJ: Princeton University Press.

Eulau, H. (1962). The American welfare state. In J. S. Rouchek (Ed.), *Contemporary political ideologies* (pp. 415–431). Paterson, NJ: Littlefield.

Fanon, F. (1965). *A dying colonialism.* New York: Grove Press.

Fitzpatrick, E. (1990). *Endless crusade.* New York: Oxford University Press.

Friedman, K. V. (1981). *Legitimation of social rights and the Western welfare state.* Chapel Hill: University of North Carolina Press.

Friedman, M. (1962). *Capitalism and freedom*. Chicago: University of Chicago Press.

George, V., & Wilding, P. (1977). *Ideology and social welfare*. Boston: Routledge & Kegan Paul.

Gouldner, A. (1976). *The dialectic of ideology and technology*. New York: Seabury Press.

Groskind, F. (1994). Ideological influences on public support for assistance to poor families. *Social Work, 39*, 81–89.

Habermas, J. (1970). *Towards a rational society*. London: Heinemann.

Handler, J. F., & Hasenfeld, Y. (1991). *The moral construction of poverty: Welfare reform in America*. Newbury Park, CA: Sage Publications.

Hansen, E. J., Ringen, S., Uusitalo, H., & Erikson, R. (1993). *Welfare trends in the Scandinavian countries*. Armonk, NY: M. E. Sharpe.

Karger, H. J., & Stoesz, D. (1994). *American social welfare policy*. New York: Longman.

Kerr, C., Dunlop, J. T., Harbison, F. H., & Myers, C. A. (1965). The industrializing elites. In M. A. Zald (Ed.), *Social welfare institutions: A sociological reader* (pp. 73–101). New York: John Wiley & Sons.

Kropotkin, P. (1969). *Mutual aid*. Boston: Porter Sargent. (Original work published 1902)

Mechanic, D. (1986). *From advocacy to allocation*. New York: Free Press.

Murray, C. (1984). *Losing ground: American social policy, 1950–1980*. New York: Basic Books.

Murray, C., & Herrnstein, R. J. (1994). *The bell curve: Intelligence and class structure in American life*. New York: Free Press.

Navarro, V. (1992). *Why the United States does not have a national health program*. New York: Baywood.

Parsons, T. (1951). *The social system*. Glencove, IL: Free Press.

Pinker, R. (1979). *The idea of welfare*. London: Heinemann.

Proudhon, P. (1969). *Selected writings of P. J. Proudhon*. Garden City, NY: Doubleday. (Original work published 1846)

Rayback, J. G. (1959). *A history of American labor*. New York: Free Press.

Rimlinger, G. (1971). *The welfare state and industrialization in Europe, America, and Russia*. New York: John Wiley & Sons.

Rose, S. M. (1992). Empowering case management clients. *Ageing International, 19*(3), 1–4.

Salamon, L. M. (1992). *America's nonprofit sector*. New York: Foundation Center.

Schoor, A. (1986). *Religion and economic action.* New York: Basic Books.

Snyder, D., & Kick, E. (1979). Structural position in the world-system and economic growth, 1955–1970: A multiple network analysis of transnational interactions. *American Journal of Sociology, 84,* 1096–1126.

Specht, H., & Courtney, M. E. (1993). *Unfaithful angels.* New York: Free Press.

Stoesz, D. (1989). A theory of social welfare. *Social Work, 34,* 101–107.

Titmuss, R. M. (1950). *Problems of social policy.* London: George Allen & Unwin.

Titmuss, R. M. (1958). *Essays on the welfare state.* London: George Allen & Unwin.

Titmuss, R. M. (1968). *Commitment to welfare.* London: George Allen & Unwin.

Titmuss, R. M. (1969). *The gift relationship.* London: George Allen & Unwin.

Titmuss, R. M. (1974). *Social policy.* London: George Allen & Unwin.

Tropman, J. E. (1989). *American values and social welfare.* Englewood Cliffs, NJ: Prentice Hall.

Waitzkin, H., & Waterman, B. (1974). *The exploitation of illness in capitalist society.* Indianapolis: Bobbs-Merrill.

6

WELFARE IS A CAMOUFLAGE FOR CLASS, GENDER, OR INTEREST–GROUP CONFLICT: 1

> Distribution seems to antedate and to determine production in another way as well, as a pre-economic fact, so to say. A conquering people divides the land among the conquerors, establishing thereby a certain division and form of landed property and determining the character of production; or, it turns the conquered people into slaves and thus makes slave labor the basis of production. Or, a nation, by revolution, breaks up large estates into small parcels of land and by this new distribution imparts to production a new character. Or, legislation perpetuates land-ownership in large families or distributes labor as a hereditary privilege and thus fixes it in castes.
>
> In all of these cases, and they are all historic, it is not distribution that seems to be organized and determined by production, but on the contrary, production by distribution.
>
> Marx, *The Essential Writings*

A number of disciplines—social work, sociology, history, and economics—and the new multidisciplinary field of feminist theory use conflict theory to explain the development of the welfare state. In this chapter, I review the thesis that welfare is a camouflage for several types of conflict by discussing the following issues: (1) what is meant by conflict, (2) which groups are parties to conflict, and (3) the ways in which such conflict can be understood.

WHAT IS CONFLICT?

I start with a heuristic definition: Conflict is a hostile encounter or struggle that originates in an existing order, either within or between persons, roles, or groups, owing to actual or perceived differences in status, resources, or opportunities. Conflict may lead to violent or nonviolent efforts to resolve it.

If the conflict is resolved, then a new order (with its own inherent differences in status, resources, or opportunities) is instituted. If no resolution is attained, then the existing order continues (see Figure 6-1). In this heuristic definition, conflict is an intermediary between two types of social orders, as in the following example of an interpersonal conflict.

> Two boys in a schoolyard have maintained an uneasy rivalry for leadership over the other boys (neither boy is a clear leader of the group). One day, a fight breaks out between them, and one boy clearly wins. After the fight, a new social order of the school's boys' group emerges, in which the winner is the new leader and the defeated boy has the option of accepting a subservient status in the group, leaving the group, or preparing for another fight.

In this example, the existing order (in Figure 6-1) represents the situation before the fight, the rivalry for leadership (2) represents a conflict, and the fight (4) represents a violent outcome of the rivalry. One boy winning the fight represents, at least for the time being, a temporary resolution, leading to a new order (5). If the fight ended in a draw or could not be completed because of intervention by others, then the situation would have gone on with no resolution, and the existing order (1) would have been maintained.

Figure 6-1.

Conflict as an Intermediary between Two Orders

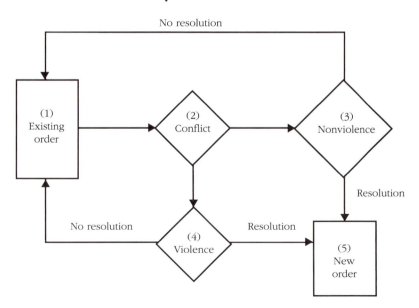

This is an example of the violent resolution of conflict. In an alternative scenario the conflict is resolved without a fight, but the same boy still becomes the leader of the group. This scenario represents the nonviolent resolution of conflict.

Figure 6-1 is an elementary representation of real-time conflict situations. In real life, such conflict situations range from those in the interpersonal realm (as in the preceding example) to the realm of various roles, to small groups, and finally to large groups. For convenience, I refer to conflicts within and between persons, roles, and small groups as *microlevel* conflict and conflicts within and between large groups, such as communities; organizations; interest groups; ethnoracial, ethnolingual, or ethnoreligious groups; social classes in one nation; and among nations themselves as *macrolevel* conflict.

Conflicts within persons (such as the one depicted in Hamlet's soliloquy, "To Be or Not to Be"), roles (like a person in a parental role torn between punishing or ignoring an unruly child), or small groups (for instance, stepfamilies) are of marginal interest for understanding the welfare state. So are conflicts between persons (like the two schoolboys), roles (such as a woman who wishes to have more time with her child in her role as a mother but who requires time away from her child in her professional role as an attorney), and small groups (like two adolescent street gangs in a dispute over their neighborhood territory), unless the parties to the conflict represent larger constituencies. Thus, for example, a conflict between two small groups, one representing labor and the other representing management, may mean a conflict between two larger interest groups: owners of capital versus providers of labor, the working class versus the upper class, or believers in state protection of labor versus believers in a free market. Such cases would be of interest because they are likely to contribute to an understanding of the development of the welfare state.

On the other hand, conflicts within and between large groups, such as communities, organizations, ethnic groups, interest groups, and nations, are of substantial interest. In this macrolevel category I have included, for convenience, interests owing to socioeconomic status, class position, or gender under the term "interest group."

Parties to Conflict

Microlevel and Macrolevel

Microlevel

Among the social and behavioral scientists who have studied microlevel conflict (intra- and interpersonal conflict and intra- and intergroup conflict) have been Dollard and Miller (1950), Freud (1922), Lewin (1948), and Simmel

(1902/1950). Lewin also developed social techniques for resolving conflict in small groups. Business schools in the United States and other First World countries often include these techniques in their curricula, and businesses and nonprofit social agencies use them to do conflict resolution.

Macrolevel: Communities

Conflicts at the community level have been studied by many scholars from several perspectives. Park (1936), an early Chicago school sociologist, classified conflict inherent in human communities as being symbiotic or the commensalistic. Barth (1956) found that such conflict was inherent among the peoples of northwest Pakistan and Afghanistan. Trivers (1971) showed how unrelated members of a community tacitly engage in mutual support, which he called reciprocal altruism (an idea similar to Kropotkin's mutual aid, discussed in chapter 5). A central theme in all this subsocial conflict at the community level is that conflict resolution requires some form of altruism or mutual aid.

Macrolevel: Organizations

Conflicts at the organizational level are of two types: intra-organizational and interorganizational. The field of intraorganizational conflicts was defined, to a great extent, by Lewin (1948; see also Newstrom & Davis, 1993), whereas the field of interorganizational conflicts is vast, and scholars of many disciplines have contributed to it. Interorganizational conflict occurs when established organizations that fail to provide adequate services or to represent their members are challenged by new organizations or when two or more organizations are competing for an increased share of the market in a given territory or community (see Klenk & Ryan, 1974).

Macrolevel: Ethnic Groups

Conflict between ethnolingual groups (like the Bengali-speaking versus the Urdu-speaking groups in Bangladesh in 1972), ethnoracial groups (like whites and blacks in the United States in 1964), or ethnoreligious groups (like the ongoing conflicts between Serbs and Muslims in Bosnia or Arabs and Jews in the Middle East) are often a result of the actual or symbolic efforts of one group to achieve dominance over the other or of the competition of two or more groups for a given territory.

Macrolevel: Interest Groups

Conflicts between groups representing special interests are common in First World countries, but may occur in Second or Third World countries as well (Kerr, Dunlop, Harbison, & Myers, 1965). These conflicts may be due to actual or potential economic gain, political gain, class interests, role interests, gender interests, or ideological positions. These six levels of conflict are not mutually exclusive and may overlap.

Chapin (1994) showed how these levels of conflict are played out between alcohol-producing groups and alcoholism-treatment groups, two interest groups that represent the alcohol-production industry and the alcoholism-treatment industry, respectively. In capitalist societies, both groups operate in the marketplace. Thus, the first level of conflict between them is for economic gain because, on the surface, it appears that the more one group gains economically, the more the other group loses. However, the situation is essentially non-zero-sum, so both groups tacitly cooperate to make alcohol use a politically visible issue. Both sides also represent class interests, because the profits of the alcohol-production industry enrich upper- and upper middle-class people (those in a position to invest capital in the industry), as do the profits of the treatment industry (upper middle-class professionals in the hospital business and in the treatment professions). Both sides also represent role interests (Dahrendorf, 1959) because they occupy roles in either the production industry or the treatment industry.

Feminist groups, another type of special-interest group, may become parties to the conflict between the two alcohol-related groups by protesting that the alcohol-production industry is increasingly pitching its advertising at women, especially women of color, and that the treatment industry is not offering more services to treat women with alcohol problems. Finally, there may also be a conflict of ideologies; temperance groups may demand that the production and consumption of alcohol be banned (delegitimated), whereas public health and adult education groups may argue that prohibition does not work and that the problem should be dealt with by improving the level of adult education.

Macrolevel: Nations

Conflict between nations can lead to three types of outcomes: master–subject, trader–independent client, and trader–captive client. In the first type, one nation is the colonizer and the other is the colony. In the second type, two nations share a legacy of conflict, but both retain the privilege of doing business elsewhere. In the third type, one nation becomes a captive client of another nation and cannot choose to do business elsewhere. Examples of these three types of conflict are presented later.

THEORIES OF CONFLICT

CLASS CONFLICT: THE LEGACY OF MARX

Conflict between classes is essentially a Marxist view. According to Marx, society is polarized between two classes: the workers and the capitalist (also called the proletariat and the bourgeoisie) (see Israel, 1971). Marx believed that most history is a history of class struggle.

One important hypothesis in the Marxist view is that in all societies, one class "appropriates" or "extracts" the value of the unpaid labor of another class. In capitalist societies, subclasses may engage in this process, and the basic structure of society is a hostile relationship between the performers (the proletariat) and the extractors (the bourgeoisie) of labor.

Another key hypothesis is that "consciousness is influenced by social conditions. . . . [That is], the social situation of a man determines his system of ideas" (Israel, 1971, pp. 71–72). It follows, then, that a humble or low life situation may lead to a different ideological orientation than may a high and privileged life situation, and the greater the disparity in social positions, the more the ideologies will differ.

Hence one type of conflict is the result of ideological cleavages. Marx elaborated on this idea with his theory of alienation, in which he delineated three types of ideological conflict: religious alienation, political alienation, and economic alienation. With regard to religious alienation, Marx (quoted in Israel, 1971, p. 32) wrote: "Religion is the sign of the oppressed creature, the sentiment of a heartless world, and the soul of soulless conditions. It is the opium of the people."

According to this view, religion serves as an instrument of social control by those in the upper stratum of society (the privileged) in that a religious ideology justifies both their privileged position and the misery of those at the bottom stratum. In religious alienation, there is a built-in ideological conflict: Those who are privileged find happiness in the here and now, but those who are not must wait for happiness in some other promised land.

Marxists believe that whereas religious alienation occurs because of people's need to escape the demand for loyalty to and the pretentious promises of a religion, political alienation is the result of a similar need to escape the demands of a political system, such as a nation-state that demands nationalism. The political ideology of nationalism disguises the inequalities inherent in that system and serves the interests of the elite. Nationalism makes those at the bottom of society surrender their labor and life (in case of war) to serve the interests of those at the top.

With regard to economic alienation, Marx eloquently portrayed how human beings become alienated from their "most important activity": human labor (Israel, 1971, p. 37). It is through the use of labor that people transform the world around them. However, certain socioeconomic conditions, legitimated by accompanying ideologies (capitalism, for example), transform this most basic human attribute into another commodity to be sold in the marketplace. Selling one's labor without being creatively and affectively attached to the fruit of that labor is like selling one's body to a person without being creatively and affectively attached to him or her. The basic conflict is between one's need to find meaning and creativity in one's work (labor) and an economic ideology that converts that work or labor solely into an economic exchange. This process is referred to as alienated labor.

In all three conflicts, the ideologies (religious, political, and economic) of those at the top of a society serve as the means of legitimating the status quo. The conflict lies in humanity's struggle to free itself from the stranglehold of these idea systems, or ideologies. As was discussed in chapter 4, Mannheim (1936) formulated the following paradigm: Ideologies are the idea systems of those at the top of the stratification ladder, or the ruling classes, and utopias are the idea systems of those at the bottom. Ideologies are the fictions that are used to stabilize the social order, whereas utopias are the idea systems with which the existing order is challenged.

Furthermore, Mannheim stated, when people from the bottom of a stratification ladder (black slaves in the pre-Civil War American South, for example) embrace an ideology (Christianity as taught by their masters), as they often do, they also endorse an instrument of their oppression. Their embracing the idea systems of the ruling class, that is, subscribing to ideologies instead of utopias, gives rise to false consciousness, that is a consciousness alien to their struggle for freedom, a concept also used by Marx and Engels (see Israel, 1971).

Within the Marxist tradition of class oppression, Lukacs (1971) observed the powerlessness and alienation of the working people and the poor people in all institutions of society. He saw commodification in all institutions and noted that the ideology of commodification, with its phantom objectivity, defines relationships in capitalist societies.

Habermas (1970; see also Turner, 1993), a scholar of the Frankfurt school (see chapter 4), labeled the technocratic consciousness in capitalism a form of ideology and stated that it contributes to the commodification of most objects. Friere (1970, pp. 76–77) suggested that every human being, no matter how ignorant or "submerged in the culture of silence," is capable of seeing this ideology of commodification, or the inherent conflicts and contradictions in society.

FUNCTIONS OF CONFLICT AND ROLE: COSER AND DAHRENDORF

The ideas of Coser (1956, 1967), another major macrolevel conflict theorist, are not intellectually close to those of Marx. In fact, some of his metaphors seem to be borrowed from structural-functionalism in that Coser focused on the functions of conflict for the body politic of the entire social system, as well as for parties engaged in conflict. Summarizing the works of Coser, Turner (1986) proposed that Coser's work covers the (1) causes, (2) functions, and (3) duration of conflict. In addition, it also covers the use of violence in conflictual situations.

The causes of conflict, according to Coser (1956), may be the closeness of relationships; the need for cohesion within a group, because "conflict with out-groups increases internal cohesion" (p. 87); and the need to define the structure of the group (which emerges during a conflict). Sometimes these needs may lead to a "search of enemies" (p. 104). In addition, the representation of collectivities and groups for ideological reasons may give rise to intense conflict (rather than conflict ensuing from personal animosities).

The functions of conflict are to (1) unify the group, (2) define the nature and structure of relationships between the conflicting parties, (3) provide a safety valve for hostile impulses inherent in humanity, and (4) unify the parties when they come together to engage in conflict with a third party. The duration of conflict depends on the ability of the leaders of conflicting parties to define the goals of the conflict, interpret the adversary's goals and gestures, locate the adversary's means of triumph, and to persuade the followers to end the conflict (Coser, 1967; Turner, 1986). Coser (1956) also noted that there is a greater potential for violence when conflict emanates from unrealistic issues (unobtainable goals) (realistic issues, or obtainable goals, are less likely to lead to violence) and when the system has no built-in ritual or activity for channeling hostility and simultaneously fosters inequality within the system.

Dahrendorf (1959), also not a Marxist, offered a reformation of macrolevel conflict theory. According to him, both macroconflict theorists and functionalists create a utopia—the functionalists by claiming that society rests on consensus, and the macroconflict theorists by claiming that it is based on continuous conflict. He agreed that conflict is a permanent part of society, but stated that it is not between classes (as Marx thought) but between interest groups: those that are dominant and privileged and those that are subjected and underprivileged. There may be some consensus within groups and conflict among groups, but at times there is also consensus among groups and conflict within groups. Conflict emanates not from class positions or class interests but from roles occupied in a dynamic industrial society and role interests. Thus, according to Dahrendorf, roles acquired from the occupational structures of an industrial society and roles inherited from an existing stratification system lead to role interests that are sometimes in conflict with the role interests of others.

CONFLICT OF KNOWLEDGE: FOUCAULT AND BOURDIEU

A central theme that runs throughout the works of Foucault (1965, 1969, 1975, 1979) is that knowledge leads to power and that transitions from one system of knowledge to another have occurred throughout history. According to Foucault, the essential conflict in society is not so much between classes (though it may appear to be) as it is between knowledge systems. In this conflict, the medical–psychiatric disciplines, for example, have become "gigantic moral enterprises" that have fostered society's control over people. Foucault referred to the *Panoptican* (a device similar to a watchtower in a prison that permits complete observation) and wondered whether it could be a way of building an entire society. He warned that the state's possession of a thorough inventory of knowledge about individuals may lead to its complete control of them. His warning about the danger of a Panoptican-based state is indeed applicable to the welfare state, which has a large inventory of knowledge about the recipients of transfer.

Bourdieu's (1977, 1984, 1989) convictions about the relationship between knowledge and power are similar to Foucault's in that he contended that the human condition is in a dialectical relationship between habitus and field. *Habitus* is the cognitive structure of humans through which they deal with the social world. It is a product of history, and it produces and is produced by the social world (see Ritzer, 1992). Habitus constrains, but does not determine thought and action, and existing customs, or practice, act as arbiters between it and the social world.

In contrast, *field* is a network of relations that exist apart from individual consciousness and will. There are several overlapping fields in the social world (such as the artistic, the economic, the religious, and the mass media), each of which has its own logical structure, although there are similarities in the logical structures of the fields. Some people know these logical structures better than do others. The reason for the superior knowledge of some groups (classes) is their class origin. People of higher class origins have a greater amount of cultural capital (a concept comparable to economic capital). Cultural capital refers to a composite of linguistic, aesthetic, normative, and behavioral preferences in a given situation (Haydn over the blues, vintage wine over beer, or an opera over a Hollywood movie, for example), which those from higher social classes know about. Regarding the welfare state, those with higher cultural capital are more likely both to define it and to demand a higher share from it than are those with lower cultural capital.

CIVIL DISOBEDIENCE: GANDHI AND KING

Mohandas K. Gandhi and Martin Luther King, Jr., built two of the largest mass movements the world has ever seen—Gandhi's in India (1919 to 1947), and King's in the United States (1960 to 1968). The initial objective of Gandhi's movement was to gain India's independence from British rule (or, in terms of the concepts discussed in chapter 2, to seek liberty). As the mass movement was gaining strength, Gandhi added the objectives of equality (between the British and the Indians, between the ethnoreligious groups of the Hindus and the Muslims, and between the upper-caste and lower-caste Hindus) and community (an ashram that served as the fountainhead of the movement).

In comparison, King started his movement with the objective of equality (of black people in the United States). His initial efforts reflected the quest for political equality, but his later efforts (as in the Poor People's March) also reflected the goal of economic equality. One can argue that King was also interested in liberty because black people in the United States had not attained liberty in the spheres of social life. Another important theme that pervaded King's efforts was the building of community (the foundation of the black church). Both mass movements were built on Henry David Thoreau's concept of civil disobedience, and both used nonviolent tactics as a means of conflict resolution (pursuing the pathway from 2 to 3 in Figure 6-1).

The ideology behind Gandhi's efforts (often called Gandhianism) combined the pursuit of liberty under an agrarian society (with cottage industries, homespun goods, and mutual aid) and communal socialism, legitimated under the name of the mythical Hindu King Rama. It united the Hindu masses, but, for the most part, alienated the Muslim masses. It was useful for uniting most of India against the British, but less so in building a modern state after India's independence. The founding ideology of the state of India, under the leadership of Jawaharial Nehru, was central planning and Fabian socialism. (Nehru had been educated in England, where he was influenced by the Fabians and the incrementalist Marxists.)

The ideology behind King's efforts can be called a variant of traditional Christianity. It combined the pursuit of liberty and equality with the aid of urban institutions, basically legitimated by both traditional Christianity and civil rights–oriented democracy. Although this mass movement brought about political liberty, the majority of the black population in the United States from the late 1970s onward had formed a massive underclass (Wilson, 1979, 1987) in American society whose position in a reluctant welfare state was later questioned (see Murray, 1984).

It may be suggested that the efforts of both Gandhi and King produced political liberty. However, they did not contain the formula to attain economic equality with the industrial societies (in the case of India, as a struggle between nations) or with the urban middle class (in the case of minorities of color, as a struggle within a nation, that is the United States).

CONFLICT IN WORLD SYSTEMS: WALLERSTEIN AND SKOCPOL

Wallerstein's (1976, 1980, 1989) work (introduced in chapter 3) focuses on the conflicting relationships between nations as they emerged macrohistorically. The basic thesis is that there are essentially two types of world systems: one based on conquest, resulting in empires, and one based on mercantile relationships, leading to an economic hierarchy among nations, in which the losses are absorbed by political entities while the gains flow to a small group (mostly at the core). Between 1450 and 1640, there was a worldwide shift from conquest relationships among nations. During that time, the economic hierarchy became linear, with the most powerful mercantile countries absorbing positions at the core; the less powerful, at the semiperiphery; and the powerless, at the periphery. "The flow of surplus from the lower strata to the upper, from the periphery to the center, and from the majority to the minority" (Wallerstein, 1976, p. 15) resulted in a worldwide division of labor, whereby the major sources of labor were in the semiperiphery and the periphery and the major source of capital was in the core.

England and France competed for leadership of the core, and England won. The Industrial Revolution in England, the French Revolution, and the American Revolution "represented further consolidation" (Wallerstein, 1989, p. 256) of the transition from empire to mercantile hierarchy.

A great portion of what is termed the Third World today (see chapter 3), Wallerstein (1989) noted, was in the "external zones," that is, the semiperiphery and the periphery, until about 1757 (the year the East India Company won the war against Siraj-ud-daulla and established a base in India). Between 1757 and about 1948, countries in the external zones were incorporated into the periphery or the semiperiphery. The result was the globalization of the division of labor (which would give rise to issues of immigration and the responses of the welfare states in the 20th century), the flow of capital from the external zones to the core, and power-dependent relationships. This historical development led to the formation of class systems and class conflict both within and among nations.

An inference that can be drawn from Wallerstein's analysis is that the upper-class people of the core nations assumed the position of world dominators, middle-class people of the core nations became the key idea persons (professionals and white-collar workers) of the world, and upper- and middle-class people of the semiperiphery and the periphery became the agents (also called the liaison elite) of the upper- and the middle-class people of the core. Furthermore, the working-class people (and sometimes the poor people) of the core nations and some nations in the semiperiphery were protected by the welfare state, and the working-class and poor people in the nations of the periphery and sometimes in the semiperiphery were left with a choice between poor recompensement for labor, the welfare family (see chapter 1), or living on the streets.

Skocpol (1979, 1986; see also Ritzer, 1992) differed from Wallerstein by asserting that political, not economic, development at the transnational level over time explains the conflicts of the 20th century. According to Skocpol (1979, p. 27), the state "is a structure with a logic and interests of its own not necessarily equivalent to, or fused with, the interests of the dominant class," and even Marx failed to see the power (and the interests) of the state. Thus, social revolutions (as in France, Russia, and China) occur more because of the structural positions of those states in a set of power relationships among states than because of ideologies or class interests.

An inference that can be drawn from Skocpol's thesis is that the interests of the state and the state's position in a dynamic power relationship with other states should be an important focus of study. Furthermore, the emergence of the welfare state is an outcome of this dynamic power relationship. Other works by Skocpol that are directly related to the development of the welfare state are discussed in chapter 9.

CONFLICT IN STYLES OF PRODUCTION

A group of neo-Marxist scholars, conflict theorists, and students of the welfare state (mostly from western Europe) have conceptualized two overlapping but different technological bases of society: *Fordism* and *post-Fordism* (see Gould, 1993; Ritzer, 1992). At times, these two bases are in conflict, and this conflict has sometimes been superimposed on or replaced the class interests and class conflicts of an earlier epoch.

Although the concept of Fordism and post-Fordism is similar to those of modernism and postmodernism or industrialism and postindustrialism, the disciplinary and national origins of the three concepts are different. The concept of Fordism and post-Fordism is popular with the theorists of the London school (see chapters 4 and 5) and with many neo-Marxists and is basically British in origin. The concept of modernism is popular among many non-Marxist American sociologists, whereas the concept of postmodernism was devised by several philosophers, architects, and social scientists in France. The idea of industrialism is perhaps the oldest and is known to social scientists all over the world. In contrast, the idea of postindustrialism was first articulated by Bell (1973), an American social scientist. I discuss Fordism and post-Fordism in this chapter and modernization, postmodernization, industrialization, and postindustrialization in chapters 8 and 9.

Henry Ford's system of the mass manufacturing of automobiles on an assembly line, coupled with Taylor's (1911) "scientific management" of the assembly line, form the basic idea for Fordism. Ritzer (1992) and Clarke (1990) delineated the attributes of both, which are summarized in Table 6-1.

There are numerous conflicts inherent in Fordism and post-Fordism. In Fordism, the conflicts are between social classes and between interest groups (elites versus the working class, capital versus labor, management versus unions, and those in the transfer sector versus the interest groups that support or oppose the population in the transfer sector). In post-Fordism, the conflicts are between interest groups (elites versus groups that are knowledgeable about new technologies, capital versus [skilled] labor, and management versus groups representing the diverse knowledge groups).

CONFLICTS FROM GENDER–BASED OPPRESSION

Although there have been numerous debates about the historical and intellectual origins of the concept of equality for women, it is generally agreed that the feminist notion of gender oppression and its relation to other

Table 6-1. Attributes of Fordism and Post-Fordism

ATTRIBUTES	FORDISM	POST-FORDISM
Products	Mass produced and homogenized	Specialized production individualized
Technology	Assembly line	Smaller and more diversified process
Management	Time management	Output management
Productivity	Quota per time unit	Total quality per product
Workers' skills	Homogenized	Diversified, flexible
Workers' groups	Unionized	Too many small groups for effective unionization
Market	For homogenized products and services	For specialized products and services

SOURCES: Clarke, S. (1990). The crisis of Fordism or the crisis of social democracy? *Telos, 83,* 71–98; Ritzer, G. (1992). *Contemporary sociological theory.* Boston: Allyn & Bacon.

forms of conflict dates back to the late 18th century, about the time of the American and French revolutions (Spender, 1983). The works of Abigail Adams, Judith S. Murray, and Mary Wollstonecraft were the pioneering position papers on women's rights and women's roles in the formation of social policy (Rossi, 1974). Included in this legacy are later works on gender equality and its overlap with democracy, international conflicts (pacifism), class conflict (socialism versus capitalism), and problems of human existence (existentialism).

The publication of *The Second Sex* (de Beauvoir, 1957) and *The Feminine Mystique* (Friedan, 1963) launched the current movement about gender-role oppression and conflicts emanating from gender-related issues. Nes and Iadicola (1989) noted that there seem to be three intellectual traditions within the feminist movement: the liberal tradition, the radical tradition, and the socialist tradition. The liberal tradition advocates the elimination of gender inequality and patriarchy from capitalist society and giving women the same opportunities to pursue the ends ordinarily pursued by men. The radical tradition calls for separatism and the building of alternative institutions. The goal of radical feminism is the construction of a matriarchy, although it is not clear whether such a society should be based on market (capitalist) principles or on collectivist (socialist) principles. The socialist tradition also advocates the elimination of patriarchy, but under collectivist, rather than capitalist, principles.

THEORIES OF CONFLICT: SUMMARY AND METHODOLOGY

It is clear that numerous theories of conflict at the macrolevel cover conflicts within and between communities, organizations, ethnic groups, interest groups, and nations. Within this framework, Marxists have contributed the ideas of class conflict, the dominance of nonelites by elites, and conflict among different types of consciousness and ideologies. Non-Marxist conflict theorists have added the idea of conflict between interest groups and between knowledge structures and between groups with different levels of knowledge (Foucault and Bourdieu); between dominant groups and oppressed groups in the civil disobedience tradition (Gandhi and King); between nations owing to differential economic and political positions (Wallerstein and Skocpol); between interests emanating from Fordism and post-Fordism; and among pro-market, separatist, and pro-state feminism. All these types of conflict can be used to understand the social policies of the welfare state, and the details of such positions are explored in chapter 7.

With regard to methodology, it seems that studies of macrolevel conflicts, as do studies of ideology (see chapter 4), frequently use qualitative historical methods. Although Lewin (1948) pioneered studies of microlevel conflict at the positivistic level and the use of experimental and quasi-experimental designs (see Forsyth, 1990), for the most part studies of macrolevel conflict remain dependent on qualitative historical data.

CONFLICT AND SOCIAL WELFARE: FIVE PROPOSITIONS

Both Marxist and non-Marxist conflict theorists suggest that an existing form of distribution is due to a short-term or long-term compromise between parties in conflict and that the compromise may camouflage the presence of conflicts. Such conflicts may be among the payers of transfer, the organized interests generated by the types of transfer used, the various forms of transfer agents, the various forms of transfer recipients, and the different transfer providers (see chapter 2).

On the basis of the levels of conflict discussed in this chapter, I suggest the following theses:

1. The welfare state may serve as a camouflage for several types of community-level conflict.
2. The welfare state may serve as a camouflage for several types of organizational-level conflict.

3. The welfare state may serve as a camouflage for several types of ethnic conflict. This hypothesis may overlap with the first one when ethnicity also means an ethnic community.
4. The welfare state may serve as a camouflage for several types of interest-group conflict, including class conflict, ideological conflict, role-interest conflict, knowledge-base conflict, conflicts owing to gender oppression, and conflicts generated by changes in technology.
5. The welfare state may serve as a camouflage for several types of international conflict.

Chapter 7 explores several examples of such macrolevel conflict.

REFERENCES

Barth, F. (1956). Ecological relationships of ethnic groups in Swat, north Pakistan. *American Anthropologist, 58,* 1079–1089.

Bell, D. (1973). *The coming of post-industrial society.* New York: Basic Books.

Bourdieu, P. (1977). *Outline of a theory of practice.* Cambridge, England: Cambridge University Press.

Bourdieu, P. (1984). *Distinction: A social critique of the judgment of taste.* Cambridge, MA: Harvard University Press.

Bourdieu, P. (1989). Social space and symbolic power. *Sociological Theory, 7,* 14–25.

Chapin, M. (1994). Functional conflict theory, the alcohol beverage industry, and the alcoholism treatment industry. *Journal of Applied Social Sciences, 18,* 169–182.

Clarke, S. (1990). The crisis of Fordism or the crisis of social democracy? *Telos, 83,* 71–98.

Coser, L. (1956). *The functions of social conflict.* New York: Free Press.

Coser, L. (1967). *Continuities in the study of social conflict.* New York: Free Press.

Dahrendorf, R. (1959). *Class and class conflict in industrial society.* Stanford, CA: Stanford University Press.

de Beauvior, S. (1957). *The second sex.* New York: Vintage Books.

Dollard, J., & Miller, N. (1950). *Personality and psychotherapy.* New York: McGraw-Hill.

Forsyth, D. (1990). *Group dynamics.* Belmont, CA: Brooks/Cole.

Foucault, M. (1965). *Madness and civilization: A history of insanity in the age of reason.* New York: Vintage Books.

Foucault, M. (1969). *The archaeology of knowledge and the discourse on language*. New York: Harper & Row.

Foucault, M. (1975). *The birth of the clinic: An archaeology of the medical perception*. New York: Vintage Books.

Foucault, M. (1979). *Discipline and punish: The birth of the prison*. New York: Vintage Books.

Freud, S. (1922). *Beyond the pleasure principle*. London: Hogarth Press.

Friedan, B. (1963). *The feminine mystique*. New York: Dell.

Friere, P. (1970). *The pedagogy of the oppressed*. New York: Seabury Press.

Gould, A. (1993). *Capitalist welfare systems*. London: Longman.

Habermas, J. (1970). *Towards a rational society*. London: Heinemann.

Israel, J. (1971). *Alienation: From Marx to modern sociology*. Boston: Allyn & Bacon.

Kerr, C., Dunlop, J. T., Harbison, F. H., & Myers, C. A. (1965). The industrializing elites. In M. N. Zald (Ed.), *Social welfare institutions: A sociological reader* (pp. 73–101). New York: John Wiley & Sons.

Klenk, R. W., & Ryan, R. M. (Eds.). (1974). *The practice of social work*. Belmont, CA: Wadsworth.

Lewin, K. (1948). *Resolving social conflicts*. New York: Harper & Bros.

Lukacs, G. (1971). *History and class consciousness*. Cambridge, MA: MIT Press.

Mannheim, K. (1936). *Ideology and utopia*. New York: Harcourt, Brace & World.

Marx, K. (1986). The general relation of production to distribution, exchange, and consumption In F. L. Bender (Ed.), *Karl Marx: The essential writings* (pp. 307–319). Boulder, CO: Westview Press. (Original work published 1859)

Murray, C. (1984). *Losing ground: American social policy, 1950–1980*. New York: Basic Books.

Nes, J. A., & Iadicola, P. (1989). Toward a definition of feminist social work: A comparison of liberal, radical, and socialist models. *Social Work, 34*, 12–22.

Newstrom, J. W., & Davis, K. (1993). *Organizational behavior: Human behavior at work*. New York: McGraw-Hill.

Park, R. E. (1936). Human sociology. *American Journal of Sociology, 42*, 1–15.

Ritzer, G. (1992). *Contemporary sociological theory*. Boston: Allyn & Bacon.

Rossi, A. (1974). *The feminist papers: From Adams to de Beauvior*. New York: Bantam Books.

Simmel, G. (1950). *The sociology of Georg Simmel*. Glencoe, IL: Free Press. (Original work published 1902)

Skocpol, T. (1979). *States and revolutions*. Cambridge, England: Cambridge University Press.

Skocpol, T. (1986). The dead end of metatheory. *Contemporary Sociology, 16*, 10–12.

Spender, D. (1983). *Feminist theorists: Three centuries of key women thinkers*. New York: Random House.

Taylor, F. (1911). *The principles of scientific management*. New York: Harper & Bros.

Trivers, R. L. (1971). The evolution of reciprocal altruism. *Quarterly Review of Biology, 46*, 35–57.

Turner, J. (1986). *The structure of sociological theory*. Belmont, CA: Wadsworth.

Turner, J. (1993). *The structure of sociological theory* (2nd ed.). Belmont, CA: Wadsworth.

Wallerstein, I. (1976). *The modern world-system*. New York: Academic Press.

Wallerstein, I. (1980). *The modern world system II: Mercantilism and the consolidation of the European world economy, 1600–1750*. New York: Academic Press.

Wallerstein, I. (1989). *The modern world system III: The second era of great expansion of the capitalist world economy, 1730–1840*. New York: Academic Press.

Wilson, W. J. (1979). *The declining significance of race*. Chicago: University of Chicago Press.

Wilson, W. J. (1987). *The truly disadvantaged*. Chicago: University of Chicago Press.

7

Welfare Is a Camouflage for Class, Gender, or Interest–Group Conflict: 2

The discovery [by John Stuart Mill], like so many great insights, was very simple. It consisted in pointing out that the true province of economic law was production and not distribution.

The laws of economies have nothing to do with distribution. . . . The distribution of wealth, therefore, depends on the laws and customs of society. The rules by which it is determined are what the opinions and feelings of the ruling portion of the community make them.

Heilbronner, *The Worldly Philosophers*

In this chapter, I review evidence to support or refute the five theses on conflict and social welfare presented at the end of chapter 6. An examination of the five theses yields two questions that are applicable to all:

1. Where is the locus of conflict? Is it at the community, organizational, ethnic group, interest-group, or international level?
2. What is the role of the state in relation to this conflict? Is it to be a neutral arbiter, an uninterested third party, a contestant, or an ally (implicitly or explicitly) of one of the parties?

Thesis 1: Welfare Is a Camouflage for Community–Level Conflicts

There are many examples of community-level conflict. I start with the case of the Ik tribe in Kenya and the efforts of the Kenyan government to relocate the entire tribe (Turnbull, 1972).

The IK, a hunter-gatherer tribe in the mountains of Kenya, had no concept of a state, of the state's intervention in local communities, or of the state's engagement in some form of central planning. They had a tribal culture based on a primitive technology (hunting small game and gathering fruits and berries).

For its own reasons, the Kenyan government decided to relocate this tribe from its ancient habitat to an area in which the tribe would have to learn agricultural techniques to farm and live off what they produced. The Ik were not prepared to adjust to a totally different culture within one generation and, after their forced relocation by the government, began showing numerous signs of anomie and cultural breakdown, including men abandoning their families and families abandoning or abusing their children. In the early 1970s, when Turnbull studied this tribe, it appeared that the entire culture was about to become extinct.

The demise of the Ik is an example of community-level conflict, in this case between the interests of a primitive culture (the Ik) and those of several nearby communities with more advanced cultures. In the name of welfare for the entire nation (and that of the communities near the Ik territory), the state initially appeared to take the role of an arbiter (it was acting in the best interests of most of its people and did not realize that it was acting against the interests of a primitive culture that would not readjust after forced relocation). In the end, however, it adopted the role of an adversary or contestant (for liquidating the Ik's resources).

The case of the Ik is one of many examples of the welfare state intervening at the community level. If the state had not acted, it would have faced political pressure from the nearby communities and from the urban population in general about its inability to formulate social policies that would be in the best interests of the nation. When it did act, it ended up being for the best interests of the majority but against the best interests of a minority tribal population.

A second example is the efforts of the administration of U.S. President Lyndon B. Johnson in the mid-1960s. For about 300 years, the black people in the United States had been subjected to slavery, political and economic exclusion, and severe discrimination. By the 1950s, there was a small but alienated black middle class (Frazier, 1957) and many large communities of poor black people (the underclass). The problems of the black underclass were traced in Moynihan's (1965) *The Negro Family,* a short monograph published by the U.S. Department of Labor that came to be known as the Moynihan report. The preamble of the report reads as follows:

> The United States is approaching a new crisis in race relations. . . .
> There are two reasons. First, the racist virus. . . . Second, three centuries of sometimes unimaginable treatment have taken their toll. . . . [The] circumstances of the Negro American community in recent years have probably been getting worse, *not better* [italics in original]. (p. iii)

Moynihan went on to outline the conditions in the inner-city black communities: the unstable matriarchy, the increasing dependence on welfare, the rising rate of illegitimate births, the low educational achievement, the absence of fathering (and mentoring), and the high levels of delinquency and alienation.

The Moynihan report was followed by several scholarly works. Billingsley (1968) contended that the conditions were the result of the black family and low-income black culture having to expend more energy on surviving than on thriving. Wilson (1979, 1987) stated that social-class divisions since the 1960s have created two groups in the black community: a new middle class, which is relatively privileged, and an underclass, which is truly disadvantaged.

Many thought that the Moynihan report was a "racist" document because it suggested that the subculture of the lower-class black community was "dysfunctional." Although Moynihan was proposing a social policy of the American welfare state that would make this subculture "functional" for survival in the competitive U.S. society, the report was seen as an unwelcome document produced by the state because it labeled the community dysfunctional.

The controversy over the Moynihan report is another example of community conflict, in this case, between a minority and poor community that lacked the resources for dignified survival in a competitive society and the majority communities that oppressed the minority community. For a long time, the state had supported or tolerated the oppression. In the Moynihan report, the state was now proposing to adopt a paternalistic social policy.

A third example, comparable to the second, involves the gypsy communities of eastern Europe and Russia. The members of these communities, with their dark skin, nomadic lifestyle, lack of attachment to the labor force, and dependence on welfare, are usually treated with ambivalence or suspicion by members of the majority communities. During the 1990s, however, there were violent attacks on gypsies by working-class white people, specifically the "Skinheads" (a subculture of the working class) in Romania and Hungary (Fonseca, 1995; "Gypsies," 1995). It seems that in both countries, the state was slow in stopping such community conflict, and it is possible that its inability to protect minority communities was a way of encouraging the gypsies to leave.

A fourth example is the urban community-development movement, which originated in the United States in the 1960s and is still popular there. The manifest objective of this movement was the economic and social development of poverty-stricken communities of the United States, and supposedly the means to achieve it was the Community Development Corporation (CDC). The ontological assumptions behind the CDC programs were that all people are oriented to rational choice, that the profit motive is a universal phenomenon, and that the only reason that people in the United States were living in poverty conditions was their lack of capital and management skills.

If capital and management skills were provided, then certainly local communities, by using these skills and venture capital, could improve their living conditions.

However, preliminary evaluations of the CDCs and their impact on local communities suggested that most of the time, they did not produce any visible change in the economic base of poor communities (see Chatterjee, 1975; Chatterjee, Olsen, & Holland, 1977). Rather, the militant and vocal leaders of these communities, who were active in demonstrating and dramatizing the plight of these poverty communities before the inception of the CDCs, became silent after the CDCs were introduced. They had been offered well-paying jobs in the CDCs, and *their* poverty status certainly changed because of the CDCs' existence. But conditions in the communities they allegedly represented hardly changed. In other words, the CDCs created an interest group of the leaders of the poor communities, and now it was in the interest of these leaders to remain silent, to protect the benefits they had received (Chatterjee, 1975).

A fifth example is the efforts of India to popularize family planning programs in the 1970s (Bailey & Chatterjee, 1992). The motto of this program was "Stop at Two," meaning couples should have no more than two children. The Stop at Two program did not affect the Indian middle class because they were practicing family planning voluntarily. However, poor Muslim families in northern India were reluctant to comply with such a policy because their tradition encouraged them to have many children and the rate of child mortality among them was high (so that if a couple had four children, perhaps two would survive). Given this scenario, many enthusiastic state officials encouraged (and sometimes coerced) Muslim men to get vasectomies. Later, this practice led to charges that the Indian government was trying to limit the growth of a minority population, even though the government encouraged all men, regardless of religion, to get vasectomies.

A sixth example is the conflict between the Cree and the Anglo-Canadians in Ontario (near the coast of James Bay in Canada). The major cultural event of the Cree was shooting geese during the summer and preserving them to eat during the harsh winter. Furthermore, the community required that the meat harvested during this festival be shared with people who are too young, too old, or too sick to hunt. However, Anglo-Canadians are vehemently opposed to this community festival of the Cree, which seems to them like a mass slaughter of geese. The Canadian government's policies have often supported the position of the Anglo-Canadians in this matter, and the only time the Canadian government supported the Cree was when a coalition of both Cree and Anglo-Canadian environmentalists opposed building a massive hydroelectric project in James Bay ("Canadian Native Groups," 1994). Canadian policies have created dependent populations among the Cree, who now require subsidies from the state to survive.

As the six examples indicated, the state is frequently a party to community-level conflicts. Although it may appear that the state is trying to "optimize" welfare, it is clear that the state often becomes a contestant in these conflicts and sides with parties that are dominant, in the majority, or powerful. In the example of the Ik in Kenya, the state sided with the interests of the majority, engaged in inappropriate intervention, and could not foresee the demise of the Ik's hunter–gatherer culture. In the case of the Moynihan report, the state was proposing to engage in too little intervention too late, since for 300 years, it had allowed black communities to be systematically repressed. Despite the report's acknowledgment of the cumulative impact of that oppression, the state was, at best, a feeble arbiter.

In the example of the gypsies of Romania and Hungary, the state may become a beneficiary of the conflict and receive some secondary gains. With regard to the CDCs in the United States, the state's actions led, at best, to some unintended consequences, including the upward mobility of some leaders of the poor communities but not of the people in these communities, and at worst, to making the state an agent of groups who were interested in maintaining the status quo, since the state co-opted the indigenous leaders and left the communities bereft of advocates. In the examples of family planning in India and the Cree's community festival in Canada, the state became the unwitting agent of a dominant group (the Hindu middle class and the Anglo-Canadians) and acted against the best interests of a minority community (poor Muslims and the Cree).

THESIS 2: WELFARE IS A CAMOUFLAGE FOR ORGANIZATIONAL–LEVEL CONFLICTS

Organizational-level conflicts can be of three types: (1) both parties in conflict are some sort of organization; (2) one party is an organization, and another party is a community; or (3) one party is an organization, and the other party is an interest group (when this interest group has an organization, it becomes a special case of type 2). The state, with its welfare efforts, can become an ally, an arbiter, a contestant, or a third party to the conflict.

The first example of interorganizational conflict is an actual case study documented by Chatterjee (1992). In this case, the first party was a school of social work of a well-known American university in an urban area (hereafter called SSW), and the second party was a community center in a poor, black neighborhood of the same city (hereafter called CCB).

CCB was an underfunded inner-city organization that frequently engaged in advocacy for its neighborhood. SSW was an organization dedicated to social work education that wanted to use CCB as a site where its students could get some fieldwork experience. SSW received a large grant from the state to engage in a cooperative venture, which included advocacy for poor people in the community and education of social workers.

From the beginning, the venture was fraught with intense conflict. The two parties came from two different class cultures: the middle class (SSW) and the poverty class (CCB). SSW was interested in educating its students, whereas CCB was interested in advocating for the community. SSW had money and political skill, CCB did not. SSW used many Freudian terms to describe the leaders of CCB (they were acting out, they had character disorders, they needed "help," and so on), whereas CCB described the SSW as another oppressor and part of the white establishment. The SSW leaders blamed the conflict on the personalities of the CCB's leaders and used psychotherapy-oriented language to describe the situation, whereas the CCB leaders blamed the situation on the racism of the SSW leaders. Later, it seemed that neither personality nor race had anything to do with the conflict. Role (who the parties represented and what their interests were) was the key to understanding the conflict.

The case represented more than a conflict between two organizations. It also represented a conflict between two sets of role interests (described by Dahrendorf, 1959, and discussed in chapter 6) and between two sets of class interests (the middle class and the inner-city underclass). The state, by its power to reward (giving money to support a cause), unwittingly became a contestant and an ally of one party (SSW). In sum, the state acted to support the interests of the middle class and against the interests of the underclass.

The second example of organizational-level conflict was documented by Lipsky (1980). In this case, the conflict is between poor communities and state bureaucracies. Lipsky noted that the work practices of state bureaucracies that serve poor people indicate how the welfare state's public service policy is implemented and that there may well be a conflict between the state policy (to *provide care*) and the practiced policy (to *produce indifference*, as Herzfeld, 1992, called it). Here the state policy is to provide income, food vouchers, or health care to the poor. The practiced policy is to make people wait a long time, to ignore them, or to treat them without dignity. Although the state seems to be an ally of poor people, it is really an ally of its own bureaucratic arm and is indifferent to the needs of poor communities.

The third example is of private social services in the United States. These services have long been a source of civic pride and an exemplar of what nongovernmental efforts can accomplish. One such private effort, called the United Way movement, involves voluntary fundraising at the metropolitan or municipal level. After funds are raised, a municipal-level representative body decides how the money is to be distributed to supplement the budgets of selected municipal-level social agencies. During the 1990s, this model of transfer (called voluntary, private, and noncentric transfer in chapter 2) has been initiated in Israel, Canada, and several former communist countries.

In the United States, corporations are highly involved in this type of voluntary fundraising for social services, which they promote as an example of "corporate social responsibility." It is common for corporations to sponsor, support, and give leadership to these activities.

At issue, however, are several practices and procedures in this venture. First, supervisors often pressure individual employees, usually line employees, to give more money to make their company look good. When a company looks good, its owners and managers get credit for a strong sense of social responsibility. Second, the United Way executives receive high salaries and fringe benefits that are comparable to those of the executives of corporations. This practice means that the cost of fundraising rises and no standard is set about the percentage of funds that fundraisers keep as the cost of fundraising. Third, the role of the state in this venture is precarious: If the state tries to regulate this venture tightly, then it will control a voluntary civic activity. If the state does not regulate the venture at all, then the "werewolves" of the free market (to use a Marxist metaphor) will be let loose in the arena of voluntary fundraising. Because the state often grants these organizations nonprofit status (so the organizations are exempt from paying taxes), its taxation policy makes it an ally of these organizations. In short, powerful organizations decide how voluntary noncentric transfers are made.

An even more dramatic case of conflict between the values of social welfare organizations and organized private philanthropy occurs in capitalist countries (especially the United States) when successful celebrities start nonprofit organizations to deal with certain social welfare issues. Whereas the particular issue may be the manifest reason for such an organization to exist, the latent reason (see Merton, 1958) may be to develop good public relations for the celebrity and to get a tax write-off for expensive activities (such as dinners or dances) that benefit the rich. Furthermore, although some of these organizations may not meet the professional standards of the field, the state supports them by granting them nonprofit status.

The fourth example of organizational conflict, conceptualized by Piven and Cloward (1971), may be termed regulating the poor. In the 1993 edition of their book, Piven and Cloward advanced the position that poor relief in the United States is a function of civil disorder produced by large-scale unemployment. That is, when unemployment is high, the state increases poor relief, and when unemployment is low, the state decreases such relief. Thus, policies on relief are used to enforce work norms and to control poor communities. The conflict is between people of poor communities, who are unskilled and hence often cannot find jobs, and the majority communities, whose ideology is that income should be derived from work (see chapter 4 on ideology and income). In this situation, the state is not an innocent third party but an ally of the majority communities.

THESIS 3: WELFARE IS A CAMOUFLAGE FOR ETHNIC CONFLICTS

Conflicts between ethnoracial, ethnolingual, and ethnoreligious communities are perhaps as old as the documented history of human civilization. In tribal communities, according to Divale and Harris (1976), ethnic conflict and warfare were ways of regulating the population, maintaining patriarchy, and ensuring that there was enough food to feed the tribe (food–human balance). In agricultural communities, ethnic conflict took on a territorial meaning and maintained the food–population balance. Ethnic conflicts are old, territorial, and rooted in history, and members of one group are socialized to hate or suspect members of the other group from childhood onward. Furthermore, as Coser (1956, p. 87) explained, "conflict with out-groups increases the solidarity of in-groups." Often loyalty to one's ethnic group as an ethnic member is stronger than loyalty to the state as a citizen. On the surface, it may appear that ethnic conflict is more frequent in the Third World, but a better explanation is that ethnic conflicts are reduced when the groups in conflict are urbanized and middle class and have a stake in the smooth operation of the state.

Any multiethnic state faces ongoing conflicts among its ethnic groups. In this regard, there are at least four areas of potential conflict in the formulation and implementation of policies, and in most of them, the state explicitly or implicitly becomes an ally, arbiter, contestant, or uninterested third party. These conflicts involve the degree of secularism a state can adopt, welfare versus labor policy, diversity policy, and the degree of fundamentalism that a state can tolerate.

Degree of secularism. In most cases, the state is based on the cultural infrastructure of a dominant ethnoreligious group (such as Anglo-Saxon Protestants in the United States or linguistic Indo-Iranian Hindus in India) and, in its efforts to be secular, cannot escape that template. Consequently, other ethnoreligious groups in the state believe that the state has a built-in bias against them. At times this belief may be valid and a source of conflict. The conflict is heightened when the state consists of many ethnic groups and is not committed to being secular (such as Iran, Israel, or Spain).

Efforts to coordinate a welfare and a labor policy. Rimlinger (1971) showed that no modern state can envision a welfare policy without simultaneously planning its labor policy. In multiethnic states, such conflicts surface in relation to affirmative action, employee assistance, retirement benefits, maternity or paternity leave, child care support, education, and health care, which are part of a labor policy, and income maintenance, health care, and training of unskilled workers, which are part of welfare policy. Often the leaders of one ethnic group (ethnoracial, ethnoreligious, or ethnolingual) charge that members of another ethnic group are getting preferential treatment in labor policy or welfare policy. At times, the charges are true because the state is trying to support an ethnic group that has been underprivileged for a long time. The conflicts are sometimes intensified when the members of underprivileged groups begin to feel a sense of entitlement in the state's redistribution efforts, and the majority or the dominant groups become resentful of such efforts.

Diversity policy. By diversity policy, I mean the state's use of its labor policy and welfare policy to achieve assimilation (of all other ethnic groups into the dominant group), pluralism (of all ethnic groups), and separatism (of some ethnic groups) (see Farley, 1988).

The dilemma of the multiethnic state is that its political and electoral processes may demand that it move toward either a separatist or an assimilationist policy, whereas norms of equality and justice call for a pluralistic policy. Sometimes, a political outcome may be due to conflict between a *stated* policy, which may be pluralist, and a *pursued* policy, which may be ambivalence.

Ability to handle fundamentalism. Ladestro (1993) stated that almost all forms of fundamentalism have the following attributes: affirmation of patriarchy, affirmation of machismo, affirmation of ethnic (religious, linguistic, or racial) loyalty, and obsession with instruments of violence. Fundamentalism is often the response of one or more ethnic groups in conflict in a multiethnic state, and the state is faced with a serious dilemma: Should it allow the fundamentalist group to practice (which may be freedom of speech and religion), or should it suppress the group (which may be necessary to protect minority interests)?

Because the very existence of ethnic conflicts may threaten the ongoing security and legitimation of the state, the state is constantly under pressure to examine its role in an ethnic conflict: Should it be an ally, an arbiter, a contestant, or an uninterested third party? Many ethnoracial, ethnoreligious, or ethnolingual conflicts (such as between the Hutus and the Tutsis in Rwanda, the Ibos and the Hausas in Nigeria, the Hindus and the Muslims in India, the Kurds and the Turkish in Turkey, or the descendants of Europeans and the descendants of African slaves in the United States) are long standing, but the state has not developed a political formula to manage them. In the short and the long run, the state cannot remain an uninterested third party in these conflicts. As a result, it is left with only three choices: to be an ally, an arbiter, or a contestant.

THESIS 4: WELFARE IS A CAMOUFLAGE FOR INTEREST–GROUP CONFLICTS

Interest-group conflict and the role of the welfare state in such conflicts can originate in at least six known contexts (outlined in chapter 6): class conflicts,

ideological conflicts, conflicts in levels of knowledge, conflicts in role interests, conflicts owing to gender-related oppression, and conflicts generated
by technology.

CLASS CONFLICT

From a Marxist or neo-Marxist view, almost all the conflict scenarios
identified in this chapter can be seen from the perspective of class conflict.
Mills (1956), for example, argued that the state is often either an agent or an
ally of the upper classes in capitalist societies, and both Domhoff (1978) and
Piven and Cloward (1971) supported this contention.

Pohlmann (1990) developed the idea of conduit capitalism, which
is built on a model of class conflict introduced by Charles V. Hamilton in
1972. In this model, the state acts as an ally of the upper class (or, as Pohlmann
called it, the "owning class," meaning the class that owns capital). The general population of the capitalist state falls into one of the following four
social classes: the upper class, the middle class, the working class, and the
poor class, or as Pohlmann called it, "welfare recipients" (the conceptual
model is the same as the one presented in Figures 1-3 and 1-4). Figure 7-1
depicts this model of class conflict.

In Figure 7-1, there are basically five parties: the four social strata
and the state. Figure 7-1 indicates that the middle and working classes pay
taxes to the state (a reminder that the welfare state is built essentially on
income transfer) and their activities send corporate profits to rich people
(the upper class). The state continues to provide subsidies to a category of
recipients in the upper class (referred to as protected entrepreneurs in Figure 2-5) and transfer payments to poor people. Many forms of income transfer and services that are aimed at the poor class yield hidden benefits (called
conduit capitalism) to the upper class (such as rent from slum dwellings and
health and other services provided through various third-party plans). In the
meantime, the anger of the middle and the working classes is directed at the
poor class because transfers to poor people are highly visible and subsidies
to rich people are not. In terms of class conflict, then, Pohlmann outlined a
three-way conflict: between the middle mass (the middle and the working
classes) and the poor class, between the middle mass and the upper class,
and between the upper class and the poor class. Of the three, the first is an
open conflict and highly visible, whereas the second and the third are not
easily visible and may even be subjected to denial or false consciousness
(see chapter 6).

Although the Pohlmann paradigm of class conflict follows the classical Marxist template, it generates certain conceptual problems. For example, the conduit-capitalist benefits that flow from the poor (welfare recipients) to the rich (welfare beneficiaries) are hard to trace, unless one
includes the upper middle class. It is usually upwardly mobile members of

Figure 7-1.

The Beneficiaries of Conflict in a Welfare State

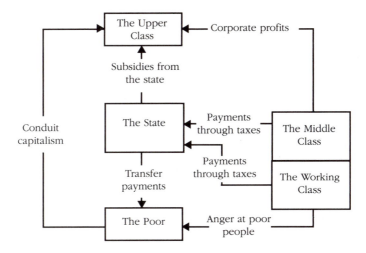

SOURCE: Pohlmann, M. (1990). *Black politics in conservative America*. New York: Longman.

the middle class who own rental property in the slums and provide medical, legal, dental, or other services to poor people (and are reimbursed by the state for doing so). Sometimes these persons are immigrants or second-generation citizens and can hardly be seen as elites or members of the upper class. Gans (1972) proposed that poverty is functional and benefits the middle class (discussed in chapter 9)—a thesis that is perhaps more valid than the contention that poverty benefits the upper class. Thus, Figure 7-2 presents a revised view of Pohlmann's thesis.

The idea of welfare as a camouflage for class conflict has also been advanced by other authors, such as Bernstein (1968), Levine (1988), and Piven and Cloward (1993). Bernstein and Levine both reviewed the New Deal (which Eulau, 1962, claimed was the achievement of "mature politics"; see chapter 5) and concluded that the introduction of social welfare measures by the administration of U.S. President Franklin D. Roosevelt in the 1930s was due less to sympathy for the poor and the marginal populations than to the need to help the capitalist class (the upper class). As Levine put it, "the manner in which the New Deal industrial recovery program attempted to maintain and further conditions for profitable accumulation was shaped by dynamics of the class struggle in the U.S. during the 1930's" (pp. 4–5).

Hence, the New Deal was a solution to a crisis in capitalism caused by contradictions in the process of accumulating capital: too high a rate of

Figure 7-2.

The Beneficiaries of Conflict in a Welfare State: Revised View

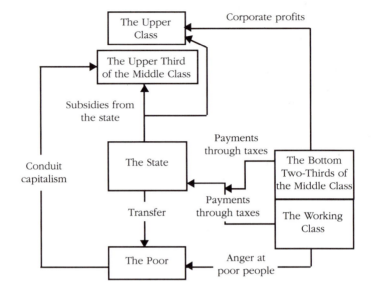

SOURCE: Pohlmann, M. (1990). *Black politics in conservative America*. New York: Longman.

labor exploitation and unregulated competition that caused problems in investment. The New Deal eliminated these contradictions, facilitated the accumulation of monopoly capital, diffused the militancy of labor, and incorporated organized labor into a national political bargaining process.

Levine's (1988) thesis (and the positions of the other authors just mentioned) is that public policies are not rationally based or established to achieve social equilibrium, but are shaped to deal with the presence of antagonism among the social classes. The state is often an ally of the elites or the upper classes and develops public policies that facilitate their interests.

IDEOLOGICAL CONFLICT

Habermas's (1970) position, that ideological conflict is like a conflict in story lines, was discussed in chapter 4. From this perspective, traditional society depended on one major coordinated story line, and using it to legitimate social action was easier than in modern society, where multiple story lines compete with each other for legitimation. It is the competition and conflict between multiple story lines (to appease the masses) that contribute to ideological conflicts.

Such ideological conflicts are present in the struggles between patriarchy and feminism, between the commodification and decommodification of goods and services (as is done by market forces), and between medicalization (knowledge based on the medical model and applied under market principles) and the concept of health as a social utility (knowledge of health leads to collective responsibility). They also are present in conflicts between the family as an agent of transfer and social control and the state as an agent of transfer and social control and between illness as an opportunity to be subjected to market forces and illness (and other human misfortunes) as a known and almost probabilistic crisis to be responded to with social utilities. These ideological conflicts can be seen in Table 5-1, where several ideologies (story lines) are in conflict. For example, at the beneficiary level (there is nobody to blame), there is a different type of legitimation than at the sick, suspect, or problem level (there is something or someone to blame).

Ideological conflicts are also manifest when the state is faced with several ways of responding to a given role. In all societies, two such common roles are the child and the aged person (see Aries, 1962). The demands of the multiple story lines may result in a policy to assist children, such as the one shown in Figure 7-3, which depicts the state's dilemmas about enacting this type of policy. Once the child role is clearly established (and the state has thus moved away from the role ambiguity shown in box 1), then one can trace all possible outcomes after the yes answer to the child role. If the child needs income support and such provisions are available from the state, then one ends up in box 3, where child assistance is available. Conversely, if the state has no provisions for income support to children, then one would end up in box 4.

In addition to or instead of an income-support policy for children, a state may enact (or ignore) a policy to protect children that includes correction. If a child needs protection (from incest, abuse, criminal association, being treated as an adult after committing a deviant act, and so on) and the state has no provision for doing so, then one ends up in box 5. On the other hand, if the state has provisions responding to the need to protect children, then one ends up in box 6.

Depending on the cultural, political, and economic setting, a state may face policy options designated individually in boxes 3, 4, 5, or 6; a combination of 3 and 5 (income support by the state and child care by the family or community), a combination of 3 and 6 (both income support and child protection by the state), a combination of 4 and 5 (both child support and child care by the family or community), or a combination of 4 and 6 (child support by the family or community and child protection by the state). All this is due to the various story lines (ideological conflicts) about how to respond to children and their needs.

The state may face some similar sets of dilemmas in relation to a policy for the aged. Figure 7-4 illustrates the conflicts related to such a policy.

Figure 7-3.

Six Ways of Defining a Child-Assistance Policy

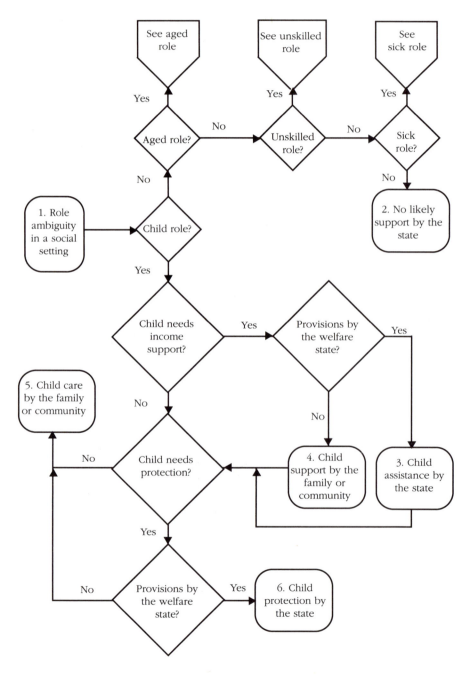

Figure 7-4.

Seven Ways of Defining an Aged-Assistance Policy

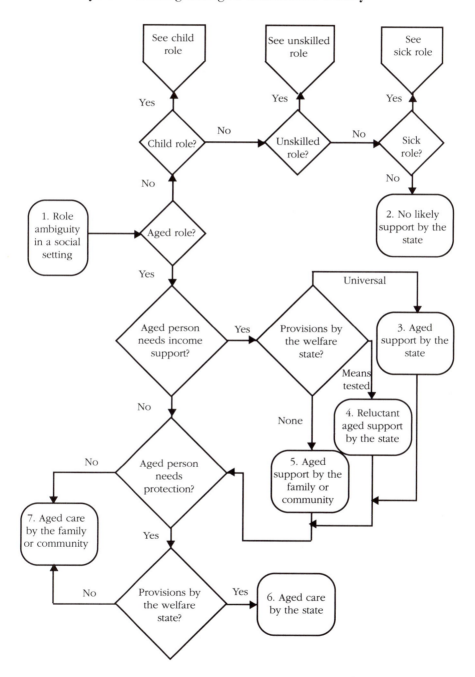

It shows that once one is culturally defined as an aged person (has been accorded an aged role), then several options follow. The matter of income support can be answered in one of three ways—there is support on a universalistic basis, there is only means-tested support, and there is no income support—boxes 3, 4, and 5, respectively. The options depicted in boxes 3, 4, and 5 each designate a different outcome in relation to income support, and they all appear in different combinations with the options noted in boxes 6 and 7.

The different outcomes shown in Figures 7-3 and 7-4 reflect conflicts about ideologies of income (outlined in chapter 4) and ideologies of personal social services for children and aged people. The next section traces how conflicts of ideologies can also operate in combination with conflicts in levels of knowledge—the positions of Michael Foucault and Pierre Bourdieu (knowledge leads to power) discussed in chapter 6.

CONFLICTS IN LEVELS OF KNOWLEDGE

Dunlap (1994, p. 37) stated that "conflict arises when communities lack tangible or intangible resources. . . . Conflict also emerges when two communities espouse different norms, values, or expectations. For example, conflict may arise when teachers expect parents to supply additional resources while parents expect schools to provide all materials." Dunlap then applied Bourdieu's concept of cultural capital to show that groups from higher social classes have more cultural capital and that the possession of such capital puts them in a more advantageous position than groups from lower social classes. Her research focused on whether a poorly educated low-income black population in North Carolina could be helped to develop cultural capital through training sessions and whether the accumulation of such capital would reduce conflicts between them and persons with high cultural capital. It found that, as Bourdieu suggested, knowledge structures have an almost linear relationship with social-class structures (the higher the class position, the more information available, and the more the information available, the more the cultural capital). Dunlap's work also established that training programs that provide lower-class people with important information and social skills help them accumulate some amount of cultural capital.

In regard to cultural capital at the community level, Kozol (1991) showed that low-income black communities in the United States are subjected to "savage inequalities," whereas middle-income communities of other groups are not. When one group, community, or social class has insufficient or lower cultural capital than another group, community, or social class, what should be the policy of a welfare state? The stated policy may be to provide compensatory packages to the disadvantaged group, but the pursued policy may not follow through on that promise.

Differences in the knowledge or beliefs of different groups in a national culture may also lead to conflicts in policy alternatives. For example, with respect to health, there may be competition among the paradigms of the allopathic, homeopathic, osteopathic, and other "schools" of knowledge. Which school is "superior," and which one should a welfare state adopt when it is providing services? By supporting one school of knowledge (for example, by allowing allopathic medicine to become the only legitimate school of medicine), does the state become an ally of one group (such as practitioners of allopathic medicine) against another (such as practitioners of homeopathic medicine)?

Another way to approach the conflict of knowledge systems in a culture is to examine differences in the concept of the "sick" role (Parsons, 1951). In any given culture, there are procedures for defining this role (see Table 5-2 for an example). Assuming that there is agreement about how the role is to be assigned, there may be both ideological and knowledge differences in a culture about how to respond to this role. Figure 7-5 outlines alternative ways to define such a policy.

The assumption in Figure 7-5 is that there are two types of conflicts in knowledge systems: (1) the conflict between whether or not to assign a sick role to a person (often the conflict is more acute in assigning the mentally sick role than the physically sick role) and (2) conflicts among several ways of responding to the sick role. When one is defined as deviant (not sick), and the state has no way to manage this role, but an alternative deviant subculture does, then box 2 is an outcome. The members and subcultures of various street gangs, organized crime groups, and new religious cults may be included in this category, and subjecting them to welfare policy may cause a conflict in some national cultures. For example, a subculture of a group of Aryan Nations (a group that believes that white persons should commit violent acts against nonwhites) may be thought of as both psychologically sick and behaviorally deviant. In the United States, members of groups who fit the category indicated by box 2 (such as drug-addicted subcultures) are not a focus of welfare policy, but in the Netherlands, some of them are likely to be located in one of the boxes marked 3. Depending on the cultural context, an alcoholic ("sick"?) driver ("deviant"?) would be placed either in box 3a or 3b. When one is defined as neither sick nor deviant, then the outcomes are those depicted in boxes 4 and 5.

When one is defined as sick (yes to the question, sick role?) and not deviant, then the question of whether the welfare state has provisions for managing such a role is important. Such a scenario is outlined in box 6. Even this scenario may vary depending on the national culture. In one culture, it may mean treatment by a national health service, whereas in another culture, it may mean treatment by providers in private practice who receive third-party payments from the state.

Figure 7-6, which outlines ways of defining income maintenance policy, follows the same logic as Figure 7-5. Here the conflict is about (1) assigning

Figure 7-5.

Seven Ways of Defining Health, Mental Health, and Corrections Policy

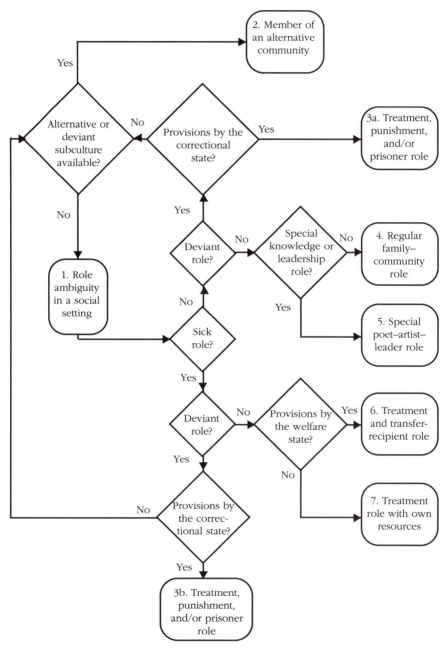

Figure 7-6.

Seven Ways of Defining Income Maintenance or Assistance Policy

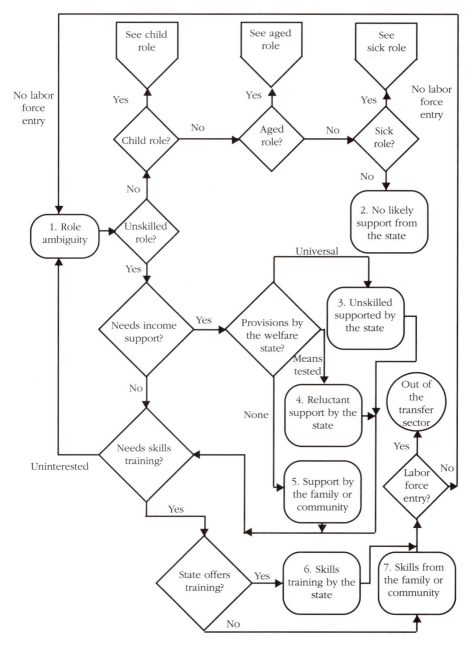

and (2) managing the unskilled role because of insufficient education, origin in a poor community, or other constraints on employment.

In most cultures, the assignment of child or aged roles by cultural templates means that one need not be judged as a skilled (capable of being employed) or an unskilled (incapable of being employed) person. Furthermore, the assignment of a sick role also means that the person is at least temporarily exempt from employment (and in chronic sick roles, one may be permanently exempt from employment, although in many cultures the assignment of a chronic sick role, especially a chronic mentally sick role, can be disputed). Otherwise, the first conflict in income maintenance or income assistance policy is, Should a person be assigned an unskilled role? The second conflict, then, is how to manage the person to whom an unskilled role has been assigned. Figure 7-6 depicts these conflicts.

A basic ideological conflict exists in assigning the four roles: child, aged, sick, and unskilled. Then there is a set of knowledge-base conflicts in defining the sick and the unskilled roles. The ideological conflicts are inherent in any role definition, regardless of whether they are supported by an established knowledge base, because two role definitions (child and aged) are based on biological roles. However, for a person to be defined as sick or unskilled, the role definition has to originate from an established knowledge base, preferably organized as an occupation or a profession (such as medicine, clinical psychology, social work, or education).

In some areas, there are conflicts or contradictions both among and within these established knowledge bases, so welfare state policymakers have to wade through these contradictions. For example, the outcome boxes 3a, 3b, and 6 in Figure 7-5 and boxes 3, 4, and 6 in Figure 7-6 can be subject to such conflicts. An example of a conflict in knowledge base (both within and between knowledgeable groups who prescribe welfare policy) was presented in Table 5-2, where suspect, sick, and problem situations are in conflict with a beneficiary situation. These different ways of managing sick or unskilled roles, in turn, generate different interest groups who are in conflict. For its own reasons, the state becomes an ally, arbiter, or contestant in such interest-group conflicts.

CONFLICTS IN ROLE INTERESTS

A conflict in role interests occurs when two or more interest groups take different or contradictory positions on a given activity. They take these positions less often because of their ideology or scientific reasoning than because their political and economic interests are advanced because of their activities.

A good example of such a conflict was cited under Thesis 2, which discussed a conflict between two organizations (see Chatterjee, 1992). In that case, one interest group was a school of social work, and the other was an inner-city community center. Both were based on the social work profession, and both shared similar (at least on the surface) ideologies. However, they got locked into a series of conflicts that were due mainly to political and economic interests.

Another good example of a conflict in role interests was Chapin's (1994) study of the alcohol-producing and alcohol-treatment industries. Both industries cite scientific studies and quote ideological positions to support their arguments, but their behavior is essentially predicated on their interests, which, for the alcohol-producing industry, is to keep the sale of alcohol legitimate and, for the treatment industry, to keep the disease concept of alcoholism in the forefront and treatment centers open. In the long run, both interest groups benefit from the situation. Chapin's thesis is also applicable to Norway, Sweden, Finland, Russia, and other countries where both alcohol consumption and alcohol treatment are prevalent.

Yet another example of a conflict in role interests was presented by Specht and Courtney (1993) with regard to the social work profession. Social work originated as a *manager of the marginalized* (the metaphors are mine, not Specht and Courtney's) meaning that it was dedicated to providing directions and services to the poor, disabled, sick, unskilled, elderly people, children, and various other marginalized groups. Since the 1980s, however, this profession has been jockeying for a position as *therapist for the middle class* (in the United States and several other capitalist countries). The latter role carries more occupational prestige, has the potential for higher earnings, and creates a social distance from clients in the lower social classes. Although it is possible that social workers can perform both roles, in reality, the better educated and the more skilled social workers perform the latter role, which leaves the less trained to perform the former role.

Conflicts Owing to Gender–Related Oppression

Whereas Richard M. Titmuss and his colleagues considered citizenship (rather than class or community membership or interest-group support) to be the only form of legitimation for social welfare, Brivati and Jones (1993) argued that the very concept of citizenship evolved using the templates of masculinity and hence relegates women to a second-class status. Although Quadagno (1990) contended that this was the case in the United States, Skocpol (1992) pointed out that the U.S. welfare state originally developed with a "maternalistic" bias in the 1860s, after the Civil War. Skocpol further noted that the maternalistic bias eroded over time, but its influence would be seen in the formation of the U.S. Children's Bureau in 1912, a governmental agency that sponsored and supported many forms of maternal and child policy in the country in the mid-20th century.

Orloff (1993) claimed that studies of the welfare state have often ignored gender-related biases and suggested, as did Korpi (1989) and Esping-

Andersen (1990), that welfare benefits are used to maintain the infrastructures of patriarchy. Noting that many welfare plans require recipients to have lost wages from the labor market, and such persons are primarily men, she stated that women who are homemakers or otherwise dependent on men can be clients of the welfare state only through their relationships with men. She added that "men make claims as worker-citizens but women make claims as worker-citizens and also members of families and they need programs especially to compensate for marriage failures and/or the need to raise children alone" (Orloff, p. 308).

Furthermore, Orloff argued, civil and political rights for women are different from those for men because women's right to control their bodies (to decide whether to engage in sexual relations and to have an abortion and to be protected from rape and other forms of violence) is continually contested, but men's is not. Thus, the presence or absence of the protective role of the state is a crucial factor.

Although Orloff contended that social policy, even in Sweden, is gender biased, Gould (1993, p. 246) stated that

> [women's] education and training opportunities [in Sweden] surpassed those of women in other countries. In terms of [women's] representation in parliament and government, their political power was significant. . . . Parental leave enabled women to undertake the dual responsibility of working in the home and in the formal economy (which in all capitalist societies is disproportionately borne by women) with less personal hardship than elsewhere and with the added possibility that it could be shared with their male partners.

Although the presence of gender-related oppression in Sweden is debatable, there is less doubt that such oppression is prevalent in other capitalist First World countries. Furthermore, gender-related oppression is much worse in Third World countries, from the Philippines to the Persian Gulf, where a combination of poverty, patriarchy, and tradition devalue women. For example, child prostitution is a source of hard-currency income in Thailand and the Philippines. In Dacca, Calcutta, Bombay, and Karachi, there are communities of cast-out women who have become prostitutes because of poverty, the lack of jobs, and social attitudes that define them as "fallen women." The underground shipment of young women from India and Bangladesh to the Persian Gulf region contributes to the supply of prostitutes in these areas.

Poverty is usually a contributory factor to such human exploitation. Other contributory factors are religious fundamentalism and a tradition that defines women as either "insiders" (of the house) or "outsiders" (of the streets). Both groups face child welfare issues, health issues, and human abuse issues. Plans for the protection of members of these communities need to be discussed in international forums.

In sum, the oppression of women seems to fall into one or more of the following categories:

1. being viewed in relation to men, rather than in relation to the state
2. being victimized by four types of hierarchies—race, class, age, and gender—whereas men are victimized by three—race, class, and age
3. being seen as persons whose labor is devalued and whose wage loss is less often compensated
4. being especially vulnerable to the "feminization of poverty" (see Ehreneich & Piven, 1984; Weitzman, 1985), both as lower-class women and as downwardly mobile middle- and working-class women
5. being able to obtain child support payments, when such payments are legally and morally owed to them
6. being able to get transfer payments from the state, indexed not after male life expectancies and labor force participation but after their own
7. being able to retain their rights to their own bodies.

Given the gendered benefit levels instituted by most states, the question is this: In two different benefit structures that have been developed on the basis of sex, what is the role of the state? Is it an ally of one party, an arbiter, a contestant, or a neutral third party?

CONFLICTS GENERATED BY TECHNOLOGY

Chapter 6 discussed how conflicts can emerge from different styles of production. This section focuses on the conflicts generated by changes from Fordism to post-Fordism. Problems generated by changes in the technological bases of society in general are discussed in chapters 8 and 9.

The form of industrial production in some countries has changed from Fordism to post-Fordism, and the group most affected by these changes is the working class. In most capitalist countries, the working classes struggled to develop collective-bargaining procedures; under Fordism, they formed unions that struggled to win benefits for their members from employers (Wilensky, 1975). With a shift to post-Fordism, the power of large-scale unions is eroding, and unions to protect new types of workers are not readily being formed. As a result, some members of the formerly wage-earning working class are now downwardly mobile.

The loss of power by large-scale unions and their lesser capacity to bargain on behalf of some members of the working class have required changes in income assistance or income maintenance plans and in health care coverage. In most European countries and Japan, the working class has been affected less than it has been in the United States, where the state is not as prompt in providing income support or health care coverage. In Europe the massive strikes of December 1995 in France showed the beginning of a conflict between the working class and the state.

In a post-Fordist economy, then, the conflict is between the working class and industry. Therefore, the question again arises: What, if any, role does the state take? Is the state an ally of one party, an arbiter, a contestant in the conflict, or a neutral third party?

Thesis 5: Welfare Is a Camouflage for International Conflicts

If citizenship is the only basis for eligibility for welfare (as Titmuss proposed; see chapters 4 and 5), then what form of legitimation, if any, should be used to offer transfers to noncitizens (or aliens)? In today's global village, is citizenship alone still a good reason for offering transfer payments or services? Furthermore, if benefits are to be offered to noncitizens, then should there be a way of categorizing noncitizens, and should there be an ordinal position of preference, on the basis of which noncitizens become eligible to receive the benefits of the welfare state?

To explore the complexity of the situation, I present five cases, some or all of which may appear at first glance to be interpersonal or intergroup transactions. A more careful examination, however, reveals that most of them are international transactions.

Case 1: A young man, neither a Dutch citizen nor of ethnic Dutch origin, who is living in Amsterdam is dependent on drugs. One day he overdoses. The Dutch welfare state treats him, no questions asked, and attempts to rehabilitate him.

Case 2: Police in California enter a Hispanic neighborhood, looking for an illegal alien who is of Hispanic origin. When they cannot find this person, they harass an American citizen who is of Hispanic origin.

Case 3: A middle-aged ethnic German man and a middle-aged ethnic Japanese man (independently) go to Thailand as tourists. They are solicited by agents of child prostitutes, and they arrive at a bargain. Both men are then serviced by two different 12-year-old Thai girls.

Case 4: An ethnic Turkish man arrives in Germany as a guest worker and fills a job category that native Germans do not like to do. After he spends some time in Germany, he wants to go to school to improve his situation, and to engage in collective bargaining to change his rate of pay. (He will have a great deal of difficulty doing either.)

Case 5: A rural farmer in India goes to Bombay looking for a laborer's job. An agent of a medical clinic tells him that he needs only one kidney to survive and that he will be rich if he sells one of his kidneys to help an ill sheik from a middle-eastern country who needs a kidney. The Indian farmer's kidney is then surgically removed, and the man is paid an equivalent of U.S. $200.

At least four types of conflicts lead to the situations inherent in these five cases, conflicts that are due to differences in citizenship, differences in ethnicity, differences in wealth, and membership in different parts of the world system. In the first case, there is a potential conflict between the payers and the recipients. The payers of health care are Dutch citizens, and the care is supported by Dutch taxpayers. A non-Dutch person who receives services is tolerated. However, what would happen if the recipients of service increasingly are from ethnically and racially different stocks? For example, more and more North Africans are coming to France, and their use of the French health care system or the welfare system is a matter of controversy. How long can the Dutch welfare state remain tolerant if it has to provide services to a large client group that is not Dutch, either by citizenship or by ethnoracial origin?

In the second case, the conflict is an ethnic conflict. The person harassed is an American citizen, but the implicit assumption, it seems, is that the citizenship of an Anglo American is more secure than that of an Hispanic American. This is a likely case of ethnic conflict (between Anglos and Hispanics), and there seems to be a tacit alliance between the state's correctional system and the Anglo community. This problem has been heightened during the 1990s because the governors of California and Florida openly stated that illegal immigrants are a drain on the economies of their states and urged that illegal immigrants be denied welfare support, health care support, and education. California had a similar history of excluding Asians only a generation ago, but it did not exclude ethnic Germans even during World War II.

The third case is an example of a multilevel transaction. First, it is an interpersonal transaction between a prostitute and her client. Second, it is an interethnic transaction because the parties are from two different ethnic groups. Third, it is a transaction between two different types of wealth holders: one (the German or the Japanese) who is wealthier than the other (the Thai girls). Fourth, it is an international transaction, given that organized prostitution and sexual junkets are a source of hard-currency income for a poor country. Fifth, it is a transaction between a child and an adult. In both Germany and Japan, this case would be seen as an example of child abuse. In Thailand, the concept of child abuse would not be invoked unless the child was much younger or was physically injured (in which case it would be construed as an assault, not child abuse). Thus, the case is an example of how the problem of child abuse is culturally constructed and of how it is more clearly defined in the First World than in Third World countries.

The fourth case reflects an ethnic conflict between Germans, who position themselves higher up the social ladder than their guest workers, for whom it is difficult even to strive for German citizenship. Thus, the case reflects a conflict of citizenship as well: One type of citizenship (German) is more valued than another (Turkish). It is also a conflict between a group with wealth and a group without and an example of international stratification, in that a First World country is engaging in restricted transactions with persons from a Third World country.

The fifth case, which can be termed body farming, illustrates the conflict between those with wealth (the sheik) and those without (the Indian peasant). Even if the customer for the kidney was a wealthy Indian the situation would be the same because the transaction would still be between a person with wealth and a person with none. However, the presence of a wealthy Arab customer for the kidney makes it a conflict between two ethnic groups, between two types of citizenship holders, and between two Third World countries.

DEPENDENCE AND INTERNATIONAL CONFLICT

An intellectual offshoot of Marxism, dependency theory explains the global hierarchy of nations (Frank, 1969; Furtado, 1970; Lenski, Lenski, & Nolan, 1991). According to this paradigm, it is difficult for Third World countries to develop economically (and to foster the development of the welfare state) because of the economic and political actions of the wealthy First World countries. The First World countries, through long imperial and colonial dominance over the Third World countries, created such conditions as massive poverty, a small wealthy and exploitive local elite, and the absence of institutions that could spur economic growth in the Third World. In this scheme, Third World countries supply raw materials and unskilled and semiskilled labor to the First World countries but face political and economic opposition when welfare benefits for their poor populations are proposed.

The counterargument to dependency theory is that Third World countries need to modernize and develop economically. It is presented in chapters 8 and 9.

CONFLICT AND THE WELFARE INFRASTRUCTURE

The conflict approach, developed in chapters 6 and 7, is well suited for understanding certain occurrences in and around the welfare state. In this regard, it is necessary to understand within- and between-group conflicts and the role of the state in them. Figure 7-7 depicts such conflicts.

In Figure 7-7, within-group conflicts refer to disputes, contradictions, or differences within payers, recipients, and providers. Similarly,

Figure 7-7.

Conflicts in the Welfare Infrastructure

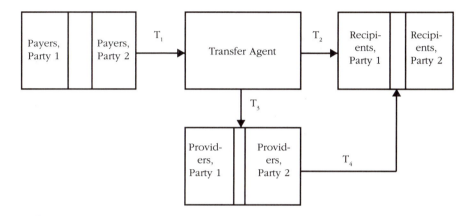

between-group conflicts refer to disputes, contradictions, or differences be-tween payers and recipients, payers and providers, and providers and re-cipients. In this series of conflict scenarios, the role of the transfer agent (the state) can be one or more of the following: ally of one party, arbiter, contes-tant, or neutral third party. Some of these within- and between-group con-flicts are discussed next.

PAYERS

At the abstract level, a conflict within payers means conflicts be-tween Party 1 and Party 2 in the figure, when both parties are payers. At the concrete level, it may mean that Party 1 is a community and Party 2 is another community, that Party 1 is an organization and Party 2 is another group, that Party 1 is an ethnic group and Party 2 is another ethnic group, or that Party 1 is one social class and Party 2 is another social class. Conflicts between these two (or more) parties may occur because one of the parties is making a higher amount of transfer payments than the other party, wants its payments to flow to an earmarked group of recipients whereas the other party does not, or avoids paying its share of transfer payments when the other party feels burdened paying its share.

TYPES OF TRANSFER

Conflicts between the payers and the transfer agent, between the recipients and the transfer agent, or between the provider and the transfer agent may develop when one group (the transfer agent, for example) be-lieves that a given method of transfer is adequate, but another group (the payer, for example) thinks that it is unfair or self-serving. Conflicts of this type may occur in centric, state-sponsored transfer (the state's pay owing to management expenses) or in noncentric voluntary transfer (the voluntary transfer agent's pay to cover administrative expenses).

TRANSFER AGENTS

Apart from the conflicts related to fundraising and the administrative costs assessed by transfer agents (discussed earlier), other types of conflicts may arise between the transfer agent and one or more of the parties involved (payers, recipients, or providers). Such conflicts may be due to differences in procedures preferred by the transfer agent, by the providers, or by the recipients or to the fact that the transfer agent prefers one type of provider and the recipients prefer another. All these conflicts may appear to be interest-group conflicts.

RECIPIENTS

Within groups of recipients, Party 1 and Party 2 can also be communities, organizations, ethnic groups, or social classes. Conflict may develop when members of Party 1 believe they are more entitled to receive transfer payments or services than are members of Party 2. This is sometimes the case when a group of retirees (Party 1) thinks that the state owes them an income (and justify that belief by an ideology of income that favors a work ethic) but that the state does not owe a group of minority children from a different ethnic group (Party 2) such an income. Similarly, members of a group who receive health care services in a given setting (Party 1) may believe that they are more entitled to such care than are members of an ethnic minority group, immigrant group, or another marginalized group (Party 2).

PROVIDERS

Intense conflict sometimes arises within groups of providers when members of Party 1 are attempting to increase their party's market share and members of Party 2 think that the efforts of Party 1 are cutting into their domain. In such cases, the conflict is essentially between two competing interests groups.

Conflicts also occur because of differences in knowledge bases, as when Party 1 represents professional social work and Party 2 represents medicine. In a health care setting, such conflicts may develop when members of Party 2 believe that they should be defining how the services delivery system should be structured and members of Party 1 help transfer recipients demand services from a different perspective. Another example of this type of conflict is when psychiatrists define homelessness as a problem of deinstitutionalized mentally ill people who need psychiatric supervision supported by the state, whereas social workers claim that only a small percentage of deinstitutionalized mentally ill people are homeless and that the homeless population also consists of victims of domestic violence, unemployment, and poverty. It should be noted, however, that conflicts in knowledge bases can often be defined as interest-group conflicts as well.

LIMITS ON TRANSFER

Often conflicts may arise because eventually there is likely to be a limit on the transfer process. Such limits (see Figure 2-7) may contribute to conflicts between recipients' groups and the transfer agent (because the quality and quantity of transfer are being limited), or between the transfer agent and the provider (because the providers' preferred services delivery structure is being compromised by the transfer agent's cost-containment procedures), or between the provider and the recipient (because the recipient blames the provider for services that were limited because of the cost-containment procedures).

CONFLICT AND THE THREE WORLDS

The foregoing conflicts usually occur in the nations of the First or Second World. In addition, conflicts may develop between a nation from the Second or Third World and a nation from the First World. Such conflicts may originate from the First World nation's immigration policy, labor policy, or welfare-eligibility policy that restricts people from the Second or Third World from migrating to, entering the labor force of, or receiving health and income assistance benefits from the First World nation.

REFERENCES

Aries, P. (1962). *Centuries of childhood*. New York: Alfred A. Knopf.

Bailey, D., & Chatterjee, P. (1992). Organization development or community development: True soulmates or uneasy bedfellows? *Journal of Sociology and Social Welfare, 19,* 17–21.

Bernstein, B. J. (1968). The New Deal: The conservative achievements of liberal reform. In B. J. Bernstein (Ed.), *Toward a new past: Dissenting essays in American history* (pp. 263–288). New York: Pantheon Books.

Billingsley, A. (1968). *Black families in white American*. Englewood Cliffs, NJ: Prentice Hall.

Brivati, B., & Jones, H. (1993). *What difference did the war make?* Leicester, England: Leicester University Press.

Canadian native groups. (1994, December 7). *Indian Country Today (Lakota Times),* p. B-9.

Chapin, M. (1994). Functional conflict theory, the alcohol beverage industry, and the alcoholism treatment industry. *Journal of Applied Social Sciences, 18,* 169–182.

Chatterjee, P. (1975). *Local leadership in black communities.* Cleveland: Case Western Reserve University Press.

Chatterjee, P. (1992). Structure and sanctions in two service organizations: A case study of interorganizational conflict. *International Journal of Group Tensions, 21,* 315–340.

Chatterjee, P., Olsen, L., & Holland, T. (1977). Evaluation research: Some possible contexts of theory failure. *Journal of Sociology and Social Welfare, 2,* 384–408.

Coser, L. (1956). *The functions of social conflict.* New York: Free Press.

Dahrendorf, R. (1959). *Class and class conflict in industrial society.* Stanford, CA: Stanford University Press.

Divale, W. T., & Harris, M. (1976). Population, warfare, and the male supremacist complex. *American Anthropologist, 78,* 521–538.

Domhoff, G. W. (1978). *Who really rules?* Santa Monica, Ca: Goodyear.

Dunlap, K. M. (1994). *Family empowerment: One outcome of parental participation in cooperative preschool education.* Unpublished Ph.D. dissertation, Case Western Reserve University, Cleveland.

Ehrenreich, B., & Piven, F. F. (1984). The feminization of poverty. *Dissent, 31,* 162–170.

Esping-Andersen, G. (1990). *Three worlds of welfare capitalism.* Princeton, NJ: Princeton University Press.

Eulau, H. (1962). The American welfare state. In J. S. Rouchek (Ed.), *Contemporary political ideologies* (pp. 415–431). Paterson, NJ: Littlefield.

Farley, J. E. (1988). *Majority–minority relations.* Englewood Cliffs, NJ: Prentice Hall.

Fonseca, I. (1995). *Bury me standing: The Gypsies and their journey.* New York: Alfred A. Knopf.

Frank, A. (1969). *Capitalism and underdevelopment in Latin America.* New York: Monthly Review Press.

Frazier, E. F. (1957). *Black bourgeoisie.* Glencoe, IL: Free Press.

Furtado, C. (1970). *Economic development of Latin America.* Cambridge, England: Cambridge University Press.

Gans, H. (1972). The positive functions of poverty. *American Journal of Sociology, 78,* 275–289.

Gould, A. (1993). *Capitalist welfare systems*. London: Longman.

Gypsies—A people apart. (1995, May 2). *The Plain Dealer,* p. A6.

Habermas, J. (1970). *Towards a rational society*. London: Heinemann.

Heilbronner, R. (1961). *The worldly philosophers*. New York: Simon & Schuster.

Herzfeld, M. (1992). *The social production of indifference*. New York: St. Martin's Press.

Korpi, W. (1989). Power, politics, and state autonomy in the development of social citizenship. *American Sociological Review, 54,* 309–328.

Kozol, J. (1991). *Savage inequalities*. New York: Crown.

Ladestro, D. (1993). Is fundamentalism fundamentally changing society? *University of Chicago Magazine, 85*(4), 16–21.

Lenski, G., Lenski, J., & Nolan, P. (1991). *Human societies: An introduction to macrosociology*. New York: McGraw-Hill.

Levine, R. (1988). *Class struggle and the New Deal*. Lawrence: University of Kansas Press.

Lipsky, M. (1980). *Street-level bureaucracy: Dilemmas of the individual in public services*. New York: Russell Sage Foundation.

Merton, R. (1958). *Social theory and social structure*. Glencoe, IL: Free Press.

Mills, C. W. (1956). *The power elite*. New York: Oxford University Press.

Moynihan, D. P. (1965). *The Negro family: A case for national action*. Washington, DC: Office of Policy Planning and Research, U.S. Department of Labor.

Orloff, A. S. (1993). Gender and the social rights of citizenship. *American Sociological Review, 58,* 303–328.

Parsons, T. (1951). *The social system*. Glencoe, IL: Free Press.

Piven, F. F., & Cloward, R. (1971). *Regulating the poor: The functions of public welfare*. New York: Pantheon Books.

Piven, F. F., & Cloward, R. (1993). *Regulating the poor: The functions of public welfare* (2nd ed.). New York: Vintage Books.

Pohlmann, M. (1990). *Black politics in conservative America*. New York: Longman.

Quadagno, J. (1990). Race, class, and gender in the U.S. welfare state. *American Sociological Review, 55,* 11–28.

Rimlinger, G. (1971). *The welfare state and industrialization in Europe, America, and Russia*. New York: John Wiley & Sons.

Skocpol, T. (1992). *Protecting soldiers and mothers*. Cambridge, MA: Harvard University Press.

Specht, H., & Courtney, M. E. (1993). *Unfaithful angels.* New York: Free Press.

Turnbull, C. (1972). *The mountain people.* New York: Simon & Schuster.

Weitzman, L. (1985). *The divorce revolution.* New York: Free Press.

Wilensky, H. (1975). *The welfare state and equality.* Berkeley: University of California Press.

Wilson, W. J. (1979). *The declining significance of race.* Chicago: University of Chicago Press.

Wilson, W. J. (1987). *The truly disadvantaged.* Chicago: University of Chicago Press.

8

WELFARE IS A BY-PRODUCT OF INDUSTRIALIZATION: 1

In a "triage" world in which it is a certainty that resources are insufficient and not all can survive, productive labor to assure survival carries greater moral density and is seemingly clear rational choice over leisure.

Lohmann, *The Commons*

Scholars who have proposed the thesis that the welfare state is a by-product of industrialization are, for the most part, from the disciplines of classical economics (with its demand-and-supply matrix), political science (especially scholars of interest-group behavior), cultural anthropology, and sociology (particularly macrosociologists with a structural functionalist, modernization, or rational-choice orientation). A few scholars from social work have also supported this thesis. In exploring this complex thesis, this chapter discusses (1) what is meant by industrialization (and related concepts, like capitalist industrialization, socialist industrialization, postindustrial societies, and post-Fordism), (2) which groups support the activities that lead to industrialization and its consequences, and (3) how the relationship between industrialization and social welfare is modeled or put forth in a cause-and-effect chain. In the organization of ideas, this chapter is similar to chapters 4 and 6 because it outlines the key ideas that are used to explain and predict the development of welfare.

WHAT IS INDUSTRIALIZATION?

Perhaps the best and simplest definition of industrialization is a technological process that involves the large-scale manufacturing of goods using machines (see Bell, 1973). Such large-scale manufacturing requires several other conditions: the availability of raw materials (which are being converted to secondary goods); a supply of adequate labor; a supply of management skills; a supply of capital to procure the raw materials, the labor, and the managers; and ways of delivering the finished goods to given markets. Blumer (1990) cited the following 13 principal attributes of industrialization:

1. production by *machines*
2. production located in *factories*
3. location of clusters of production in *cost-effective* areas
4. location of *labor nearby*
5. development of *occupational lines* to support production
6. development of *skills for the occupational lines*
7. development of *management systems* of production
8. optimization of *volume production* at a minimal cost
9. promotion of products and a push to expand *markets*
10. *ongoing movement* of capital, labor, and equipment
11. use of a *money economy,* with wage, salary, purchase, sales, rent, interest, and profit
12. development of *contractual relations* (or gesellschaft relations)
13. a *rational orientation* in production, management, and marketing.

IMPACT OF INDUSTRIALIZATION

The process of industrialization has strong effects on the family, the community, the state, and the economy.

The Family

Industrialization has important influences on the structure of the family. For the most part, preindustrial societies have extended family systems, surrounded by community and clan (Bell, 1973), whereas industrial societies have nuclear families or individuals in a personal network. Thus, in industrial societies, the family is, for the most part, "structurally unsupported" (Parsons, 1951) because it is missing the support of a multigenerational presence, of kin and clan, and of many persons during predictable and unpredictable crises. Furthermore, the family is often incapable of becoming the welfare-producing family (see chapter 1).

The Community

Industrialization also influences the nature and structure of the community (see Konig, 1968; Warren, 1969), because it transforms face-to-face human bonds to the primacy of contractual or gesellschaft-type relations (see Tonnies, 1957). Like family bonds, community bonds are weaker in industrial societies than in preindustrial societies. Janowitz (1954) observed that industrial societies usually foster "communities of limited liability." In preindustrial societies, the community is the second-line welfare provider or the transfer agent. In industrial societies, however, it is often a weak or disabled transfer agent (see chapter 1).

The State

Whereas industrialization weakens family and community bonds, it often strengthens the state. Although the state starts as an instrument of governance, it later becomes the chief protection agent and transfer agent; at times, a reluctant surrogate family; and a producer and custodian of roads, law and order, clean air and water, defense, and so on. In market economy-oriented societies, the state also becomes the overseer of the market, that is, the body that ensures that the market operates under nonmonopolistic principles, and hence a regulatory agent. In addition, industrialization supports the separation of church and state or strengthens it if the separation has already taken place.

The Economy

Industrialization may produce or coexist with two types of economies: the market economy and the centrally planned economy (often under state auspices). The two economies are legitimated by two ideologies: capitalism and socialism (see chapter 4 for detailed discussions of both). Berger (1986) referred to the two economies as industrial capitalism and socialist capitalism. Table 8-1 lists the key properties of industrial capitalism and socialist capitalism—ideal types, comparable to Weber's (1946) ideal type of rational bureaucracy.

According to Table 8-1, the interpersonal orientation is highly individualistic under industrial capitalism but collectivistic under industrial socialism. Economic productivity is lower under socialism than under capitalism. (In fact, low economic productivity is the sole reason for the demise of industrial socialism. Adam Smith's position, discussed in chapter 2, would have been that each individual, acting in his or her self-interest, ultimately fosters higher productivity.)

In the few remaining socialist economies (China, Cuba, and North Korea), both economic productivity and consumer satisfaction are low, as they were in the former Communist Bloc countries. Consumer goods are, for the most part, of inferior quality in these economies, in comparison to the superior-quality products of the capitalist economies. In fact, in the socialist economies, there is an underground economy (also known as the black market) in which consumer goods produced in capitalist economies are sold at a high premium.

Unemployment, however, is lower under socialism than it is under capitalism, partly because labor (and many other things) is more commodified under capitalism than under socialism. In capitalist countries, labor is subject

Table 8-1. Key Attributes of Two Economies

PROPERTIES	INDUSTRIAL SOCIALISM	INDUSTRIAL CAPITALISM
Intepersonal orientation	Collectivistic	Highly individualistic
Economic productivity	Lower	Higher
Consumers' satisfaction with consumer goods	Lower	Higher
Unemployment	Lower	Higher
Commodification	Low	High
Designation of deviance	Insider–outsider	Mainstreamer–marginalized
Stratification	By closeness to the Party or insiders	By position in the market
Eligibility for receipt of social welfare	By membership–citizenship	Inversely related to degrees of marginality
Professionalization of social-problem managers	Lower	Higher
Capital	Owned by the state; managed by the Party	Owned by the upper class, the upper middle class, and corporations; managed by a managerial class
Labor	Provided by most members of the society, which is labor oriented	Provided by the middle and working classes; the lower classes have poor labor force attachment; a capital-oriented society
Collective bargaining agent for labor	The state	Labor unions
Welfare plans	Prefisc, designed to protect citizens[a]	Postfisc, designed to protect the market[a]
Nonprofit sector	Less developed	Well developed and diverse

[a] Prefisc plans are developed before the taxation capacity of the state is ascertained and a budget is in place, whereas postfisc plans are established afterward.

to market pressures, and collective bargaining is done by labor unions. In socialist countries, the state itself is the employer and the collective-bargaining agent.

Both types of societies have stratification systems. In socialist societies, the closer one is to the Party insiders, the higher up one is in the stratification matrix. In capitalist societies, the more successful one is in the marketplace, the higher up one is in this matrix. The further one is from Party insiders in the stratification matrix, the more likely one is to be labeled deviant under socialism, whereas the further one is from market participation, the more likely one is to be so labeled under capitalism.

Under capitalism, capital is owned by the upper class, the upper middle class, and corporations and is managed by a managerial class, whereas under socialism, it is owned by the state and managed by the Party. Socialist society is labor oriented, and everyone is expected to provide labor. In capitalist society, labor is provided by the middle and working classes; the lower class often has low labor force attachment (and thus may be accorded a deviant status). The term *labor force attachment* refers to finding employment and remaining employed, whereas *low labor force attachment* refers to the inability to find employment or to remain employed (for whatever reason).

In socialist societies, plans for social welfare are prefisc (devised before the state ascertains its taxation capacity and develops a budget) and are designed to protect citizens, whereas in capitalist societies, they are postfisc (developed after the state's taxation capacity is determined and a budget is established) and are designed to protect the market. Eligibility for welfare in socialist societies is conferred from the rights of citizenship, whereas in capitalist societies, it is inversely related to the degree of marginality. That is, the more marginalized one is in capitalist societies, the lower the benefits; conversely, the more one is mainstreamed in capitalist societies, the higher the benefits from the state.

In capitalist societies, groups that claim they have knowledge of social problems (like poverty, deviance, personal adjustment, and mental illness) are highly professionalized, partly because this knowledge is also commodified and subjected to the market. In socialist societies, groups that claim to have such knowledge are not highly professionalized and often occupy roles in state bureaucracies as agents of social control.

The ideal types presented in Table 8-1 are two ends of a continuum of types of industrialization. The United States is close to industrial capitalism, and the Soviet Union before 1990 was close to industrial socialism. The majority of the other industrial countries fall between these two extremes, with most of western Europe, Australia, Canada, and Japan closer to industrial capitalism than to industrial socialism.

Inequality: The Kuznets Curve. Kuznets (1955) proposed that there is a curvilinear relationship between industrialization and inequality; that is, inequality of wealth and income increases during the early phases of economic growth, becomes stabilized, and then decreases substantially over time. The increase, stabilization, and the eventual decline of inequality as a function of industrialization can be plotted as an inverted U, modeled in Figure 8-1.

The Kuznets curve has serious implications for social welfare, in general, and for welfare state building, in particular. To date, it represents an accepted view of the impact of industrialization. Even though the within-group differences in industrial societies (as was noted) are important, the differences between groups (between industrial societies and preindustrial societies) are far more noticeable. That is, the building of wealth and the reduction of inequality are far greater in industrial societies than in preindustrial societies.

One implication of the Kuznets curve is that, on the one hand, industrial societies weaken the bonds of family and community but, on the other hand, generate substantial wealth and eventually new institutions of caregiving to provide for the populations who are not provided for by their families or communities. However, the emergence of this type of new institution varies from one industrial society to another. Different ways of understanding the variability of the welfare system in industrial societies, including the residual versus the institutional thesis, are discussed in chapter 9.

The Nature of Work. In industrial societies, work is centered on the wage–labor contract between the individual employee and the employer (who can be an individual, a corporate group, or the state itself). The skills required for this work can be variously obtained through apprenticeships

Figure 8-1.

A Model of the Kuznets Curve

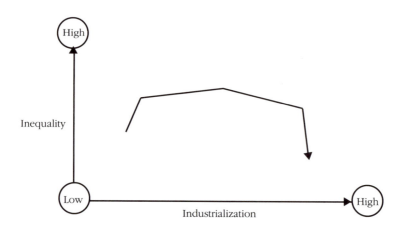

sponsored by collective-bargaining organizations, formal education, or specialized institutions. Furthermore, these skills range from low level to high level and are a strong basis for one's placement in a social hierarchy or stratification system. The levels of this stratification system, often called a class system, range from the lower class (whose members have almost no skills to participate in the workplace and hence perform unskilled labor), to the working class (whose members perform skilled labor in the trades, also called blue-collar work), to the middle class (whose members perform skilled labor in the occupations and professions, also called white-collar work), and to the upper class or the elite (whose members inherited capital or acquired it under special circumstances).

Numerous benefits, such as income protection, health care, and sometimes education, are provided through the workplace to those with labor force attachment. As these benefit systems become routinized, the state often has to step in to provide benefits to those who have little or no labor force attachment.

As industrial societies mature (see the later discussion of postindustrial societies), the nature of the workplace and the nature of the wage–labor contract begin to change. For many employers, wage-and-benefits packages become expensive (see subsection entitled "The Welfare State Is Expensive," pp. 196–200), so they offer reduced packages or lay off full-time workers to avoid paying for these packages. For some workers, reduced work or two part-time jobs (instead of one full-time job with substantial benefits) is the result.

As the nature of the workplace and of the wage–labor contract begins to change, so does the amount of income that workers earn. In many cases, the state finds itself in the role of provider of income supplements or intervenor, to ensure that such supplements are provided by business and industry. The long-cherished value of deriving income from "honest labor" becomes threatened, and members of the working and middle classes (in addition to those of the lower class) begin to receive benefits without a reciprocity network (that is, without providing productive labor for part of their lives and receiving protection when they no longer can provide this labor).

Income versus the Transfer of Wealth. The emergent welfare state in industrial societies is often dependent more on income than on the transfer of wealth. It is convenient for the state to depend on transferring (taxing) income on a systematic basis to keep up the benefit packages it delivers. On the other hand, the transfer of wealth occurs more sporadically and requires taxing death and inheritance, the voluntary giving away of wealth, the forced transfer of wealth during wartime, abrupt currency changes, or worldwide shifts in the price of key goods and services (like the price of food, petroleum, or medicine).

The transfer of wealth and a cultural tradition of voluntarism are responsible for the development of the nonprofit (nongovernment) sector under industrial capitalism. This sector is partly dependent on some form of wealth transfer. Most countries with a tradition of industrial socialism do not have a well-developed nonprofit sector. Furthermore, most Third World countries do not have enough wealth to develop and sustain a large nonprofit sector, although democratic Third World countries have small nonprofit sectors that provide voluntary social welfare services (ranging from emergency crisis assistance to socialization services) to back up whatever services the state provides.

Three Measures. The *dependency ratio*—a simple concept that requires complicated measurements—is a useful concept for examining how welfare is a by-product of industrialization. In this ratio, the numerator represents one unit of benefit paid to a recipient, and the denominator represents the number of persons in the labor force who are taxed to provide this unit of service. A formal definition of the dependency ratio is "the ratio of the population defined as dependent—those under 15 and those over 64— to the working age population, aged 15 to 64" (United Nations Development Programme, 1994, p. 219).

This concept is important because it highlights the assumptions about the demographic structure of a society and its ability to sustain a welfare state. *A high dependency ratio (close to 1) is a sign that the welfare state is in poor health, whereas a low dependency ratio is a sign that it is in good health.* If it takes one person in the labor force to pay for one person's pension or other income supplement, then the society's ability to sustain the welfare state is reaching rock bottom. However, if it takes a much larger number of workers to pay for this benefit to one person, then the welfare state is in better health. It may also mean that a society is aging, so there are not enough workers to pay a certain level of benefit for one person.

The *labor force replacement ratio,* also known as the "future labor force replacement ratio," is another concept that is important for understanding how the welfare state is dependent on income transfer. It is calculated as the population under 15 divided by one-third of the present population aged 15 to 59. *The higher the labor force replacement ratio, the greater the viability of the welfare state in the future* (since it can count on continuing income transfer plans).

The *Human Development Index* (HDI) is another measure of the impact of industrialization and welfare state development. It is formally defined as "a composite measure of human development containing indicators representing three equally weighted dimensions of human development— longevity (life expectancy at birth), knowledge (adult literacy and mean years of schooling), and income (purchasing power parity dollars per capita)" (United Nations Development Programme, 1994, pp. 108, 220). Table 8-2 summarizes relevant HDI data from key industrial countries. As the table indicates, the top HDI rates were for Lithuania and Estonia (two industrialized and former socialist countries in the Second World), followed by

Table 8-2. Human Development Indices in Industrial and Nonindustrial Countries

INDUSTRIAL SOCIALISM (SECOND WORLD)	HDI	INDUSTRIAL CAPITALISM (FIRST WORLD)	HDI	OTHER COUNTRIES (THIRD WORLD)	HDI
Lithuania	0.968	Canada	0.932	Hong Kong	0.875
Estonia	0.967	Switzerland	0.931	South Korea	0.859
Czechoslovakia	0.872	Japan	0.929	Singapore	0.836
Latvia	0.865	Sweden	0.928	Venezuela	0.820
Hungary	0.863	Norway	0.928	Malaysia	0.794
Russia	0.858	France	0.927	Iran	0.672
Belarus	0.847	Australia	0.926	Philippines	0.621
Ukraine	0.823	United States	0.925	Indonesia	0.586
Bulgaria	0.815	Netherlands	0.923	Kenya	0.434
Poland	0.815	United Kingdom	0.919	Pakistan	0.393
Romania	0.729	Germany	0.918	India	0.382
Albania	0.714	Denmark	0.912	Ghana	0.382
Cuba	0.666	Italy	0.891	Bangladesh	0.309
China	0.644			Tanzania	0.306
North Korea	0.609			Uganda	0.272

SOURCE: Data from United Nations Development Programme. (1994). *Human development report, 1994*. New York: Oxford University Press.

selected industrialized capitalist countries of the First World. The lowest HDI rates were all for the nonindustrialized countries of the Third World and, it should be pointed out, these rates were a third of those for the top-rated industrialized countries.

The foregoing discussion makes one factor clear: Despite the internal and external differences among welfare states, the welfare state is almost always a part of industrial societies. The trends discussed here support the observations made in chapter 3. A more detailed discussion of authors who support the thesis is presented in chapter 9.

The Welfare State Is Expensive

It is important to note that the welfare state is expensive, even for those countries that can afford it. Social security and health care expenditures, when measured as percentages of the gross domestic product (GDP) (the total output of goods and services produced by an economy for final use), are high under both industrial capitalism and industrial socialism but low or nonexistent in Third World countries (United Nations Development Programme, 1994). Tables 8-3 and 8-4 present some examples for 1985 to 1990.

Some interesting trends are reflected in Tables 8-3 and 8-4. For example, Cuba and China, considered "developing countries" by the United Nations even though they are part of the Second World, are somewhat laggard in social security expenditures. However, China (figures for Cuba and North Korea are not available) is not that far from other Second World countries in health care expenditures.

The high cost of the welfare state, however, does not necessarily mean high benefits. On the cost side, for example, total health care spending as a percentage of the GDP of the United Kingdom went from 5.8 in 1989 to 6.6 in 1991; in Japan, from 6.7 to 6.8; in Canada, from 8.3 to 9.9; in France, from 8.4 to 9.1; and in the United States, from 11.8 to 13.3 ("Some ABCs of Mediconomics," 1991; United Nations Development Programme, 1994). In all five industrial capitalist countries, health costs escalated. With regard to the benefits (see Table 8-3), Canada, Japan, and France had higher scores on the HDI than did the United States, the biggest spender. Also, the United States had the highest rate of infant mortality (9.7 per 1,000 live births, as reported in "Some ABCs of Mediconomics," 1991) among the five industrial capitalist countries. In 1991, then presidential candidate Bill Clinton claimed that 135 million people in the United States were uninsured for health care, although *The Economist's* (see "Some ABCs of Mediconomics") estimate was around 35 million. Even the lower number, however, is much higher than that of any other industrialized country, capitalist or socialist. Generally considered to be one of the wealthiest countries of all time, the United States had a chronic deficit by the mid-1990s. Figures 8-2 and 8-3, which show the percentages of income ($1,154 billion) and expenditures ($1,408 billion) in that country in

Table 8-3. Social Security Expenditures as a Percentage of the GDP of Industrial and Nonindustrial Countries: 1985–90

INDUSTRIAL SOCIALISM (SECOND WORLD)	% OF GDP IN SOCIAL SECURITY	INDUSTRIAL CAPITALISM (FIRST WORLD)	% OF GDP IN SOCIAL SECURITY	OTHER COUNTRIES (THIRD WORLD)	% OF GDP IN SOCIAL SECURITY
Lithuania	17.2	Sweden	33.7	Singapore	7.1
Bulgaria	15.4	Netherlands	28.7	Bangladesh	2.1
Poland	11.5	Denmark	27.8	Venezuela	1.1
Cuba	7.1	France	26.1	Philippines	0.7
China	3.4	Germany	23.0	Kenya	0.6
Albania	—	Italy	21.6	India	0.5
Belarus	—	Canada	18.8	Malayasia	0.5
Czechoslovakia	—	Norway	17.6	Ghana	—
Estonia	—	United Kingdom	17.0	Hong Kong	—
Hungary	—	Switzerland	13.3	Indonesia	—
Latvia	—	United States	12.6	Iran	—
North Korea	—	Japan	11.0	Pakistan	—
Romania	—	Australia	8.0	South Korea	—
Russia	—			Tanzania	—
Ukraine	—			Uganda	—

NOTE: A dash reflects the absence either of a program or of information.

SOURCE: Data from United Nations Development Programme. (1994). *Human development report, 1994.* New York: Oxford University Press.

Table 8-4. Health Care Expenditures as a Percentage of the GDP of Industrial and Nonindustrial Countries: 1990–91

INDUSTRIAL SOCIALISM (SECOND WORLD)	% OF GDP IN HEALTH CARE EXPENSES	INDUSTRIAL CAPITALISM (FIRST WORLD)	% OF GDP IN HEALTH CARE EXPENSES	OTHER COUNTRIES (THIRD WORLD)	% OF GDP IN HEALTH CARE EXPENSES
Hungary	6.0	United States	13.3	South Korea	6.6
Czechoslovakia	5.9	Canada	9.9	India	6.0
Bulgaria	5.4	France	9.1	Hong Kong	5.7
Poland	5.1	Germany	9.1	Tanzania	4.7
Albania	4.0	Sweden	8.8	Venezuela	3.6
Romania	3.9	Netherlands	8.7	Ghana	3.5
Lithuania	3.6	Australia	8.6	Pakistan	3.4
China	3.5	Norway	8.4	Uganda	3.4
Russia	3.0	Italy	8.3	Bangladesh	3.2
Belarus	—	Switzerland	8.0	Malayasia	3.0
Cuba	—	Denmark	7.0	Iran	2.6
Estonia	—	Japan	6.8	Indonesia	2.0
Latvia	—	United Kingdom	6.6	Philippines	2.0
North Korea	—			Singapore	1.9
Ukraine	—			Kenya	0.6

NOTE: A dash reflects the absence either of a program or of information.
SOURCE: Data from United Nations Development Programme. (1994). *Human development report, 1994*. New York: Oxford University Press.

Figure 8-2.

Sources of U.S. Income: 1993

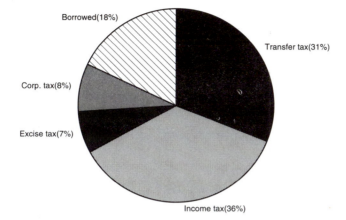

SOURCE: U.S. Internal Revenue Service. (1994). *Major categories of federal income and outlays for fiscal year 1993: Form 1040.* Washington, DC: U.S. Government Printing Office.

1993, illustrate how expensive the U.S. welfare state had become and that a welfare state is dependent on income transfer. In 1993, personal income tax represented 36 percent of the income, transfer taxes (social security and taxes for health care for older persons) represented another 31 percent, but corporate taxes in this capitalist country represented only 8 percent (see Figure 8-2). In comparison, in 1993, expenditures for welfare were 35 percent for social security and related benefits, 17 percent for social programs, and 8 percent for human development (see Figure 8-3).

One may point out that in 1993, 24 percent of the U.S. budget was spent on defense, and it was the largest defense budget in the world (Specter, 1995). In 1992–93, military spending was $298.4 billion in the United States, but $47.2 billion in Russia, $41.2 billion in the United Kingdom, $34.9 billion in France, and $34.3 billion in Japan. No other country in the world had a military budget exceeding $30 billion (Specter, 1995). The entire U.S. welfare state (and warfare state) was partly supported by borrowed money ($255 billion, or 18 percent), and 14 percent of its budget went to servicing its debts. The alternatives to this situation were, and still are: (1) to reduce the defense-related budget, (2) to reduce the welfare-related budget, or (3) to increase taxes. Almost all the western European industrial nations already have a tax base that is much higher than that in the United States, and it is this higher tax base that makes it possible for the western European welfare states to exist (Esping-Andersen, 1990). However, none of the alternatives outlined for the United States would be easy to implement because powerful interest groups are opposed to each one.

Figure 8-3.

Expenditures of the U.S. Welfare State: 1993

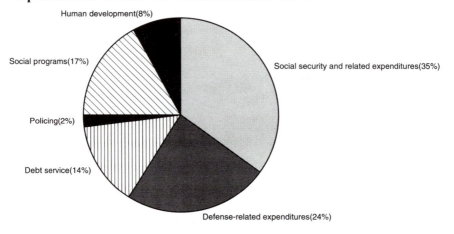

SOURCE: U.S. Internal Revenue Service. (1994). *Major categories of federal income and outlays for fiscal year 1993: Form 1040.* Washington, DC: U.S. Government Printing Office.

The problem of financing the welfare state came to a head during the massive strikes in France at the end of 1995. The French government planned budget cuts in social security for elderly people and reduced subsidies to education and health care. It also planned to freeze the wages of all public workers and to reduce their social security benefits. As a result the entire transportation system shut down, and France endured one of its most massive labor strikes (Glass, 1995). Labor unions from all European Community countries were very sympathetic to the French strike, and there was anxiety in government circles that the French situation could recur in their countries (Powell, 1995). Powell (p. 51) described the European situation:

> Government deficits are massive almost everywhere in Europe, while taxes, for the most part, are already suffocatingly high. The cost of maintaining these subsidy states has become oppressingly burdensome to European business. In Germany, for every dollar companies pay in wages to their workers—the world's highest paid, at an average of more than $20.00 an hour—management must also pay out about 80 cents in welfare benefits.

The welfare states almost everywhere seemed in financial trouble by the mid-1990s. Almost all First World countries, accustomed to a high standard of living, seemed to be living well beyond their means.

PREINDUSTRIALISM AND POSTINDUSTRIALISM

Having outlined the nature of industrialization and its impacts, I now explore the nature of preindustrial and postindustrial societies and the capacity of these societies to develop and sustain social welfare packages.

The term *postindustrial society* was popularized by Bell (1973), who used it to describe a type of society that comes after an industrial society. To differentiate preindustrial societies from industrial societies and industrial societies from postindustrial societies, Bell categorized the changes from one type of society to another along seven dimensions: (1) the economic sector, (2) the occupational slope, (3) the technology base, (4) the nature of adversaries, (5) the method of organizing experiences, (6) the society's view of itself on a temporal continuum, and (7) the primary resource on which the society depends.

Economy. According to Bell's categories, vast regions of Asia, Africa, and Latin America are preindustrial; the countries of Europe and the (former) Soviet Union, Canada, and Japan are industrial; and the United States is postindustrial. In a preindustrial country, the economy is mainly extractive (devoted to agriculture, mining, fishing, and producing timber), is dependent on the availability of raw materials, and requires vast expanses of land and relatively unskilled labor, and the occupational slope leads to work in these extractive areas. In an industrial country, the economy is primarily goods producing (manufacturing and processing), is dependent on energy to convert raw materials into secondary goods, and requires vast amounts of capital and skilled labor, and the occupational slope leads to skilled labor and engineering and management skills to oversee the skilled labor. In a postindustrial society, the economy produces mostly services and information, is dependent on knowledge and information to produce services, and requires capital and knowledge, and the occupational slope leads to knowledge and information-processing skills.

Family and community structure. The family structure in these three societies also differs. In preindustrial societies, it is often some form of the extended family; in industrial societies, the nuclear family; and in postindustrial societies, an individual within a network. The community structure of the three societies varies as well. In preindustrial societies, it is frequently a gemeinschaft type and serves as a major source of socialization and social control. In postindustrial societies, it is often a gesellschaft type, that is, a location of dwellings or a "community of limited liability" (Janowitz, 1954). In postindustrial societies, it is an ecological type, which is highly commodified and is more of a reflector of family status and position in a stratification hierarchy than an agent of socialization and social control (see Tonnies, 1957).

Social welfare. In preindustrial societies, dependent people (children; aged, ill, and disabled persons; and those who are otherwise unable to own land or to sell unskilled labor) are provided for by the welfare-providing family or the welfare-providing community (see chapter 1), and there is often no second-line provider of care for them. In industrial societies, the state is the second-line provider for dependent populations when the family cannot do so, and the community is sometimes a source of supplementary private and voluntary services. In these societies, the welfare state may already seem expensive and is subject to cutbacks. In postindustrial societies, the state is often pushed to provide a guaranteed minimum income; basic health care; and, in some cases, housing to citizens who are not capable of being in the labor force. In such cases, the state faces both a revolution of rising expectations and spiraling costs.

The differences between industrial and postindustrial societies are comparable to those between Fordism and post-Fordism (discussed in chapter 6), ideas advanced by American scholars and British scholars, respectively. Sometimes, industrialization is also called modernization, and postindustrialization is called postmodernism, ideas advanced by French scholars. Postmodernism will be discussed later in this chapter because it also represents a new theoretical paradigm. Figure 8-4 presents a visual summary of the discussions so far.

GROUPS THAT SPONSOR INDUSTRIALIZATION

The within-group variations in industrial countries and in the structures of their welfare states can be explained, in part, by the fact that different groups sponsor or usher in the process of industrialization. This idea was introduced by Kerr, Dunlop, Harbison, and Myers (1965; see also chapter 5, Thesis 1), who categorized the groups as an upwardly mobile middle class, dynastic leaders, colonial administrators, nationalist leaders, or revolutionary leaders. Rimlinger (1971) elaborated on this idea to suggest that the ideology of the sponsor of industrialization influences the labor policy of a given country, which, in turn, influences the country's welfare policy, and Esping-Andersen (1990) used it to explain the internal variations in the welfare states of First World countries.

This notion of the sponsors of industrialization is an attempt to explain not only variations in the welfare state but, in a way, variations in social development and modernization, an idea that is discussed later in this chapter. Here, I return to the idea of ideologies that justify the development of the welfare state because a central theme of the works just cited is that industrialization is an economic and wealth-building process. Once wealth has been built, several types of distribution are possible. It is these processes—wealth building followed by distribution—that need to be justified by some ideological position (especially under industrial capitalism). Thus, ideology is more often a justification for the welfare state than a reason for instituting it (see chapters 4 and 5).

Figure 8-4.

The Technology Base of the Three Worlds

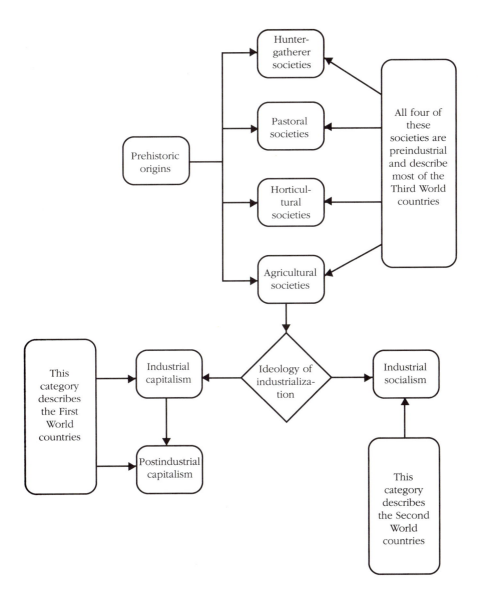

IDEOLOGIES OF THE SPONSORS

The basic sympathies of the sponsors toward capital or labor depend on the level at which the sponsors are in the stratification system of a nation (see Table 8-5 for a summary of the sponsors, their ideologies, and the consequent directions of the welfare state). For example, the three types of sponsors who are pro-capital have different attitudes toward labor. The middle-class sponsors take a pragmatic view, which calls for keeping labor placated. The dynastic leaders believe that they, an aristocratic and economically successful group, have an obligation to all who are below them, including labor, and thus have a patronizing view of labor (see Rimlinger, 1971); however, they are also seeking capital, which will be owned by the state. And the colonial administrators, who think they are superior to the people in the colony, take a hostile or at least a laissez faire view toward labor and facilitate the flow of capital from the colony to the mother country. Of the two groups that are generally pro-labor, the nationalists are also mindful of their new nation's need to build capital and hence try to placate the owners of capital, whereas the revolutionaries take a hostile view toward the owners of the capital that they are seeking to expropriate for the state.

The pro-labor/pro-capital dimension in Table 8-5 allows for an understanding of the basic sympathies of the dominant groups (elites) in a nation that are due not to ideology but to the nature of the economic alliances these groups form while their political economies are developing. Once these economic alliances are formed and the templates of the political economy are in place, various groups behave to protect their own economic interests. For example, the United States was industrialized with a pro-capital orientation, and, over time, the labor movement earned various rights to engage in collective bargaining (Rayback, 1959). The current welfare state is a result of efforts to placate labor, from the New Deal of Franklin D. Roosevelt to the Great Society of Lyndon B. Johnson. However, pro-capital (conservative) groups often ally with the Republican Party to pass pro-capital taxation policies (such as lower capital gains and corporate income taxes and reduced benefits to labor). Because it is awkward to espouse policies that favor their own interests, these groups use the political strategy of attacking pro-labor policies, including transfer programs to groups who are and are not in the labor market ("welfare chiselers"). The efforts of pro-capital groups to downsize the welfare states in the United Kingdom and in Sweden in the 1980s and 1990s were similarly driven more by economic interests than by ideologies.

Table 8-5 (last row) also includes a group that I added to accommodate historical developments since the publication of Kerr et al. (1965) and Rimlinger (1971). It is an unusual alliance between an upwardly mobile middle class and an active working class that occurred in European countries, such as Sweden, that were both geographically and intellectually proximal to the domains of the dynastic leaders to the south (Germany and Austria) and the

Table 8-5. Sponsors of Industrialization, Their Ideologies, and the Consequent Directions of the Welfare State

SPONSORS	IDEOLOGY	ORGANIZATIONAL PREFERENCE	DIRECTION OF THE WELFARE STATE
Upwardly mobile middle class (pro-capital, placate labor)	Capitalism, democracy, polite patriarchy	Privatize most efforts	Reluctant welfare state (such as the United States)
Dynastic leaders (pro-capital, patronize labor)	Capitalism, variations from democracy to autocracy, patriarchy	Privatize efforts, some nationalization	Patronizing welfare state (such as 19th century Germany)
Revolutionary intellectuals (pro-labor, seek capital)	State socialism, autocracy of groups, disguised patriarchy	Nationalize most efforts	Active welfare state (such as Bolshevik Russia)
Colonial administrators (pro-capital, hostile to labor)	Capitalism, variations between autocracy and colonialism, patriarchy	Privatize efforts in the model of the mother country	No welfare state (such as India under British rule)
Nationalist leaders (pro-labor, placate capital)	Group socialism, variations between autocracy and democracy, patriarchy	Nationalize most efforts but selectively privatize others	Active welfare state (such as Australia)
Alliance of the middle and working classes (pro-capital, pro-labor)	Capitalism, socialist democracy, apologetic patriarchy	Privatize work, nationalize most other efforts	Active welfare state (such as Sweden)

revolutionary intellectuals to the east (the former Soviet Union). Esping-Andersen (1990) termed this type of welfare state *social democratic* (his analysis of three types of First World countries is discussed later).

THE IMPLICIT CONTRACT

One major, but often unnoticed, impact of industrialization is the shift from the "status" orientation of preindustrial societies to the "contract" orientation of industrial societies, first articulated by Sir Henry Maine in 1861 (cited in Nisbet, 1966). For example, in preindustrial societies, marriage is a sacrament, whereas in industrial societies, it is a contract. In the first case, the rights and obligations of the parties are defined by tradition and legitimated by ideology (often patriarchy). In the second case, the rights and obligations of the parties are defined by both custom and law; when there is a conflict between custom and law, the law prevails. A similar orientation prevails in generational relationships: The rights and obligations of the generations in preindustrial societies are defined by tradition and ideology, whereas those in industrial societies are defined by custom and law.

The direction a welfare state takes is dependent less on ideology than on the implicit contract between the genders and between generations (and national adaptations of this contract) that guides relationships. Thus, in welfare-providing families in preindustrial societies with no welfare state, the right to be supported is based on ideology, whereas in welfare-providing states in industrial societies, the right (or gratuity) to be supported emerges from the implied contract. An implied contract between the genders may be institutionalized as a "family wage" concept, whereby men with families are paid a higher wage than women. The impact of the bias that often remains when transfer payments or services to women are indexed has been the subject of protest by feminist authors (see Orloff, 1993). Similarly, the result of an implied contract between generations may be the imposition of transfer taxes on a given generation to support another generation.

In preindustrial societies, the obligations are diffuse (see Parsons, 1951) and exist within the boundaries of kinship and community, whereas in industrial societies, they are specific (as to the amount and duration) and are applied on the basis of citizenship and society. Put differently, "status" calls for the support of family and community members according to their gender and generational roles, whereas "contract" calls for the support of fellow citizens in a society because of their gender and generational roles. In most modern welfare states, there seems to be less controversy over the notion of support on the basis of generational roles than on the basis of gender roles. For example, in Germany, the concept of a contract between generations is a popular metaphor, but the gendered basis of transfer payments is the subject of interest-group conflict, as it is in most industrial countries.

INDUSTRIALIZATION AND WELFARE INFRASTRUCTURE

The discussion of implied contract leads back to the idea of the welfare infrastructure, discussed in chapter 2.

Payers

One group of payers in the welfare state is the *working generation*. Often a major part of the budget of a welfare state is supported by taxing the income of this generation. This support base can be further divided into a voluntary–involuntary dimension; that is, the state receives payments through involuntary contributions as it encourages voluntary donations (through the community, the church, or nonprofit organizations).

A second group of payers can be categorized according to their *social class,* on a continuum from the lower class (poor people) to the working class to the middle class to the upper class (the elites). According to this classification, the payments of working-class and middle-class payers are in the form of income transfers to recipients.

A third group of payers of welfare can be seen in the *public–private* dimension. In other words, transfer flows from the public sector (a composite of all levels of government support) and from the private sector (a composite of all nongovernment support), which has tax exemptions from the state.

A fourth group of payers can be identified in the *individual–corporate* dimension, meaning both voluntary and involuntary transfers from individuals and corporations. For example, Figure 8-2 showed that individuals paid about 67 percent of the U.S. budget in 1993, whereas corporations paid about 8 percent.

Although it is possible to identify payers on the basis of gender, ethnoracial status, or ethnolinguistic status, looking at the position of payers in the class structure of a nation often reveals a nearly complete picture of who pays for welfare. For example, Wilson (1979) argued that discrimination against African Americans in the United States is declining and that the discrimination that remains is due more to their position at the bottom of the class ladder than to their ethnoracial status. The class position of a racial or ethnic group, then, is often an important indicator of the group's status as payers of welfare.

Transfer Agents

Figure 2-4 identified six common types of transfer agents: the family, the community, the church, the collective-bargaining body, the corporation, and the state. Three of these six—the collective-bargaining body, the corporation, and the state—are primary or major transfer agents in industrialized countries. Furthermore, of these three, the state is the more frequent and most dominant transfer agent in almost all First World countries and all Second World countries. Japan is the only country in which the major transfer agent is the corporation (like Mitsubishi or Yamaha). In many other countries, labor unions and professional associations act as supplementary transfer agents. The family, the community, and the church are also supplementary transfer agents in industrial countries, often operating in the voluntary arena or collecting from voluntary payers.

Recipients

At least six overlapping categories of recipients of welfare can be identified: previous payers and nonpayers, victims and vulnerable persons, senior and junior generations, privileged and unprivileged groups, insiders and outsiders, and protected entrepreneurs. Of the six, the previous-payer and nonpayer category causes substantial controversy in industrial societies. Previous payers are those who were in the labor force but are now recipients because of age or disability. They are part of a reciprocity system with the society, because they have "paid" something like club dues and are now collecting benefits as fully paid-up members and often feel entitled to these benefits. On the other hand, people who have never paid into the system (children and others, who because of illness, disability, or cultural disadvantage have never been in the labor force) can be made to feel that they are not entitled to transfer benefits.

The category of victims and vulnerable persons is culturally constructed in each society. For example, if a child or an elderly person is abused and there is a clear cultural understanding that the situation is deviant (see the model by Chatterjee & Bailey, 1993, discussed in chapter 5), then the person will be viewed as a victim and can be placed in some type of state-sponsored "protective services" and be thought of as a transfer recipient. Nonabused children in an abusive situation will be considered part of a vulnerable population. However, most industrial societies do not include able-bodied women in the category of vulnerable people (although some Third World countries do).

The senior and junior generations category is important in industrial societies. Often people in the senior generation are also in the previous-payer category and may feel entitled to a decent pension, housing, health care, and other benefits. In such cases, those in the junior generation, who are in the labor force, are the payers. On the other hand, people in a senior generation who are active in the labor force and are paying for children's allowances or child welfare services may be disgruntled if the transfer is flowing to children of poor people, of minorities, or of people who have not been in the labor force. In most European (including Second World) welfare states, these two types of recipients are not strongly differentiated, and their benefits are simply called pensions and children's allowances. In

Anglo-American democracies, however, those in this category are further broken down into "deserving" (meaning a previous payer) and "nondeserving" subcategories.

The privileged–unprivileged category is complex in industrial societies. If one assumption of the welfare state is that transfer should flow from the privileged to the less privileged, then the assumption is often violated when a recipient becomes eligible to receive transfer because of generational status (such as reaching old age) but is a privileged member of the society. In many industrial countries, people in the senior generation who receive social security and subsidized health care fall into two categories: those who have sufficient resources and those who do not. Should people in the senior generation who have substantial resources be helped with transfer payments while children (and, in some countries, children of minorities, poor persons, or immigrants) and other unprivileged people receive meager or no income transfers or health care? In this category, issues other than age also arise. For instance, should children of rich and middle-class families be allowed to obtain a higher education (in countries where higher education is highly commodified, such as the United States) in state-supported universities, while children of poor and minority families receive an inferior elementary and secondary education in state-supported public schools? Likewise, should middle-class (and rich) people be given tax subsidies or outright financing to acquire good-quality housing while poor people are relegated to substandard housing? The core problem is that many industrial societies offer what appear to be progressive transfers but are really regressive transfers (see chapter 1).

The insiders–outsiders category is also complex in industrial societies. Anthropologists and sociologists (see, for example, Merton, 1972) have noted that this concept has guided the development of all enduring small groups, organizations, cultures, and nations. In certain countries, the groups who are insiders often consist of the descendants of earlier immigrants or those who won a civil war, as well as the children and grandchildren of those who were successful in commerce or were in well-educated professional groups. In contrast, outsiders are those who are recent immigrants and whose descendants lost a civil war or were unsuccessful in commerce or in education. If the population of a nation is thought of as concentric circles of insiders and outsiders, the question arises: How far out should the welfare state reach to serve and support those who are unprivileged, aged, children, victims and vulnerable people, and those with no reciprocal relationship with the labor force? What happens when groups qualify as worthy of service but are located in an outer periphery of the concentric circles (such as guest workers in Germany, Hispanic domestic workers in the United States, and North Africans in France)?

The final category—protected entrepreneurs—consists of people who have been engaged in legitimate entrepreneurial activities that have failed and who claim that their failure in the market will lead to job losses or other hardships for many other people; it may also consist of those who are engaged in illegitimate entrepreneurial activities (such as by some wine-making or garment-producing entrepreneurs who pay unskilled workers and, in some countries, illegal aliens below the prevailing minimum wage) to whom the state finds it convenient to direct transfer payments. In either case, these groups, which may range from the highly privileged to the less privileged, are in a position to blackmail the welfare state into providing benefits.

Figures 8-5 and 8-6 depict the frequent recipients of transfer in industrial societies. Inherent in these figures are two key characteristics of recipients of transfer: (1) that vulnerability and victimization know no boundaries of privilege or social position (which Prince Siddhartha realized and which led to his transition to the Buddha) and (2) that there may be two clusters of potential recipients of transfer, both of whom are subject to vulnerability and victimization. The first cluster consists of the insiders, who may also be previous payers, members of the senior generation, privileged persons, and sometimes protected entrepreneurs. The second cluster con-

Figure 8-5.

Insiders and Outsiders in Transfer Activity, with Children (the Junior Generation) as Outsiders

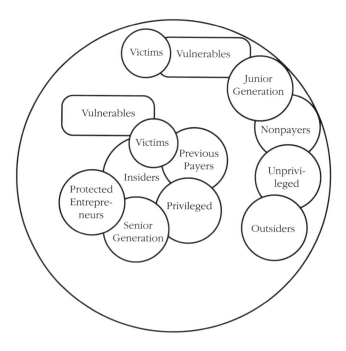

Figure 8-6.

Insiders and Outsiders in Transfer Activity, with Children (the Junior Generation) as Insiders

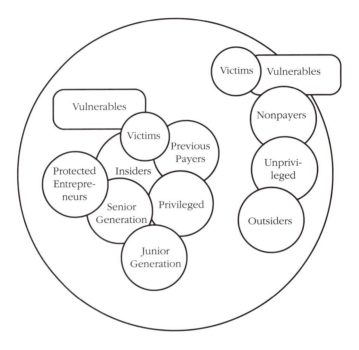

sists of the outsiders, who may be the nonpayers, members of the junior generation, and unprivileged persons.

There may be a substantial social distance between the two clusters. A dilemma of the welfare state, then, is whether social policy should treat them equally or differently. Even if the welfare state decides to formulate a social policy to treat them equally, a further dilemma is whether the two clusters are to be treated equally when social policy is implemented. This dilemma may be illustrated in the health policies of several First World countries: In the Netherlands and Denmark, the two clusters are covered by the same health policy, whereas in the United States, the insiders are treated better (metaphorically and literally) than are the outsiders. Another example is the U.S. policy for aged people (the senior generation), which is far more comprehensive (and includes privileged aged people) than is the policy for children (members of the junior generation, children of minorities, and outsiders).

Providers

In preindustrial societies, the transfer agent is often the provider of services and usually is not the state. In industrial societies, the transfer agent is not always the provider, and several complex systems develop to pay the providers. The most common way is the third-party payment system (in which the transfer agent pays the providers to render services to recipients).

There are many variations in the four-way relationship between the payers, the transfer agent, the providers, and the recipients in industrial societies. Here again, various ideologies may be used to justify the behavior of the different interest groups. For example, in industrial capitalism, giving third-party payments to providers means that the providers can continue to operate in the market system and that by paying the providers, the transfer agent keeps supporting the market system. However, several professional and mercantile ideologies, like the desirability of delivering quality-controlled services, may be used to justify such a system. Essentially, such systems are set up to produce two beneficiaries: providers and recipients, which is one reason for the skyrocketing costs of delivering such services as health care in some industrial societies.

In contrast, industrial socialism does not call for too many complex transactions among the payer, the transfer agent, the provider, and the recipients because the provider is often an agent of the transfer agent. Therefore, it appears that the cost of delivering services is lower under industrial socialism.

Limits on Transfer

Often a major dilemma in all industrial societies is how to ration the transfers that flow to recipients. Rationing is an important and necessary step in planning and delivering goods and services to designated recipients. If such rationing is not done by design, then it almost inevitably occurs by default.

Rationing can be achieved by earmarking the output (setting a limit on the maximum amount of goods and services one can get), as is done for income maintenance provisions. Or it can be done by procedures (often bureaucratic or organizational) that discourage recipients from requesting certain goods and services, as is common in the delivery of health and mental health services.

PARADIGMS OF INDUSTRIALIZATION

Given the complex nature of industrialization, the social sciences (economics, political science, sociology, and so forth) and the profession of social work have developed several paradigms to understand it. The following are the major examples of such paradigms: (1) demographic analysis; (2) demand-and-supply matrix; (3) dual labor market theory; (4) monopoly capital theory; (5) class analysis; (6) value-orientation analysis; (7) structural functionalism; (8) modernization theory, including social development and technology transfer; (9) postmodernism; (10) exchange and game theory; and (11) rational choice theory. These paradigms offer partial views of industrialization, as well as different explanations of the development of the welfare state, some that are overlapping and some that are contradictory.

These paradigms, all of which claim to be scientific theories based on empirical evidence, are attempts to explain why certain things are the way they are and to predict given cause-and-effect sequences. In contrast, normative theories are attempts to propose how things *should be* and build a paradigm around the principle. They constitute another important paradigm of industrialization, since they are concerned with how the goods and services produced under industrialization should be distributed. The role of normative theories is discussed after the empirical theories are reviewed.

Demographic Analysis

The purpose of demographic analysis, which is common in almost all disciplines, is "to identify and measure as precisely as possible the influences that underlie population changes" (Cox, 1970, p. 21). Toward that end, researchers develop rates and ratios of live births, deaths, marriages, and migration patterns, and risks of acquiring a given role or condition (marriage, divorce, pregnancy, illness, or death). They then compare these rates and ratios within and among ecological or other units, and study the behavior of different cohorts over time; the behavior of different groups (by gender, social class, ethnicity, and the like) at a given time and across a time sequence; and the stability or change of a population over time.

With regard to the model discussed in chapter 2, demographic analysis attempts to identify different categories of payers, their ability to make transfer payments, and the risk of their becoming unable to make these payments; recognizes different types of recipients and how long they are likely to remain in that role; designates the types of providers and the cost-benefit factors associated with each of them; and dynamically portrays how the model shown in Figure 2-1 may change over time. Demographic analysis is essential for developing or understanding the welfare state because it elucidates the sources and amounts of inflow (from the payers to the transfer agent), the cost of managing transfer (by the transfer agent), the cost of supporting different types of providers, and the categories of different recipients and the expected time during which they are likely to remain in that role.

DEMAND–AND–SUPPLY MATRIX

The demand-and-supply approach is the core of orthodox Western economic theory. Gordon (1972) suggested that the following key concepts form the disciplinary matrix of this approach: Income derived from a wage–labor exchange depends on the productivity of labor. Labor and commodities produced with it are valued according to their demand in the marketplace. When demand and supply are balanced, there is market equilibrium, which means there is perfect competition and individuals and groups maximize their choices under these circumstances.

Applied to the development of the welfare state, this matrix offers explanations for why the welfare state is necessary and how it should be structured. On the need for the welfare state, it suggests that persons with no capital or no productivity (from labor) may have to be supported by a transfer process (though not all proponents of this theory agree on this point). However, the social construction of "persons with no productivity" may vary from interest group to interest group and from national system to national system. Some roles, such as the child and the aged person, are defined as those that need not show productivity in most industrial (First and Second World) countries. Other roles, like the sick or the unskilled person, are not that easily defined and may vary widely from country to country. Friedman (1962), a major modern proponent of this theory, argued for a transfer that would set a minimum income for all, and Atherton (1990) stated that Adam Smith, the architect of the demand-and-supply matrix, supported a limited definition of persons with no productivity.

On how to structure the welfare state, this matrix suggests that the state should be built on one major foundation: *human incentive* (a variant of the profit motive). Thus, transfer payments should never exceed or be even equal to what a person could earn in the labor market. In other words, the welfare state should be means tested, and transfer payments should be kept at a low level, preferably slightly lower than the going minimum wage.

DUAL LABOR MARKET THEORY

Although the concept of the market (Smith's, 1776/1963, Invisible Hand) is a core concept in the demand-and-supply matrix, it is viewed as a bifurcated entity in dual labor market theory. In this paradigm, the primary and secondary markets are structured differently. The primary market offers high wages, fringe benefits, employment security, and due process, whereas the secondary market offers low wages, none or few fringe benefits, no job security, and no due process (Doeringer, 1971; Gordon, 1972; Piore, 1971). Given this bifurcated market structure, members of the middle class and some selected members of the working class operate in the primary market, and the remaining members of the working class and the lower class operate in the secondary market, as do members of most minority groups and women. Schooling and vocational training do not change this situation.

The central thesis of this theory is that there is a strong association between stratification and market structure. The higher one's position in a stratification matrix, the more likely it is that one will be located in the primary market, and vice versa. The theory supports the need for the welfare state to subsidize those who are in the secondary labor market and even to offer protection to those who are in that market (children, aged people, and sick people, as well as marginalized people). However, it does not explicitly outline how a welfare state should be structured.

MONOPOLY CAPITAL

A Marxist view of demand and supply in the market has been called radical economic theory (Gordon, 1972) or the theory of monopoly capital (Levine, 1988). In this view, the owners of capital (members of the upper class and their agents who are mostly from the upper middle class) are constantly accumulating capital, and their pursuit of capital becomes easier when they have a monopoly in the marketplace. Thus, the owners of capital are always looking for ways to develop such a monopoly. As was noted in chapter 7, the pursuit of such capital accumulation and the development of a monopoly are the bases of class conflict in industrial capitalism (Levine, 1988; Piven & Cloward, 1993). The state, according to this theory, is an ally of the capitalists or the corporate interests.

When there are barriers to or problems in the accumulation process, the state creates devices to make the process barrier or problem free. One such device is the welfare state, which placates the middle and working classes by offering them transfer payments. In capitalist societies, the motive for such transfer payments is not altruism, but facilitation of the development of monopoly capital.

CLASS ANALYSIS

At its simplest core, class analysis is the assessment of the impact of class position or stratification (in industrial societies) on such outcomes as health or mental health condition, life expectancy and life chances, political participation, and even ways of thinking. Although the classical Marxist theoreticians were responsible for popularizing class analysis, this paradigm is not unique to Marxist scholars. Anglo-American sociologists, especially American sociologists (including Marxist scholars), have studied the impact of social class and life outcomes since Sorokin's (1927) work was first published in the United States. Beeghley (1988), who summarized these efforts, contended that much of what human beings experience in modern societies is a function of social class.

Applied to welfare state analysis, this theory may take two opposing positions. The first position is that the state is essentially an ally of the owners of the means of production (the upper classes), often engages in heavy subsidies to them (see Huff & Johnson, 1993), and offers only small amounts of transfer to poor people to avoid major disruptions in the social order. The second position is that the state has no innate position but is responsive only to organized interest groups who can exercise political power. According to the second perspective, the more the political power of given groups, the greater the flow of transfer toward them.

VALUE–ORIENTATION ANALYSIS

Rokeach (1973, p. 5) stated that human values are enduring beliefs "that a specific mode of conduct or end-state of existence is personally or socially preferable to an opposite or converse mode of conduct or end-state of existence. A value-system is an enduring organization of beliefs concerning preferable modes of conduct or end-states of existence along a continuum of relative importance." Seen from this perspective, value-orientation analysis offers some understanding of the end-states preferred by payers, transfer agents, providers, and recipients.

Offe (1984) and Tropman (1989) noted that there are built-in conflicts and contradictions in values in the welfare state. Offe outlined one such conflict between the Right and the Left. The Right, for example, is usually against welfare state programs because it imposes a disincentive to investment for the holders of capital and a disincentive to work for the providers of labor. The Left, in turn, is against the welfare state because "it is a step to stabilize, rather than a step in the transformation of, capitalist society" (Offe, p. 154). According to Tropman, the welfare state poses seven policy dilemmas: work versus leisure, struggle versus entitlement, equity versus adequacy, independence versus interdependence, personal versus family orientation, secular versus religious positions, and public versus private support for solving problems. Karger and Stoesz (1994) echoed these views, stating that at least in the United States, the welfare state represents a dynamic compromise between the values of the conservatives and the liberals.

In the United States, where the value-orientation approach is popular, welfare state spending is called the liberal approach, and cutbacks in welfare state spending are called the conservative approach. In Europe, welfare state spending is often considered a pro-labor position, and cutbacks are seen as a pro-capital position. However, this latter terminology implies that political behavior about the welfare state is driven not by values but by political interests.

STRUCTURAL FUNCTIONALISM

Structural functionalism, a theoretical paradigm in anthropology and sociology, was developed in England around World War I and quickly became popular as a dominant paradigm in these two disciplines. Although its popularity waned in the 1970s, it is still one of the important paradigms in the social sciences and is undergoing a revival under the name neofunctionalism (see Ritzer, 1992; Turner, 1993).

The basic premise of structural functionalism is that all societies or national cultures must perform certain key functions to survive as cultural entities. These functions are universal, regardless of where the societies are located. However, the macrostructures that perform these functions may take different shapes in different cultures. In other words, functions are constant, but structures vary.

Malinowski (1955), an early scholar of this paradigm, believed that the following functions are universal for human societies—reproduction, socialization, reciprocity, mutual support, governance, production, consumption, and social control—and that the institutional structure of the family, the government, the world of work, and religion variously share these functions in different societies. In preindustrial societies, the family performs the reproduction, socialization, mutual-support, consumption, and social-control functions and may also perform key production functions. In industrial societies, the family is no longer an important factor in production, and it shares the socialization, mutual-support, and social-control functions with other institutional structures.

Other early proponents of this paradigm (see Davis & Moore, 1945) stated that each society ensures that all functionally important positions are filled with qualified personnel because these positions are important for the survival of the society as a whole. However, these positions are rewarded in inverse proportion to their availability. That is, the easier it is to fill these positions, the lesser the reward structure attached to them. (The demand-and-supply matrix seems to be integrated into this theory.) It is the attachment of reward structures to performing key societal functions that leads to a form of social hierarchy, or stratification, in all societies.

Parsons (1951), a major architect of this paradigm, noted that the following four functions are universal in all social systems, whether they are societies, communities, organizations, or smaller groups: *adaptation* with the environment; *goal setting and governance; integration* of the different parts; and *maintenance and replication* of cultural styles over time. In a society, the economy performs the goal-setting function, the religious and educational institutions (including social services institutions) perform the integration function, and the family performs the pattern-maintenance or replication functions. Parsons is also credited with developing the concept of the sick role, which creates a structure and a procedure for managing illness in societies. Many modern societies are conflicted about extending the concept of the sick role to certain behaviors that are not traditionally construed as illness, such as alcohol or drug abuse, because doing so requires an expansion of the domain of the welfare state, whereas defining the same behavior as deviance necessitates an expansion of the domain of the correctional state.

Merton (1958), another major architect of this paradigm, added that social roles and the social structures that constitute them often simultaneously perform functions they were intended to perform, and those they were not intended to perform. For example, professional social work roles under capitalism originated to manage the marginal members of society but, over time, became therapeutic roles for many nonmarginal members of society. Managing the marginal members of society was the intended function, whereas providing psychotherapy was the unintended function.

Applied to welfare state analysis, this paradigm suggests that although the creation of the sick role gives the social structure a humane way to manage illness, it also creates many unforeseen and sometimes unintended markets or opportunities for given professionals. One example is the argument that "poverty is functional" (see Gans, 1972), which is similar to Durkheim's (1950) argument that "crime is functional." The existence of poor people ensures that society's "dirty work" is done, that there is an ongoing supply of cheap labor, and that those in certain middle-class occupations and professions are employed.

The works of Parsons and Merton formed the basis of social problem analysis in many countries, especially in the United States, Britain, and some parts of Europe. This paradigm has been used to understand problems like poverty, family instability, crime, delinquency, and substance abuse (see Cloward & Ohlin, 1960; Merton & Nisbet, 1965; Neubeck, 1991).

MODERNIZATION THEORY

Modernization theory and dependency theory evolved in competition with each other. Dependency theory, which originated mainly in Latin America, attempts to explain why there is a global level of stratification among nations (see Frank, 1969; Furtado, 1970; Lenski, Lenski, & Nolan, 1991). It overlaps somewhat with the views of Immanuel Wallerstein (discussed in chapter 3), and takes the position that the "wealth of [some] nations" (to paraphrase Smith, 1776/1963) develops because of the "poverty of [other] nations," especially nations from the Third World. The nations from the first group are wealthy because they have succeeded in exploiting the developing nations. Capitalist industrialization, the argument goes, has used the Third World countries as sources of raw materials and cheap labor.

Modernization theory, which was developed primarily by U.S. scholars, suggests that the problems of the Third World nations are due to the values, attitudes, and behavior of the people in these countries (see Eisenstadt, 1960; Inkeles & Smith, 1974; Moore & Feldman, 1960; Parsons, 1971; Rostow, 1962). Such values and attitudes include the preference for large families and extended families, the use of child labor and primitive technology, and the absence of information. The lack of capital and skilled labor also contribute to the lack of "modern" status. Modernization theory builds on the classic premises of Weber (1922/1958, discussed in chapter 4) and of structural functionalism. Thus, modernization means the *resocialization* of the Third World countries with the values, information, and institutions of the First World countries. The assumption is that such a resocialization will lead to industrialization, which, in turn, will lead to the development of wealth. Programs of community development and technology transfer, it is believed, will contribute to this resocialization. Furthermore, a *motif of rationality* is a necessary condition for modernization. (Weber, 1922/1958, was interested in the study of the rational motif and used it as a basis of his studies of bureaucracies, which make the operation of modern societies possible.)

Steward (1958) observed that cultural development can be understood from one of three perspectives: (1) unilinear development, (2) universal development, or (3) multilinear development. Unilinear development follows from the 19th century assumptions of the European and North American elites that there are stages of cultural development (comparable to the biological stages of human development) and that at a given time, any culture can be located in one of these stages. Proponents of this view believe that contemporary North American and European cultures are in the "most evolved" stage. Universal development is a modification of unilinear development advocated by White (1949) and Childe (1951). This perspective states that a culture can be placed in a stage according to its ability to incorporate new technological and social features to survive. Multilinear development, on the other hand, does not assume that different cultures can be placed on a single linear historical continuum. This school of thought, supported by Steward, assumes that there are parallel developments in two or more cultures that make cross-cultural comparisons possible. However, two or more cultures should not be placed on one linear scale.

Midgley (1984) reviewed three paradigms of cultural changes: (1) the modernization school, (2) the dependency school, and (3) the Marxist school. He concluded that the modernization school follows the intellectual templates of the universalistic development of cultures. The dependency theorists seem to agree, but argue that the reasons for poverty and the underdevelopment of certain cultures are imperialism, colonialism, and capitalism because these three forces have transferred substantial amounts of resources from the areas that are now underdeveloped. The Marxists are in partial agreement with the dependency theorists, except that they single out capitalism as the most exploitive form and state that its removal and replacement with a centrally planned economy would lead to more desirable cultural change.

These paradigms of cultural change are relevant for social welfare planners who are interested in community development and social change, both within and among nations. Within-nation efforts, like the urban community development efforts and the enterprise-zone programs in the United States, are aimed at the subcultures of a rich nation that are trapped in cultures of poverty, matriarchy (feminist theorists are silent about the relationship among poverty, underdevelopment, and female-headed households on a world scale), and underemployment and unemployment. The multinational efforts, such as the massive regional community development programs in African, Asian, and Latin American countries, are aimed at nonliterate peasants and other populations who are trapped in lifestyles at the subsistence level.

POSTMODERNISM

Postmodernism started out as a theory of how language is a definer of knowledge, as well as a vehicle of communication (Lyotard, 1984; Pardek, Murphy, & Choi, 1994; Wittgenstein, 1921/1963). According to this theory, language (linguistic symbols), not the culture in which a given language appears, constructs meaning, identity, and reality. Consequently, groups who feel oppressed (because of gender, class, race, sexual preference, or whatever) must *deconstruct* the linguistic symbols that are the instruments of their oppression.

Postmodernism assumes that cultural developments are specific to given localities (that is, what happens in one local culture is not necessarily a part of either a universal or a unilinear pattern of development) and are not always cumulative. Applied to welfare state analysis, postmodernism suggests that the empowerment of an oppressed group has to begin with the deconstruction of demeaning linguistic symbols, the acquisition of superior language skills, and the conversion of interactions into discourses. Friere (1970) established that the discourse method can be used to empower even illiterate peasants. Finally, postmodernism deromanticizes the concept of rationality that is uniform and universal in nature—the basis of modernization theory. In postmodernism, there may be several types of rationalities, depending on the locality and language structure of a culture.

EXCHANGE AND GAME THEORY

A variant of classical exchange theory, which originated in economics, was made popular in sociology and political science by Blau (1964) and Emerson (1981). Nye (1984) and Martin and O'Connor (1989) applied this theory to social services issues. In this paradigm, all interactions between persons, groups, communities, organizations, or nations are transactions. These transactions may be ends to themselves (as in gemeinschaft-type relations) or means to ends (as in gesellschaft-type relations). Furthermore, transactions are symmetrical when the resources held by both parties are even but asymmetrical when the resources held by the parties are uneven.

The basic assumption of exchange theory is that all transactions are exchanges; that exchanges are guided by conscious rationality; that exchanges may involve material resources, information, roles, attractiveness, or the ability to commit violence; that exchanges are even or uneven; and that uneven exchanges lead to imbalances of power. Most social or personal problems, it is believed, originate in such a power imbalance. Applied to welfare state analysis, exchange theory suggests that social problems (requiring state intervention) occur when exchanges are uneven, when the rules of exchange are unclear, or when there is substantial status incongruity in the transactions. These conditions are likely to contribute to substantial inequalities over time unless the state implements policies to reduce uneven exchanges, to make the rules of exchange clear, and to reduce status incongruities in most transactions.

RATIONAL CHOICE THEORY

Rational choice theory, which was devised mainly by Hechter (1987), is intellectually close to exchange theory. In this paradigm, an essential function of any cultural group is production. Goods produced may be *public goods* (to be consumed by all people, regardless of whether they participated in its production) or *private goods* (to be consumed either by a selected few according to the principles of market exchange or by groups chosen by the producer). Examples of public goods and services are roads, defense, and police services, whereas private goods are most other goods that, when consumed by one person, decrease their capacity for consumption by others (see Turner, 1993). The production of public goods is extremely important, and people can either be forced to produce them (by being required to participate in their production or to pay taxes that make their production possible) or rewarded for producing them (by being paid wages or given respect or affection). An assumption of this theory is that because some persons are likely to avoid any role in the production of public goods, the state must decide who, if any, should be allowed to do so.

Applied to welfare state analysis, rational choice theory would suggest that social control in the production of public goods and equity across communities and social classes in sharing this responsibility should both be increased. For example, the production of nationalized health services (as in the United Kingdom or Canada) can be considered a public good, offered as one possible solution to the problems of delivering health care services in the United States. Because it is an expensive public good, how should all segments of the population be asked to contribute to its continued production? In chapter 2 it was pointed out that one current means of social control in health care usage is rationing. Rational choice theory would call for some contribution to health care costs from most segments of the population and some kind of rationing of health care delivery.

NORMATIVE THEORY

Normative theories are formalized positions (prescriptive action schemes) about what should be done in given circumstances. Goldhammer (1978) described the action schemes recommended by such wise men throughout history. For example, Chinese philosopher Mo-tzu (also written as Motse) advised the king to be consistent; the Hindu philosopher Kautilya suggested that the king get things done without regard to how he did so; English theologian Sir Thomas More required the king to be a moral exemplar to his people; and Italian scholar Niccolo Machiavelli recommended that the king should either caress or destroy people, but caressing was preferable (Goldhammer, 1978). The constitutions of most modern nations are another example of formalized normative theories. The essential idea of normative theory is the specification of one or more goals, such as equality, protection, and justice, to be pursued by the actions of a monarch or a state.

Nozick (1974) and Rawls (1971) took opposite positions regarding the concept of justice. According to Nozick, the state should not engage in redistribution, because its function should be restricted to the protection of individual rights and justly acquired property. According to Rawls, the state should engage in redistribution, especially if it benefits "the truly disadvantaged" (Wilson, 1987). Barry (1990, p. 88) referred to Rawls as "a muted egalitarian."

Modern feminist theorists are partly immersed in normative theory. Although they may disagree about the reasons for the subjection of women (Nes & Iadicola, 1989), they agree that there *should be* a better redistribution scheme across gender lines and that state action should be geared toward the attainment of equality, protection, and justice for women. Classical Marxists and neo-Marxists have argued in favor of a better redistribution across class lines and proposed state action to facilitate that end.

Applied to welfare state analysis, normative theory contributes to the controversies over whether there should be a welfare state and, if so, what domains it should cover. One position is that there should be no welfare state because the state is not meant for redistribution. The opposite position, calls for the presence of a well-designed welfare state that engages in large-scale redistribution.

ONTOLOGICAL ISSUES IN THE PARADIGMS

All 12 paradigms of industrialization (the empirical ones plus normative theory) cluster around one central issue—ontology—when they are applied to welfare state analysis. In some way or other, all the paradigms and their subsets make some basic assumptions about human nature and the factors that influence human behavior. Therefore, the controversies about the welfare state are not due just to the application of different theoretical paradigms, but to different ontological assumptions. The following are examples of these ontological issues.

RECIPROCITY

Structural functionalism explicitly states that the expectation of reciprocity in human relations is an important part of human nature and a governing force in human behavior, but seven other paradigms of industrialization either implicitly or explicitly depend on this concept. These paradigms are the demand-and-supply matrix, class analysis (the inability of certain classes to engage in reciprocity), value-orientation analysis (the norm of reciprocity, as Gouldner, 1960, called it), modernization theory (culturally prescribed modes of reciprocity), postmodernism (reciprocity as a basis for local knowledge), exchange theory, and rational choice theory.

Given the importance of reciprocity in human nature and behavior, a key question is, Should the welfare state extend its benefits to those who cannot engage in reciprocity? If the answer is yes (when the economy can afford to do so and the polity allows it), then the following questions must be clarified:

1. Among the various subgroups who are not capable of reciprocity, which should be candidates for the benefits? In this context, children are a subgroup who are likely to enter the reciprocity network in the future; aged people are a subgroup who were part of the network in the past; and people who are chronically ill (including those who are chronically mentally ill), developmentally disabled, or poor and unskilled are a subgroup who are not likely to enter the network.
2. How are all these subgroups to be treated? If they are to receive benefits, then how much and in what order?

PROFIT MOTIVE

If there is support for extending welfare state benefits to the subgroups who are not capable of reciprocity, then what is the motive behind such support? Is it altruism, or is some profit to be derived in the future from extending such benefits? Put a different way, does extending welfare state benefits create a market, profits, or a constituency for some group? These concepts are inherent in many of the paradigms.

Is Behavior Value Driven or Interest Driven?

Does the providers' support for welfare state benefits come from a basic human value or from a clear interest of some kind? Is it true that when providers' reasons for supporting such benefits are both value and interest driven, the chances of legitimating the benefits are high; when the reasons are driven only by one or the other, the chances of legitimating the benefits are low; and when neither value nor interest can justify providing the benefits, the chances of legitimating them approach zero?

Recipients' acceptance of welfare state benefits can also be viewed from this perspective. Given that accepting the benefits is in the recipients' interest, does making them a gratuity reduce their acceptability, and, conversely, does making them an entitlement enhance their acceptability?

Is Behavioral Change Externally Induced?

Many types of tax policies, welfare policies, and other efforts by the state are devised to achieve certain behavioral objectives. For example, in many cultures, payers can use donations to charity as tax write-offs, so a tax write-off policy is supposed to be an inducement for voluntary giving. In addition, some income maintenance or other welfare benefits are set up in a manner that should discourage their usage. These examples of a state's attempt to promote certain types of behavior (to have payers donate money or to discourage recipients from consuming welfare benefits) represent the use of rewards and punishments (from classical behaviorism) as external inducements. However, they raise the following questions: To what extent can the state provide inducements to engage in certain types of behavior? Do these inducements succeed when the community values of the payers or recipients are against such behavior? And do they fail when these community values are in favor of such behavior?

The Market

The market is an important concept in several paradigms of industrialization. In some, such as the demand-and-supply matrix, it takes on godlike features (Smith's, 1776/1963, Invisible Hand, for example) and is used as a source of all sanctions. In others, like dual market theory, it is viewed as two or more entities that have separate domains. In welfare analysis, the market and the state are frequently used as determinants of two types of welfare states. Sen (1981) stated that a perfect operation of the market could not prevent the famous Bengal famine of 1941–42. I add that the Great Depression of the 1930s in the United States and the famine in Ethiopia in 1993 also could not be prevented despite the regular operation of the market. Sen further noted that "in the market economies of the West, if people do not go begging for food it is only because of the social security system that the state has offered" (quoted in Barry, 1990, p. 67). It seems that by "the social security system," Sen meant the social welfare system. The implication is that there are times when the market does not or cannot be a perfect agent of distribution, and state intervention is necessary. Barry (1990), seemingly a believer in the ability of the market system, conceded that either intervention from the state or a strong voluntary system or a combination of the two are needed to supplement a system of market distribution.

MAKING RATIONAL CHOICES

With regard to external inducements for behavior, one can question a basic assumption of several of the paradigms—that individuals, families, communities, and subcultures make rational choices from available alternatives. Rather, the question is, Is making such ratioal choices a result of cultural conditioning? For example, women in Nepal cook on traditional stoves that are extremely labor intensive. However, when they are offered fuel and labor-saving modern stoves, they tend not to use them (Pandey, 1989). If people do not make rational choices in one area because of cultural conditioning, it follows that they are not likely to do so in other areas as well. Thus, a question related to welfare state analysis is, Under what circumstances are payers, providers, and recipients of state welfare benefits guided by rational choices, and when is their decision making influenced by impulse, affect, or cultural conditioning?

IS RATIONALITY UNIVERSAL?

Rationality is a powerful and widely used concept in the German and Anglo-American social sciences, especially among social scientists who are intellectually indebted to Weber (1946). In the modern social sciences, rational action is considered to be action that is maximally effective (Haas & Drabek, 1973). Simon's (1957) concept of "bounded rationality" was perhaps the first to point out that all the major decisions made by key leaders and their follower groups are only partly rational and that many nonrational elements enter into the decision-making process of groups.

Furthermore, postmodernists, such as Mestrovic (1992), have noted that rationality is multidimensional and varies from place to place and from culture to culture, so that what may be a rational action for one group may not be so for another. Herein lies the possibility of cultural clashes. A powerful example of such a clash of cultures is the historical story of the pursuit of the Rajput queen Padmini by the Moslem conqueror Alauddin, which has been the subject of many books and operas (Brosolo, 1984).

Alauddin, sultan of Delhi (1296–1316), was a mighty ruler of a large portion of northern India. During a visit to Chitore, a small Rajput kingdom, he caught a glimpse of Padmini, the queen of Chitore. After returning to Delhi, he demanded that Padmini be sent to him as his mistress. Padmini and the people of Chitore refused to submit to this demand, and Alauddin invaded Chitore with an enormous military force and conquered it after a mass destruction. As he approached the palace in Chitore to claim Padmini, she walked into a huge funeral pyre.

In this account, both Alauddin and Padmini engaged in rational action from their perspectives and for different purposes. Alauddin's use of military maneuvers was rational and goal-directed behavior to achieve his goal: to maximize ownership. Likewise, Padmini's suicide by walking onto a huge funeral pyre was a rational act to achieve her goal: to maximize honor. But the means they used were different: mass destruction versus self-destruction. Furthermore, Alauddin used a rational organization of soldiers, whereas Padmini used an intra- and interpersonal rational organization of attitudes.

Many centuries later, during the Vietnam War, Vietnamese monks used the same type of rationality that Padmini used to publicize the invasion of Vietnam by foreign powers by immolating themselves on huge funeral pyres. This is another example of the fact that rationality is tied to group membership and locale.

UNINTENDED CONSEQUENCES

The term *unintended consequences* is an important construct of structural functionalism. Although it is not an ontological matter in itself, the structural functionalists introduced it because they believed that the observable unintended consequences of certain decisions are due mostly to ontological reasons. Moynihan (1968, 1973) wrote that some of the intended consequences of the administrations of U.S. presidents Lyndon B. Johnson and Richard M. Nixon (such as the reduction of poverty) could not be accomplished because of their unintended by-products, namely, interest-group politics, or to put it badly, the politics of greed. Group politics and greed politics are both ontological matters.

Even when separated from greed politics, group politics contributes to an understanding of the unintended consequences of industrialization in general and welfare state analysis in particular. For example, in labor policy, support of the concept of the "family wage" simultaneously increases the value of labor, especially men's labor, and supports the concept of patriarchy because it increases the economic power of male heads of households. Feminists (see, for example, Ehrenreich & Piven, 1984) have argued, however, that the incorporation of the family wage concept in labor policy led to the empowerment of men and reduced the power of women. Thus, a welfare policy that is based on this concept is also likely to make women relatively powerless.

INDUSTRIALIZATION AND SOCIAL WELFARE: 10 THESES

The paradigms of industrialization have, in some combination, generated the following 10 theses:

Thesis 1: The welfare state is a by-product of industrialization (demand-and-supply matrix, class analysis, value-orientation analysis, structural functionalism, modernization theory, exchange theory).

Thesis 2: The welfare state is a by-product of industrialization but is justified by ideology (class analysis, value-orientation analysis, structural functionalism).

Thesis 3: Poverty is functional in industrial capitalism (class analysis and structural functionalism).

Thesis 4: Industrial socialism leads to prefisc welfare states, whereas industrial capitalism leads to postfisc welfare states (demand-and-supply matrix, value-orientation analysis, modernization theory, normative theory).

Thesis 5: Postfisc welfare states are better than are prefisc ones (demand-and-supply matrix, exchange theory, rational choice theory).

Thesis 6: Cost containment is a major problem in the welfare state, in general, but is a greater problem under industrial capitalism (demographic analysis, demand-and-supply matrix, dual labor market analysis, class analysis, normative theory).

Thesis 7: Cost containment in welfare states is managed better by indexing welfare expenditures than by deficit financing (demographic analysis and demand-and-supply matrix).

Thesis 8: The operation of a free-market system of capitalism, not modernization efforts, can build a welfare state and perhaps a welfare society in the Third World and can sustain welfare states and welfare societies in the First and Second Worlds (demand-and-supply matrix, class analysis, structural functionalism).

Thesis 9: In industrial capitalism, human vulnerability is commodified and subjected to a market system, which leads to a provider class that is part of the middle class (class analysis, structural functionalism, rational choice theory).

Thesis 10: The more individualized the polity, the greater the commodification of human vulnerability. The greater the commodification of human vulnerability, the more the medicalized vision of problem solving (demand-and-supply matrix, class analysis, rational choice theory).

REFERENCES

Atherton, C. R. (1990). Adam Smith and the welfare state. *Arete, 15,* 24–31.

Barry, N. (1990). *Welfare.* Minneapolis: University of Minnesota Press.

Beeghley, L. (1988). *The structure of social stratification in the United States.* Boston: Allyn & Bacon.

Bell, D. (1973). *The coming of post-industrial society.* New York: Basic Books.

Berger, P. (1986). *The capitalist revolution.* New York: Basic Books.

Blau, P. (1964). *Exchange and power in social life.* New York: John Wiley & Sons.

Blumer, H. (1990). *Industrialization as an agent of social change.* New York: de Gruyter.

Brosolo, A. (1984). *Nei giardno di Padmini.* Udine, Italy: Brosolo.

Chatterjee, P., & Bailey, D. (1993). Ideology and structure of nonprofit organizations. In P. Chatterjee & A. Abramovitz (Eds.), *Structure of nonprofit management* (pp. 3–26). Lanham, MD: University Press of America.

Childe, V. G. (1951). *Social evolution.* London: Schuman.

Cloward, R., & Ohlin, L. E. (1960). *Delinquency and opportunity.* New York: Free Press.

Cottingham, P., & Ellwood, D. T. (1989). *Welfare policy for the 1990s.* Cambridge, MA: Harvard University Press.

Cox, P. R. (1970). *Demography.* Cambridge, England: Cambridge University Press.

Davis, K., & Moore, W. (1945). Some principles of stratification. *American Sociological Review, 7,* 242–249.

Doeringer, P. B. (1971). *American ideologies.* Chicago: Markham.

Durkheim, E. (1950). *The rules of sociological method.* Glencoe, IL: Free Press.

Ehrenreich, B., & Piven, F. F. (1984). The feminization of poverty. *Dissent, 31,* 162–170.

Eisenstadt, S. N. (1960). *Modernization.* Englewood Cliffs, NJ: Prentice Hall.

Emerson, R. M. (1981). Social exchange theory. In M. Rosenberg & R. H. Turner (Eds.), *Social psychology* (pp. 30–65). New York: Basic Books.

Esping-Andersen, G. (1990). *The three worlds of welfare capitalism.* Princeton, NJ: Princeton University Press.

Frank, A. (1969). *Capitalism and underdevelopment in Latin America.* New York: Monthly Review Press.

Friedman, M. (1962). *Capitalism and freedom.* Chicago: University of Chicago Press.

Friere, P. (1970). *The pedagogy of the oppressed.* New York: Seabury Press.

Furtado, C. (1970). *Economic development of Latin America.* Cambridge, England: Cambridge University Press.

Gans, H. (1972). The positive functions of poverty. *American Journal of Sociology, 78,* 275–289.

Glass, P. Y. (1995, December 3). France's famed rail system is on brink of bankruptcy. *The Plain Dealer,* p. 6-A.

Goldhammer, H. (1978). *The adviser.* New York: Elsevier.

Gordon, D. (1972). *Theories of poverty.* Lexington, MA: D. C. Heath.

Gouldner, A. (1960). The norms of reciprocity. *American Sociological Review, 25,* 161–178.

Haas, J. E., & Drabek, T. A. (1973). *Complex organizations.* New York: Macmillan.

Hechter, M. (1987). *Principles of group solidarity.* Berkeley: University of California Press.

Huff, D. D., & Johnson, D. A. (1993). Phantom welfare: Public relief for corporate American. *Social Work, 38,* 311–316.

Inkeles, A., & Smith, D. (1974). *Becoming modern.* Cambridge, MA: Harvard University Press.

Janowitz, M. (1954). *The community press in an urban setting.* Chicago: University of Chicago Press.

Karger, H. J., & Stoesz, D. (1994). *American social welfare policy.* New York: Longman.

Kerr, C., Dunlop, J. T., Harbison, F. H., & Myers, C. A. (1965). The industrializing elites. In M. A. Zald (Ed.), *Social welfare institutions: A sociological reader* (pp. 73–101). New York: John Wiley & Sons.

Konig, R. (1968). *The community.* New York: Schocken Books.

Kuznets, S. (1955). Economic growth and income inequality. *American Economic Review, 45,* 1–28.

Lenski, G., Lenski, J., & Nolan, P. (1991). *Human societies: An introduction to macrosociology.* New York: McGraw-Hill.

Levine, R. (1988). *Class struggle and the New Deal.* Lawrence: University of Kansas Press.

Lohmann, R. (1992). *The commons.* San Francisco: Jossey-Bass.

Lyotard, J. (1984). *The postmodern condition: A report on knowledge.* Minneapolis: University of Minnesota Press.

Malinowski, B. (1955). *Magic, science, and religion.* New York: Doubleday Anchor Books.

Martin, P. Y., & O'Connor, C. G. (1989). *The social environment.* New York: Longman.

Merton, R. (1958). *Social theory and social structure.* Glencoe, IL: Free Press.

Merton, R. (1972). Insiders and outsiders. *American Journal of Sociology, 78,* 9–47.

Merton, R., & Nisbet, R. (1965). *Contemporary social problems.* New York: Harcourt, Brace & World.

Mestrovic, S. G. (1992). *Durkheim and postmodern culture.* New York: de Gruyter.

Midgley, J. (1984). Social welfare implications of development paradigms. *Social Service Review, 58,* 181–198.

Moore, W., & Feldman, D. (1960). *Labor commitment and social change in developing areas.* New York: Social Science Research Council.

Moynihan, D. P. (1968). *Maximum feasible misunderstanding.* New York: Basic Books.

Moynihan, D. P. (1973). *The politics of a guaranteed income.* New York: Basic Books.

Nes, J. A., & Iadicola, P. (1989). Toward a definition of feminist social work: A comparison of liberal, radical, and socialist models. *Social Work, 34,* 12–22.

Neubeck, K. J. (1991). *Social problems.* New York: McGraw-Hill.

Nisbet, R. A. (1966). *The sociological tradition.* New York: Basic Books.

Nozick, R. (1974). *Anarchy, state and utopia.* Oxford, England: Basil Blackwell.

Nye, F. I. (1984). *Family relationships and delinquent behavior.* New York: John Wiley & Sons.

Offe, C. (1984). *Contradictions of the welfare state.* Cambridge, MA: MIT Press.

Orloff, A. S. (1993). Gender and the social rights of citizenship. *American Sociological Review, 58,* 303–328.

Pandey, S. (1989). *Some factors determining the level of use of improved stoves by Brahmin and Chhetri women in central Nepal.* Unpublished Ph.D. dissertation, Case Western Reserve University, Cleveland.

Pardek, J. T., Murphy, J. W., & Choi, J. M. (1994). Some implications of postmodernism for social work practice. *Social Work, 39,* 343–346.

Parsons, T. (1951). *The social system.* Glencoe, IL: Free Press.

Parsons, T. (1971). *The system of modern societies.* Englewood Cliffs, NJ: Prentice Hall.

Piore, M. J. (1971). The dual labor market: Theory and implications. In D. M. Gordon (Ed.), *Problems in political economy: An urban perspective* (pp. 162–180). Lexington, MA: D. C. Heath.

Piven, F. F., & Cloward, R. (1993). *Regulating the poor: The functions of social welfare* (2nd ed.). New York: Random House.

Powell, B. (1995, December 11). Days of rage in Paris. *Newsweek, 126,* 51–52.

Rawls, J. (1971). *A theory of justice.* Cambridge, MA: Harvard University Press.

Rayback, J. G. (1959). *A history of American labor.* New York: Free Press.

Rimlinger, G. (1971). *The welfare state and industrialization in Europe, America, and Russia.* New York: John Wiley & Sons.

Ritzer, G. (1992). *Sociology: A multiple paradigm science.* Boston: Allyn & Bacon.

Rokeach, M. (1973). *The nature of human values.* New York: Free Press.

Rostow, W. (1962). *The process of economic growth.* New York: W. W. Norton.

Sen, A. (1981). *Poverty and famines.* Oxford, England: Clarenden Press.

Simon, H. (1957). *Administrative behavior.* New York: Free Press.

Smith, A. (1963). *An inquiry into the nature and causes of the wealth of nations.* New York: Modern Library. (Original work published 1776)

Some ABCs of mediconomics. (1991, July 6). *The Economist.*

Sorokin, P. A. (1927). *Social mobility.* New York: Harper & Bros.

Specter, G. (1995). *Creating a common agenda: Strategies for our communities.* Northampton, MA: National Priorities Project.

Steward, J. H. (1958). Evolution and process. In A. L. Kroeber (Ed.), *Anthropology today.* Chicago: University of Chicago Press.

Tonnies, F. (1957). *Community and society.* New York: Harper & Row.

Tropman, J. E. (1989). *American values and social welfare.* Englewood Cliffs, NJ: Prentice Hall.

Turner, J. (1993). *The structure of sociological theory* (2nd ed.). Belmont, CA: Wadsworth.

United Nations Development Programme. (1994). *Human development report, 1994.* New York: Oxford University Press.

U.S. Internal Revenue Service. (1994). *Major categories of federal income and outlays for fiscal year 1993: Form 1040.* Washington, DC: U.S. Government Printing Office.

Warren, R. L. (1969). *The community in America.* Chicago: Rand McNally.

Weber, M. (1946). *From Max Weber: Essays in sociology* (H. H. Gerth & C. W. Mills, Trans.). New York: Oxford University Press.

Weber, M. (1958). *The Protestant ethic and the spirit of capitalism.* New York: Charles Scribner's Sons. (Original work published 1992)

White, L. A. (1949). *The science of culture.* New York: Farrar, Straus.

Wilson, W. J. (1979). *The declining significance of race.* Chicago: University of Chicago Press.

Wilson, W. J. (1987). *The truly disadvantaged.* Chicago: University of Chicago Press.

Wittgenstein, L. (1963). *Tractatus logico-philosophicus.* London: Routledge & Kegal Paul. (Original work published 1921)

9

WELFARE IS A BY-PRODUCT OF INDUSTRIALIZATION: 2

The reduction of human suffering rather than its increase is the proper goal of human society.

Moore, *Reflections on the Causes of Human Misery*

You give a man a fish, you feed him for a day. You teach a man how to fish, you feed him for a lifetime.

Japanese proverb

In a manner similar to chapters 5 and 7, this chapter examines the evidence available to support or refute the 10 theses presented at the end of chapter 8. The following questions help clarify the examination of these theses:

1. Is industrialization a sufficient condition for the development of the welfare state? If yes, then why? If not, why not?
2. If industrialization is a sufficient condition for the development of the welfare state, then what explains the variability of the welfare state from nation to nation?

THE 10 THESES

THESE 1: THE WELFARE STATE IS A BY-PRODUCT OF INDUSTRIALIZATION

The first scholar to support this thesis in a clear and forceful voice was Schumpeter (1950). In his book, *Capitalism, Socialism, and Democracy,* he noted that Marx stated that capitalism will destroy itself because of its failure to deliver a better economic condition to the masses. Marx was correct, Schumpeter observed, but his reasoning was wrong. Rather,

Schumpeter concluded, capitalism is not likely to survive because of its overwhelming success in providing a better life for the masses. When capitalism destroys itself, it will be replaced by a form of socialism.

On the face of it, this prediction seems not to have proved true, what with the collapse of state socialism in the former Soviet-Bloc countries and the success of free-market economies over planned economies. So, is there any value to it as the 21st century nears?

After carefully rereading Schumpeter, I found that he never used the terms *social welfare* or *welfare state*. Moreover, during Schumpeter's time, the very concept of the welfare state was known as socialism. The state, by developing policies to distribute goods and services to nonproductive populations (known today as social welfare policies), engages in acts that are clearly socialist. Or, put a different way, any effort by the state to distribute goods and services through some sort of central planning is socialism and is not consistent with free-market capitalism, in which the market is the agent of distribution. Thus, in announcing that socialism will eventually triumph over capitalism, Schumpeter was at least partially right. All industrial countries have some kind of welfare state. Even among the capitalist states, the last country to convert to welfare statism—the United States—is, despite many cutbacks and procapital politics, still an ambivalent convert to welfare statism.

The other parts of Schumpeter's prediction rest on the idea that "control over the means of production and over production itself [will be] vested with a central authority" (p. 167). In this regard, one sees a parallel development that is consistent with the prediction: arbitration, regulation, intervention, and the formation of coalitions by the state (central authority) in the production process in all industrial countries. In other words, the state is not a neutral bystander in the production process. Thus, here, too, Schumpeter was close to the mark.

With these caveats, Schumpeter's prediction can be restated as follows: *Industrialization and industrial capitalism are responsible for building a decent surplus (wealth building), which, in turn, makes socialistic distribution (social welfare) possible. Ideology does not contribute to this process.*

In addition to supporting Thesis 1, Schumpeter's prediction is an ideal type of analytical tool, as shown in Figure 9-1. In this figure, the group responsible for production is on the horizontal axis, and the group responsible for distribution is on the vertical axis. In this mode of analysis, outcomes in boxes 7, 8, and 9 clearly do not lead to a welfare state. Outcome 1 reflects classic socialism and does not seem to be a viable state (given the breakup of the Soviet Bloc). Outcome 2 may reflect China during the 1990s, but its viability in the long run is not clear. Thus, outcomes 2, 3, 5, and 6 are possible welfare states. Most of the First and Second World welfare states discussed in chapter 3 fall within outcomes 1 and 6. During the 1990s, the Scandinavian countries would be in box 3; most of

Figure 9-1.

Variations in the Welfare State

DISTRIBUTION BY

		State	Combination	Market
PRODUCTION BY	State	1 (Classic socialism— not a viable state)	4 (Not a viable state)	7 (Neither a viable state nor a welfare state)
	Combination	2	5	8 (Not a welfare state)
	Market	3	6	9 (Classic capitalism— not a welfare state)

the Second World countries, in box 2; the United States, in box 6; and the other First World countries, in either 2 or 5.

Given that industrialization changes the structure of the family, community, and other primary institutions (see chapter 8), many new forms of vulnerable groups emerge. At this point, Wilensky and Lebeaux (1958) picked up Schumpeter's thesis and, influenced by the work of Richard M. Titmuss (discussed in chapters 4 and 5), suggested that industrialization, in turn, may lead to the development of two types of social welfare systems: (1) a *residual type,* in which no planned intervention structure is in place to manage vulnerable populations, and the (2) *institutional type,* in which planned intervention structures are in place. In this approach, the outcomes in boxes 1 through 6 in Figure 9-1 are close to institutional social welfare.

Wilensky's (1975) ambitious study of the growth and variability of the welfare state, entitled *The Welfare State and Equality,* concluded that the welfare state is a by-product of industrialization (wealth building), emerges from the needs of the population, and is maintained by the age of the population and of the social security system. In his view, ideology has nothing to do with the formation of the welfare state. Given industrialization, the key contributors to the development of the welfare state are the demographic structure of the nation and the interest groups that arise with the introduction of a social security system. Although some scholars (such as Zald, 1976) have questioned Wilensky's use of causal modeling, the work is still provocative.

In addition to the work of Schumpeter, an economist, and Wilensky, a sociologist, two scholarly works in social work openly supported Thesis 1: Wolins (1967) and Gilbert and Specht (1974). Wolins argued that the welfare state (the structure of social welfare) emerges to maintain or strengthen the existing structures of an industrial society (again, as a by-product of industrialization). In any society, there are normally four institutions (the family, economy, polity, and informal reciprocity) that meet human needs (the influence of Malinowski, 1955, and Parsons, 1951, is clear here). In industrial societies these four are often not adequate to meet predictable human crises, so one of two types of welfare state may arise to do so: Type A, in which benefits are available to individuals because of their *membership* in a collectivity (like citizenship of a state), and Type B, in which individuals who seek to obtain benefits are seen as deviants (as in the sick role of Parsons, 1951) but that form of deviance is considered *acceptable deviance.*

Following the same analytical tone, Gilbert and Specht (1974) added to Wilensky and Lebeaux's typology: In a residual social welfare state, there is no planned infrastructure to act as a "safety net" to deal with predictable crises; therefore, the family or the church is expected to do so. In the institutional social welfare system, however, a fifth institution (in addition to the family, religion, economy, and the polity) emerges to meet predictable human needs: the welfare state.

THESIS 2: THE WELFARE STATE IS A BY-PRODUCT OF INDUSTRIALIZATION, BUT IS JUSTIFIED BY IDEOLOGY

The first scholar to put this popular position in a clear and coherent form was Rimlinger (1971). Using comparative case studies of England, France, Germany, the Soviet Union, and the United States, Rimlinger maintained that social welfare is a system of secondary income distribution that is legislatively superimposed on and must be coordinated with a country's economic system. Furthermore, social welfare can be used to influence several parts of the economy: (1) the supply side, by ensuring that there are sufficient high-quality human resources (by increasing the geographic availability of workers, providing adequate training, and motivating people to work by limiting benefits to a subsistence level; (2) the demand side, by transferring money to populations who will increase the demand for consumer goods; and (3) the social environment, by creating an atmosphere of economic and social stability (it has also been used to suppress discontent and mass hostility). As industrialization occurs, the social welfare system becomes more organized.

In a step-by-step fashion, Rimlinger argued that the development of social welfare (Rimlinger used the term *social security*)

1. is a by-product of industrialization
2. occurs more rapidly in cultures that have upper-class traditions of "protecting" lower-class people
3. is introduced and maintained more by authoritarian (like communist, fascist, or monarchical) governments than by democratic governments
4. is related to a country's labor policy and the level of skills of its labor force
5. is related to the prevalent idea in a given country about the relationship between the individual and the state.

About 20 years after the publication of Rimlinger's work, Skocpol's (1992) *Protecting Soldiers and Mothers* provided some support for Thesis 2. Skocpol noted that the Civil War in the United States led to "precocious social spending" from the 1860s to the 1890s that was also fueled by the massive industrialization that was taking place. By the end of the 19th century, the United States seemed to be headed toward a "paternalistic" welfare state, comparable to the ones that were to develop in Europe. However, the leadership of several women thinkers (discussed in chapter 4) converted it into a "maternalistic" welfare state. Civil War pensions, which were modest in the 1870s, were liberalized by Congress to consume almost 42 percent of federal spending by the 1890s. This was the time when women activists won key social provisions. However, their hard-fought gains had eroded by World War I.

Katz (1993, p. 776) suggested that the absence of working-class solidarity in the United States may be a better explanation for the lack of development in the 20th century U.S. welfare state. He pointed out that "Skocpol pays little attention to the social bases of conflicts over 'social provisions' other than their relation to gender," and her work is a story of "elite women's clubs."

Esping-Andersen (1990), on the other hand, depended on survey research of welfare states, rather than the case study method of Rimlinger and Skocpol. In a study of 18 industrialized capitalist countries (14 countries in western Europe, plus Canada, the United States, Australia, and New Zealand), he essentially supported Thesis 2. He sorted these First World countries into three welfare regimes—conservative, liberal, and socialist—and rated them on each category.

According to Esping-Andersen, conservative (also called corporatist–statist) cultures respond to socialistic threats by devising social policies that support middle-class loyalties to the state. They are strongly influenced by church (often European Catholic) policies and are committed to the preservation of traditional patriarchal families and motherhood. Their benefits exclude nonworking wives.

The belief of the liberal states is that the market is a major source of benefits, so these states try to support a market orientation even in their welfare policies. They usually have means-tested programs for poor people, and offer benefits to nonpoor people on the basis of their past contributions.

The socialist states have "universalistic" social welfare policies that do not depend on a recipient's past or present ability to pay; in addition, the benefits are usually not means tested and are tied to middle-class standards. Nonworking wives and other people who are not in the labor force are included as welfare beneficiaries.

In addition to categorizing the First World welfare state according to their ideological orientations, Esping-Andersen used two key concepts as devices for analyzing welfare states: decommodification and stratification. Built on the Marxist concept of commodification (see chapters 4 and 5), decommodification is a society's ability to liberate its employees' basic requirements of living independent of the market structure. Socialist states are usually high in decommodification, which is consistent with their policy of including nonworking adults as welfare beneficiaries and not having means-tested social policies. On the other hand, liberal states (such as the United States and other English-speaking democracies) are low in decommodification and place a high value on the ability of the market to optimize human welfare.

With regard to stratification, Esping-Andersen observed that conservative social policy is aimed at maximizing traditional class, status, and gender relations; liberal social policy is aimed at maximizing individual freedom and equality of opportunity; and socialist social policy is aimed at increasing the solidarity of the labor movement.

In a comparative case study of Japan, Britain, and Sweden, Gould (1993) essentially also supported Thesis 2. Although Japan is close to the conservative (or corporatist–statist) position identified by Esping-Andersen, Gould pointed out some differences between Japan and Europe. In Europe, the changes in social welfare were driven first by industrialization and then by post-Fordism (see Table 6-1). They included the following factors: curtailment of public expenditures and demands for further curtailments; increased fees for social welfare services in areas where the state was the provider; tightening the eligibility of recipients by shortening the circle that separates the "insiders" from the "outsiders" (as shown in Figures 8-5 and 8-6); privatization of many services; pushing many state-produced services into the market; and increasing means-tested benefits. In contrast, Japan had a small public sector and low taxation rates, and many of its welfare benefits were tied to the large corporations that were the recipients' employers.

Gould also critiqued some of Pierson's (1991) basic hypotheses about the welfare state. These hypotheses and Gould's responses to them are summarized in Table 9-1.

Table 9-1. Gould's Comments on Pierson's Hypotheses about the Welfare State

PIERSON'S HYPOTHESES	GOULD'S COMMENTS
The weflare state is a product of industrial societies.	Capitalist societies need welfare systems, and such needs are met in a variety of ways, including a combination of state, voluntary, and other systems.
The welfare state is a product of successful mobilization to attain full citizenship in the context of industrialization.	This hypothesis is true only in relation to a handful of European countries until the 1980s.
The welfare state embodies the success of the social democratic political project to transform capitalism.	This thesis is dated. Even in Sweden, capitalism is transforming social democracy.
The welfare state is a product of a struggle between the political powers of the industrial state and the economic powers of capital that makes the transition to socialism possible.	The alliance of the holders of capital, the bourgeoisie, and the electorate made the transition to socialism not feasible during the 1990s.
The welfare state is an ill-conceived and unprincipled intrusion on the welfare- and liberty-maximizing imperatives of a market economy.	This philosophy conceals how public-sector workers, in demanding more resources, often ask for the unjustifiable in pursuit of their own interests.
The welfare state functions to secure the long-term interests of capital accumulation.	The welfare state would be still with us (and thriving) if it were so, but it seems to be declining.
The welfare state embodies the contradictory nature of developed capitalism and chronic crises.	Capitalism has resolved this contradiction and has gained support from the middle classes.
The welfare state is an accommodation of capitalism and social democracy.	The terms, *organized* and *disorganized capitalism* seem synonymous with Fordism and post-Fordism.
The welfare state secures the interests of capital and men at the expense of women.	Evidence varies; in Sweden it is not true, but in Japan it is.

(Continued)

Table 9-1. *Continued*

The welfare state secures the interests of capital and of white people, at the expense of the interests of ethnic minorities (and people of color).	Evidence varies; in Sweden it is not true (but it may be true in the United States, Germany, and several other countries).
The welfare state is an instrument of control by the capitalist state.	This statement seems to be true, as evidenced by the welfare systems of Japan and Britain from 1980 to 1993.
The welfare state should be understood in a historical context and against the interplay of unique national and local forces.	This statement does not seem to be true; trends in the development of the welfare state in capitalist countries since World War II were similar.

SOURCES: Gould, A. (1993). *Capitalist welfare systems.* London: Longman; and Pierson, C. (1991). *Beyond the welfare state?* University Park: Pennsylvania State University Press.

THESIS 3: POVERTY IS FUNCTIONAL IN INDUSTRIAL CAPITALISM

The emergence of the welfare state in the First and Second Worlds leads to a number of observations about the functions of the welfare state. Table 9-2 lists some of the intended and unintended functions from the structural functionalist perspective. One important point is that the structure of the First World welfare states may have been more conducive to the performance of the intended functions than that of the Second World welfare states, which explains why the First World countries still have welfare states. In the long run, the labor and other policies of the Second World countries did not generate enough economic productivity to support either the planned economies or the welfare states of these nations, but the structure led to unintended consequences that were of lasting duration.

Gans (1972, p. 278) pointed out that the existence of poverty in the First World "makes possible the existence or expansion of respectable professions and occupations, for example, penology, criminology, social work, and public health." He also noted that the continued existence of poverty in the First World performs 13 functions, almost all of which are unintended (see Table 9-3 for a summary).

THESIS 4: INDUSTRIAL SOCIALISM LEADS TO PREFISC WELFARE STATES, AND INDUSTRIAL CAPITALISM LEADS TO POSTFISC WELFARE STATES

Although there is a minor controversy regarding the terms *prefisc* and *postfisc,* to many welfare theorists (see Goodin, 1988; Moon, 1988; Plant, 1988) the nature of fiscal policy making and the consequent budget

Table 9-2. Intended and Unintended Consequences of the Welfare State: The Structural Functionalist View

INTENDED CONSEQUENCES

First World	Second World
To support a market economy and a labor policy that requires means-tested benefits as much as possible (to get people back into the labor market)	To support a planned economy and a labor policy that offers universalistic benefits as much as possible
To support a labor policy that commodifies labor	To support a labor policy that partially decommodifies labor
To support a health policy that makes health care a commodity to be purchased in the market	To support the substantial decommodification of health care, so it is a social utility equally available to all
To support a housing policy that commodifies housing	To support the partial decommodification of housing

UNINTENDED CONSEQUENCES

First World	Second World
To create another market for the upper and middle classes whose business is to work with poor and marginal people	To use the welfare state as a device to give the appearance of full employment
To achieve social control by upper- and middle-class norms and by the impact of these norms on formal social control devices	To achieve social control by the state
To give the political elite, through the enormous structure of the welfare state, the opportunity to establish a patronage system for providing welfare-related jobs to middle-class workers	To give the political elite, through the enormous structure of the welfare state, the opportunity to establish a patronage system for providing welfare-related jobs to middle-class workers

Table 9-3. The Functions of Poverty in First World Countries

FUNCTION	HOW IT WORKS
1	"The existence of poverty ensures that society's dirty work is always done" (Gans, 1972, p. 278).
2	By working for low wages, poor people subsidize affluent people. For example, maids from the poverty class, who work for low wages, support the cultural, recreational, and other activities of their affluent employers.
3	Poverty supports a number of occupations and professions, such as penology, police work, and social work, and activities, including faith healing, work in the armed forces during peacetime, and pawnbrokering. Poorly trained professionals, who would not be acceptable to others in society, often work with poor people.
4	"The poor buy goods which others do not want" (Gans, 1972, p. 279). For example, used clothes, used automobiles, and slum housing.
5	Poor people can be used as exemplars of criminals or deviants to make other members of society feel morally and spiritually superior.
6	Middle- and upper-class people may participate vicariously in the entertainment activities of poor people.
7	Middle-class people often enjoy art, artifacts, and music created by poor people. Examples include spirituals, rock music, and rap music.
8	The presence of poor people in their environment reminds nonpoor people that their living conditions are far removed from the unhealthy and dangerous conditions under which poor people live.
9	The presence of poor people makes it easier for people in higher social strata to pursue upward mobility.
10	The presence of poor people makes it possible for middle- and upper-class people to have a cause to which they can donate money and time and feel good about helping "the unfortunate."
11	Poor people absorb the costs of change and growth in societies. During industrialization (in England and the United States), they

(Continued)

Table 9-3. *Continued*

	did all the backbreaking work of building cities and railroads. During the 20th century, they are forced out of their neighborhoods to make way for urban renewal efforts, or their neighborhoods are destroyed by expressways.
12	Poor people do not vote or participate in the political process in general. Consequently, they become captive constituencies of political groups and parties that claim to represent them.
13	Poor people are used as examples of what happens to people who do not work or otherwise participate in the marketplace.

SOURCE: Gans, H. (1972). The positive functions of poverty. *American Journal of Sociology, 78,* 275–289.

construction are the bases of this typology. In prefisc welfare states, benefits to given populations are promised *before* the taxation capacity of the state is ascertained and a budget is in place, whereas in postfisc welfare states, benefits to given populations are itemized *after* the said taxation capacity and budgetary provisions. Table 9-4 presents the main features of the two systems.

For the most part, a prefisc system creates entitlements, whereas a postfisc system may create a continuum, ranging from various combinations of gratuities and entitlements. Furthermore, the entitlements in prefisc systems call for universalistic provisions, whereas the combination of gratuities and entitlements in postfisc systems calls for both universalistic provisions and social insurance systems. Thus, prefisc systems end up with universalistic benefit structures, whereas postfisc systems have both universalistic and means-tested benefit structures.

In addition, prefisc systems are designed to optimize equality and, in a way, fraternity or community, thus pursuing two noble goals inspired by the French and the Russian revolutions. Postfisc systems are designed to optimize liberty, thus pursuing a noble goal inspired by the American Revolution. In their versions of the theory of justice, Rawls (1971) endorsed state activity to achieve equality, whereas Nozick (1974) endorsed state activity to achieve liberty. In the pursuit of liberty (also endorsed by Milton Friedman and Friederich Hayek, among others), the primary task of the state is to ensure the liberty of all individuals by protecting their legitimately earned and accumulated property, whereas in the pursuit of equality and fraternity (community) (endorsed by such theorists as Richard M. Titmuss and T. H. Marshall), the primary task of the state is to ensure that all citizens enjoy certain levels of benefits. The main argument against the pursuit of liberty is that there are always people in a state who, because of

Table 9-4. Characteristics of Prefisc and Postfisc Welfare States

PREFISC	POSTFISC
Benefits promised before wealth building occurs.	Benefits allocated after wealth building occurs.
Benefits promised before the capacity of the state is known.	Benefits allocated after the taxation capacity of the state is known.
Benefits promised before the budget is established.	Benefits allocated during or after the budget is in place.
Recipients are entitled to the benefits.	Some recipients are entitled to some benefits, and others are given gratuities; thus, the system is a combination of entitlements and gratuities.
Provisions are universal.	Provisions are universal for some and gratuities for others.
The benefit structure is universal.	The benefit structure is universal for some and means tested for others.
The state atttempts to promote equality and community.	The state attempts to protect liberty and sometimes to promote equality.
Common under socialism.	Common under "compromised" capitalism.

some disability or another, are unable to pursue liberty because they cannot exercise their rights of citizenship. The main argument against the pursuit of equality and fraternity is that it leads to an oppressive state that thwarts liberty.

For the most part, prefisc models approximate industrial socialism and postfisc models approximate industrial capitalism. However, they are two extreme ends of a continuum, rather than a dichotomy. Most postfisc states represent an accommodation to socialism (as in compliance with the predictions of Schumpeter, 1950, discussed earlier) and can be called "compromised" capitalism. Almost all the capitalist welfare states of the First World studied by Esping-Andersen (1990) are in this category, whereas the socialist welfare states are closer to the prefisc model that to either industrial capitalism or compromised capitalism. On the other hand, most of the Second World states would have been classified as prefisc before the breakup of the Soviet Bloc, although they are now moving closer to the postfisc model.

At this point, it is important to note two worldwide trends that seem to be occurring. First, most Second World states are moving from the prefisc to the postfisc model. Second, even the most ardent capitalist states are moving from the postfisc model of industrial capitalism to the postfisc model of compromised capitalism. Therefore, the majority of the welfare states in the 21st century are likely to be variations of the postfisc model.

THESIS 5: POSTFISC WELFARE STATES ARE BETTER THAN PREFISC ONES

The health care system of Cuba has been a model for Third World nations (Castro, 1983). Cuba also has modest income maintenance provisions and is close to a prefisc welfare state. It makes health care coverage an entitlement for everyone, which is certainly not the case in the United States, which is a postfisc welfare state. It seems that patients (especially those from humble backgrounds) who seek health care have more dignity in Cuba than in the United States.

If dignity were the only criterion for assessing the desirability of a welfare state (or considering one better or worse than another), then the Cuban welfare state would certainly be thought of as better than the U.S. one. However, economically stagnant Cuba cannot keep proper equipment in its health care settings. A "dignified" health care system cannot be desirable if its hospitals and clinics do not have such staples as boric acid and disposable syringes on their shelves or medicines in their pharmacies. The "undignified" U.S. health care system (although health care in the United States is not really undignified from a worldwide perspective) does not lack medicines, equipment, and facilities. Thus, dignified health care in a poor country is inferior health care, whereas undignified health care in a wealthy country is superior health care. In short, although the intention to deliver dignified health care is noble, it is the productivity base of a system that defines whether the care is better than that of other systems.

THESIS 6: COST CONTAINMENT IS A GREATER PROBLEM IN INDUSTRIAL CAPITALISM

In the 1990s, containment of the costs of social welfare services (especially health care services) has been a problem in almost all postfisc welfare states, whereas inflation contributed to the problem in prefisc welfare states ("Canada Dry," 1991; "Eastern Europe and the World," 1991). In the postfisc states, political movements have advocated the reduction or elimination of health and welfare expenditures, especially those for poor people ("Last of the Big Spenders," 1991).

Janowitz (1976), who foresaw this trend, warned the postfisc welfare states that effective social control of the welfare state was necessary. He noted that welfare expenditures had increased substantially since the 1930s; that no state could afford the limitless growth of welfare expenditures; that the economic surplus that supported social welfare (in the United States and Britain) had been declining substantially; that "the necessities of industrial development create the welfare state; and [that] the welfare state generates a set of economic equity claims that are complex, diffuse, and even mutually contradictory" (p. 86). Mechanic (1986), a health care theoretician, observed the same trend. He suggested that health care should be considered a national resource and that it increasingly faces problems of allocation (how it should be distributed). The only way to deal with such problems, he stated, is effective rationing strategies (discussed in chapter 2).

The concept of rationing (of both income maintenance and health care services) is unattractive to many interest groups. However, given the high cost, dissatisfaction of many groups, and chronic budget deficits, rationing may be the only solution. If rationing is not done by design, then it occurs by default. Therefore, the task of policymakers in the 21st century may well be to devise clear and explicit rationing policies for social welfare.

THESIS 7: COST CONTAINMENT IS MANAGED BETTER BY INDEXING WELFARE EXPENDITURE THAN BY DEFICIT FINANCING

John Maynard Keynes (cited in Heilbronner, 1961) taught the state to "manage capitalism" by using its power of spending as an instrument to inflate or deflate the volume of investment. The New Deal was one such instrument. Far from being a socialist scheme, the New Deal (together with World War II) was an instrument of deficit spending, which revived capitalism. Thus, the welfare state, in conjunction with the warfare state, nursed capitalism back to health.

Hence, the origins of the welfare state, at least in Britain and the United States, were tied to the deficit financing of the state. After World War II, Beveridge (1945) promoted the idea of a full-blown welfare state in Britain because it would make the labor market a sellers' market, preserve liberty, and support full employment. Mishra (1984), who agreed that the modern welfare state may have originated with the ideas of Keynes and Beveridge, called the original one the differentiated welfare state, but noted that over time, it gave way to the integrated welfare state. A differentiated welfare state is relatively autonomous (in the prefisc style) and emerges as a response to the demand side of the economy. An integrated welfare state, in contrast, is responsive to both demand and supply, and its welfare expenditures are indexed to the spending capacity of the state and the purchasing capacity of the currency.

It is important to note here that indexing social welfare expenditures had two concealed objectives: to ration social welfare expenditures but to retain their value. The value-retention objective, according to Janowitz (1976), was never accomplished because more and more welfare provisions were added, and thus the number of claimants soared. However, such rationing can be done only if the demographic structure of the population remains stable. With changing dependency ratios (see chapter 8) in most postfisc welfare states, it seems that even rationing is not likely to keep the welfare state stabilized.

The welfare state, it appears, has gone from deficit financing to indexed financing and is now headed toward uneven (or arbitrary) rationing. I call it uneven because entitlements are harder to eliminate in politically responsive postfisc states, and hence it is the gratuities that are likely to be the targets of rationing.

THESIS 8: THE OPERATION OF A FREE–MARKET SYSTEM, NOT MODERNIZATION EFFORTS, CAN BUILD OR SUSTAIN A WELFARE STATE

Presenting a combination of historical and empirical evidence, Berger (1986) contended that the postfisc welfare states and industrial capitalism do not have the glamour or intrinsic moral appeal of industrial socialism or the prefisc welfare states. However, the prefisc welfare states base their claim to be a viable political and economic system more on philosophy than on empirical evidence. The empirical evidence is clear that industrial capitalism and the postfisc welfare states are in a better position to promote human happiness than are industrial socialism and the prefisc welfare states.

According to Berger, a unique natural experiment took place between 1945 and 1985. In this natural experiment, the Four Dragons (Hong Kong, Taiwan, Singapore, and South Korea) from the larger group of Third World nations opted for industrial capitalism, and almost all the other Third World nations that were emerging from colonialism or other forms of foreign dominance opted for socialism or mixed economies. The four nations that chose industrial capitalism have completed their baseline wealth building and are contemplating the imposition of postfisc welfare states. All the other Third World nations, which were opposed to capitalism as a means of social development, were, as of the mid-1980s (and, it may be added, still are), caught in an economic quagmire and were in no position to develop any form of welfare state.

At the same time, another natural experiment took place between the paired countries of North Korea (industrial socialism and a prefisc orientation) and South Korea (industrial capitalism and a postfisc orientation) and between China (industrial socialism and a prefisc orientation) and Hong

Table 9-5. Natural Experiments in Social Development in the Third World: 1945–85

GROUP OF NATIONS	TIME 1	PATH CHOSEN	TIME 2	STATUS
The Four Dragons (Hong Kong, Taiwan, Singapore, and South Korea)	1945–55	Industrial capitalism	1985	Wealth
Other Third World countries	1945–55	Mixed economy	1985	Poverty

SOURCE: Berger, P. (1986). *The capitalist revolution.* New York: Basic Books.

Kong and Taiwan (industrial capitalism and a postfisc orientation). Tables 9-5 and 9-6 present the designs of these natural experiments. The reader is also referred to Figures 3-2 and 3-3 in chapter 3.

Clear conclusions can be drawn from these two natural experiments. First, capitalism is a better means of social development than is any other political economy. Second, it is industrial capitalism that makes wealth building possible, and wealth building, in turn, makes postfisc welfare states possible. Industrial socialism has not been able to build wealth and hence has not had viable welfare states. The Third World countries that opted for mixed economies or socialist economies have not been able to build any form of welfare states. But the Four Dragons that chose market economies and industrial capitalism were in a position to contemplate the development of welfare states in 1985.

Table 9-6. Natural Paired Experiments in Social Development between Second and Third World Countries: 1945–85

GROUP OF NATIONS	TIME 1	PATH CHOSEN	TIME 2	STATUS
North Korea	1945–55	Industrial socialism	1985	Poorer
South Korea	1945–55	Industrial capitalism	1985	Richer
China	1948–55	Industrial socialism	1985	Poorer
Hong Kong and Taiwan	1948–55	Industrial capitalism	1985	Richer

SOURCE: Berger, P. (1986). *The capitalist revolution.* New York: Basic Books.

THESIS 9: IN INDUSTRIAL CAPITALISM, HUMAN VULNERABILITY IS COMMODIFIED AND A CLASS OF MIDDLE–CLASS PROVIDERS IS FORMED

This thesis is an elaboration of Function 3 in Table 9-3, in which it was proposed that the existence of poverty supports a number of occupations for middle-class workers. Only a slight change is needed here: The existence of welfare state expenditures creates a group of providers who meet the needs of both poor and nonpoor persons. This volume of spending supports a select group of professionals: social workers, physicians, nurses, and the like. Although professionals claim that they can police themselves, in reality, professional groups do a poor job of regulating their members (Bergthold, 1990; Freidson, 1986; Gray, 1991; Kornblum & Smith, 1994; Larson, 1977). The provision of a large amount of resources by the welfare state to professionalized providers, in turn, gives these professionals opportunities to become more and more professionalized and to increase their profits. It creates a new market, captured by a group of professions, which is enjoyed not by the owners of capital but by holders of selected skills. And the holders of these selected skills are often from the entire span of the middle class: physicians from the top, nurses and social workers from the middle, and others from the bottom. In sum, the welfare state creates a market for the middle class.

THESIS 10: THE MORE THE COMMODIFICATION OF HUMAN VULNERABILITY, THE MORE MEDICALIZED THE VISION OF PROBLEM SOLVING

This thesis is an extension of Thesis 9, which suggested that human vulnerability is commodified in industrial capitalism. It claims that the liberal form of industrial capitalism (in Esping-Andersen's 1990, typology) is the closest to individualism on a continuum from individualism to collectivism and is where the vision of solving human problems by medicalized (see chapters 4 and 5) and professionalized psychology is most common.

Frank, Meyer, and Miyahara (1995) found that the professionalized psychological orientation as a way of comprehending the human condition is more legitimated and more frequent in the liberal industrial capitalist states. This orientation leads to the assumption of a "sick role" (see Parsons, 1951) to problems of addiction, marriage, interpersonal orientation, and many other areas of human behavior. The presence of these sick roles, in turn, leads to the emergence of a number of occupations and professions that claim that they have "scientific knowledge" to "treat" these problems. These claims based on "science" are often a means of defining, gaining, and retaining a share of the market that emerges from the activities of the welfare state under liberal industrial capitalism.

The Three Worlds in the 21st Century

In this section, I return to the idea of the world system discussed in chapter 3 and present some conclusions.

Roads Open to the Third World

During the latter half of the 20th century, many countries in the Third World emerged from foreign domination. Some of them have remained committed to cultures that were adaptive in earlier centuries, but do not seem to be so in the global world system of the late 20th century. The revolution of rising expectations has created a great demand for high-quality consumer goods in this part of the world. In addition, there is a need for income maintenance plans, high-quality health care services, and protective services. The lesson of the 20th century is that only massive industrialization under industrial capitalism can generate enough wealth to make such developments possible.

Lasting Contributions of the Second World

The collapse of the communist system has led to the replacement of centrally planned economies with market economies in the Second World. At the end of the 20th century, most Second World countries (except China) are facing serious economic problems that are posing problems for the future of their cherished welfare states. Given this situation, did the Second World countries make any viable long-term contributions to the world?

Borrowing a metaphor from Schumpeter (1950), I suggest that the Second World countries performed two historic functions well. The first function was to offer protection and hope to the Third World countries. At the time of World War I, the white capitalist Eurocentric countries (including those of North America and Australia) were engaged in a great conflict over which faction (the Teutonic or Anglo-Saxon) would be the colonial masters of the world. By the end of World War II, however, it was clear their colonial mastery of the world was no longer viable, and these powerful capitalist countries had to court or negotiate with the poor, nonwhite Third World countries. This change in the power structure of the world was partly a result of the presence of the Second World countries. For example, during the Suez Canal crisis of 1956, it was the Soviet Union that supported Egypt's right to control its own resources (although the Suez Canal was built by the British and French, it was constructed in Egyptian territory). The point is that both the First and Second Worlds were predatory, but their mutual presence gave the relatively powerless Third World countries some protection.

The second function of the Second World was to force the capitalist First World to develop welfare states. The New Deal in the United States, the promise of full employment in Britain, and the development and politicization of the labor movement in post-World War II Europe were efforts to co-opt the poor class, the working class, and even the middle class in the cause of capitalism. In short, they were the capitalists' bribes to labor that might not have been necessary without the presence of the Second World.

ROADS OPEN TO THE FIRST WORLD

In the 21st century, with the Second World relatively powerless, the political economies of the First World countries will become more powerful. Against this backdrop, and buttressed by the argument that the welfare state is too expensive (which it is), too contradictory (which it also is), and too wasteful (which it sometimes is) and that it supports the "wrong" kind of people (which means a struggle to define the boundaries between outsiders and insiders), the movements to reduce or dismantle the welfare state in the First World will grow even stronger. The further development of post-Fordist economies and weakening of many large labor unions will contribute to the efforts to curb the First World welfare states. Such efforts are likely to have one or more of the following consequences:

1. an alliance among capital, the state, and labor against poor people
2. the bribery of labor (with welfare state provisions) and propa-ganda (that other groups want to claim the same provisions), which are likely to create hostile encounters with outgroups, such as immigrants, people of color, and people in Third World countries
3. the placating of elderly retired people in the middle or working classes.

The future of most of the First World welfare states is more likely to be defined by class interests than by race, ethnicity, or gender interests. Thus, members of minority races or ethnic groups (as well as women) will probably be included in welfare state provisions if they are from the middle or working classes. In sum, it is likely that the First World welfare states will increasingly become instruments in the hands of an alliance of the state, capital, and labor against poor people, people of color, and the Third World.

REFERENCES

Berger, P. (1986). *The capitalist revolution*. New York: Basic Books.

Bergthold, L. (1990). *Purchasing power in health: Business, the state, and health care politics*. New Brunswick, NJ: Rutgers University Press.

Beveridge, W. H. (1945). *Full employment in a free society*. New York: W. W. Norton.

Canada Dry, pot-pourri and sushi. (1991, July 6). *The Economist,* pp. 13–15.

Castro, F. (1983). *The world economic and social crisis: Its impact on the underdeveloped countries, its somber prospects and the need to struggle if we are to survive.* Havana: Council of State.

Eastern Europe and the world. (1991, July 6). *The Economist,* p. 69.

Esping-Andersen, G. (1990). *The three worlds of welfare capitalism.* Princeton, NJ: Princeton University Press.

Frank, D. J., Meyer, J. W., & Miyahara, D. (1995). The individualist polity and the prevalence of professionalized psychology: A cross-national study. *American Sociological Review, 60,* 360–377.

Freidson, E. (1986). *Professional powers: A study of the institutionalization of formal knowledge.* Chicago: The University of Chicago Press.

Gans, H. (1972). The positive functions of poverty. *American Journal of Sociology, 78,* 275–289.

Gilbert, N., & Specht, H. (1974). *Dimensions of social welfare policy.* Englewood Cliffs, NJ: Prentice Hall.

Goodin, R. E. (1988). Reasons for welfare: Economic, sociological, and political—but ultimately moral. In J. D. Moon (Ed.), *Responsibility, rights, and welfare: The theory of the welfare state* (pp. 19–54). Boulder, CO: Westview Press.

Gould, A. (1993). *Capitalist welfare systems.* London: Longman.

Gray, B. H. (1991). *The profit motive and patient care.* Cambridge, MA: Harvard University Press.

Heilbronner, R. (1961). *The worldly philosophers.* New York: Simon & Schuster.

Janowitz, M. (1976). *Social control of the social welfare state.* Chicago: University of Chicago Press.

Katz, M. B. (1993). Roads not taken: Failed alternatives for American social welfare. *Contemporary Sociology, 22,* 775–777.

Kornblum, W., & Smith, C. D. (1994). *The healing experience: Readings on the social context of health care.* Englewood Cliffs, NJ: Prentice Hall.

Larson, M. S. (1977). *The rise of professionalism.* Berkeley: University of California Press.

Last of the big spenders. (1991, July 6). *The Economist,* pp. 9–11.

Malinowski, B. (1955). *Magic, science, and religion.* Garden City, NY: Doubleday Anchor Books.

Mechanic, D. (1986). *From advocacy to allocation.* New York: Free Press.

Mishra, R. (1984). *The welfare state in crisis.* New York: St. Martin's Press.

Moon, J. D. (Ed.). (1988). *Responsibility, rights, and welfare: The theory of the welfare state.* Boulder, CO: Westview Press.

Moore, B., Jr. (1973). *Reflections on the causes of human misery and on certain proposals to eliminate them.* Boston: Beacon Press.

Nozick, R. (1974). *Anarchy, state and utopia.* Oxford, England: Basil Blackwell.

Parsons, T. (1951). *The social system.* Glencoe, IL: Free Press.

Pierson, C. (1991). *Beyond the welfare state?* University Park: Pennsylvania State University Press.

Plant, R. (1988). Needs, agency, and welfare rights. In J. D. Moon (Ed.), *Responsibility, rights, and welfare: The theory of the welfare state* (pp. 55–74). Boulder, CO: Westview Press.

Rawls, J. (1971). *A theory of justice.* Cambridge, MA: Harvard University Press.

Rimlinger, G. (1971). *The welfare state and industrialization in Europe, America, and Russia.* New York: John Wiley & Sons.

Schumpeter, J. (1950). *Capitalism, socialism, and democracy.* New York: Harper & Row.

Skocpol, T. (1992). *Protecting soldiers and mothers.* Cambridge, MA: Harvard University Press.

Wilensky, H. (1975). *The welfare state and equality.* Berkeley: University of California Press.

Wilensky, H., & Lebeaux, C. (1958). *Industrial society and social welfare.* New York: Russell Sage Foundation.

Wolins, M. (1967). The societal function of social welfare. *New Perspectives: The Berkeley Journal of Social Welfare, 1,* 1–18.

Zald, M. (1976). Review of Wilensky's *The welfare state and equality. American Journal of Sociology, 81,* 942–945.

Part 3

SUMMARY AND CONCLUSIONS

P art 3 first summarizes most of the important information from the previous chapters (some of which is contradictory) and asks, Which claimant is right? It then builds on the answer to this question in the final chapter and speculates what ideas should be considered to envision a future welfare state.

10

APPROACHES TO THE WELFARE STATE: WHO IS RIGHT?

I had gone out begging, when

they told me: "Hey, move! On this day

the King will pass by. Don't stand on the street!"

I moved to a corner of the sidewalk

as I saw Him come by.

First came some horses, then all those men.

His carriage was so big, and sunshine

reflected off His wheels. There were more

horses and more men behind Him!

He looked at me—and out of habit—

I extended my hands, hoping

He would throw something my way.

His carriage stopped!

Looking straight at me, He extended His hand,

and said: "Why don't you give Me something!"

"What a joke," I thought, and picked

one grain of rice from my beggar's pouch,

and threw it at Him. He smiled, and thanked me

as His carriage moved away.

At the end of the day,

after I returned to my little hut,

I emptied my beggar's pouch on the bed:

there lay my day's collections!

Some copper coins, a small piece of silver,

grains of this, grains of that, and

shining among them, there was

one little grain of gold!

I began to cry:

"Why didn't I give You all of what I had!"

Rabindranath Tagore, *Rabindra-Rachanabali*

I n the preceding chapters, it was evident that scholars do not agree about how or why the welfare state develops or is sustained. Some scholars suggest that the welfare state evolves or is sustained by ideological cleavages and compromises, others see it as a camouflage for inherent conflicts in society, and still others believe it is a by-product of industrialization.

A review of the three perspectives indicates that the proponents of the first two are more advocates than scholars or, put differently, are committed more to advocacy for or against state spending (the welfare state) than to conducting scholarly studies of the subject. For example, the thesis that welfare is a function of ideology was supported by adherents of the London school, Anglo-American social workers, and several other groups that were already against or for state-sponsored social programs. Similarly, the thesis that the welfare state is a conflict-resolution device has been popular with various advocacy groups. Of the proponents of the various paradigms that try to explain the development of the welfare state as a by-product of industrialization, some are also partisans for or against the welfare state. This chapter summarizes most of the contradictory ideas about the welfare state and then asks, Given that there are so many contradictions about the welfare state, who is right?

THE WELFARE STATE: POINTS OF AGREEMENT AND DISPUTE

The central problem faced by the welfare state is *whether* and *how* to respond to problems of human dependence and vulnerability. This question troubled Prince Siddhartha, when he went for a carriage ride and saw people who were poor, aged, ill, disabled, and abandoned. His life-long search for solutions to such dependence and vulnerability made him the Buddha.

The discussions so far have covered how and why social responses to certain problems of vulnerability have varied widely, from no response to many levels of organized responses; how different national social systems have designed similar or different responses to the same problem (such as income maintenance, health care, and protection of vulnerable populations); how responses have been comprehensive or piecemeal; how responses have emerged in the face of crises like war, natural disasters, and economic depression or developed to prevent crises; and how such responses have been institutionalized or are in a forever-transient state and are subject to challenges and cutbacks. In short, I have presented competing hypotheses about how the welfare state emerges and is sustained. Among these hypotheses, there appear to be 12 points of agreement, which I have ordered in the following coherent scheme:

1. Social welfare responses are more frequent in nations that have a surplus or in which a certain amount of wealth has been generated. All the great religions of the world include prescriptions for providing social welfare, in the form of the welfare community or the welfare church or temple, when there is a surplus. Of the three worlds, the First World, with a foundation of industrial capitalism, has generated the greatest surplus and the most elaborate welfare states.

2. Social welfare responses are plans for distributing or, as I have called it, transferring resources. Even insurance plans are supported by transfer. Furthermore, these responses have usually been plans to transfer income, rather than wealth, from those who are active in the labor market to those who are not.

3. Because social welfare responses are transfer plans, the social sciences cannot answer questions about the ends of the welfare state. Therefore, the questions about the welfare state (whether or not to have a welfare state and who should be its recipients if there is one) are normative, not scientific.

4. Given that scientific answers to questions about the ends of the welfare state are not possible, welfare responses are often justified by ideological positions. That is, once wealth has been generated to make transfer possible, powerful interest groups and elites use ideological systems to justify transfer plans.

5. Norms of justice, equality, liberty, and protection form the structure of ideological systems that are used to justify social welfare. Often these norms are contradictory.

6. Various forms of rationing are used to implement the transfer plans instituted by welfare states. Sometimes rationing is done by design, and sometimes it occurs by default.

7. Many types of conflict emerge and are embedded in the social welfare systems when the rationing schemes are implemented. Although it may be possible to replace one form of conflict with another, it is not possible to eradicate conflict per se.

8. Industrialization requires the location of social welfare at the state level and sometimes at the corporate level (as in Japan), rather than at the family, community, or church level.

9. In the First World, social welfare provisions support or supplement market distribution. In the Second World, social welfare systems were planned to preempt market distribution. In the Third World, state-level social welfare systems have not yet emerged.

10. In addition to ideological justifications, welfare responses are further justified as a means of protecting the internal security of the state, much like military expenditures are justified as a means of protecting external security.

11. Income transfer in a welfare state is based on certain assumptions about the demographic structure of a given state. Because transfers are often made from those who are in the labor market to those who are not, a low dependency ratio maintains the surplus, whereas a high dependency ratio threatens the surplus.

12. Welfare state provisions have been moving from a deficit-spending base to an indexed-payments base. There are tensions between the provision of means-tested gratuities and universal entitlements, and there has been a tendency to move incrementally from the former to the latter. Entitlements afford dignity to individual recipients but are rarely cost-effective at the collective (state) level. Gratuities reduce the dignity of individual recipients but help make the collective budget more cost-effective. Therefore, entitlements are directly related to human dignity and are inversely related to cost-effectiveness.

There are also some strong points of disagreement about how the welfare state develops and is sustained, as was evident in the competing hypotheses presented in Part 2. Additional points of disagreement include whether the welfare state is desirable in the first place, how the political system can direct it, whether its base should be means-tested gratuities or entitlements, and what types of social organizations it should contain. The remaining sections of this chapter deal with these various areas.

THE WELFARE STATE: WHO IS RIGHT?

This discussion is organized according to four aspects or levels of the term *right:* the moral, political, legal, and scientific or technological. At the *moral level,* distinctions are made between right and wrong, and the interest is in the moral foundations that support or oppose the idea of the welfare state. At the *political level,* the difference is between the Left and the Right, and the issue is what drives political behavior regarding the welfare state. At the *legal level,* the discussion relates to whether social welfare benefits are a matter of entitlement or gratuity. At the *scientific* or *technological level,* the distinction is between accurate and inaccurate, and the interest is in activities that resemble hypothesis testing in science.

In addition, the moral level is *value driven* because the goal is to render judgments about the desirability of social welfare. The political level is *interest driven* because the major goal is to support one's interests. The legal level is *legitimation driven* because the goal is to give formal sanction to certain claims over others. The scientific or technological level is *information driven* because the goal is to increase knowledge on the assumption that increased knowledge will facilitate decision making.

Any effort to understand the development of social welfare, in general, or the welfare state, in particular, is complicated by conflicts between these four levels of right. The following example may clarify the four levels:

> Mrs. S, a frail American woman in her late 80s, has been living alone in a small apartment and supporting herself by income from two sources: social security and a small pension left by her deceased husband. After she fell and broke her hip for the second time, her three grown children—Henry, Julia, and Robert—began to quarrel about how and where she should live.
>
> Henry is in his early 60s, is approaching retirement, and is financially comfortable. He lives with his second wife in a house. His three children from his first marriage are independent adults and have homes of their own, and he and his second wife have no children. Julia, who is in her late 50s, is a professional social worker, divorced, and lives alone. Her only daughter lives nearby and visits her often. Robert is in his late 40s and lives with his wife and two children. He is a salesman, and his wife is a professional nurse. Their oldest son is in college, and their daughter is finishing high school.
>
> Both Henry and Robert say that their mother cannot live with either of them because they do not have the facilities or the space to house her and take care of her. They

both think that Julia should take their mother in because she is not married and has the space.

Julia feels guilty that she cannot take care of their mother because she has a job and does not have the time to supervise an elderly person. Henry and Robert often say that because Julia is the professional social worker, she should have the answer to this problem.

In this case, the matter of surplus is not an issue because there are enough resources in the family to ensure the continuing survival of Mrs. S. The realm of moral behavior is manifested in the conflict between whether she should live with one of her adult children (the traditional moral position is that she should) or in a nursing home (the revised moral position is that in industrialized societies, it is acceptable for elderly people to live in nursing homes). The realm of political behavior is manifested in the reluctance of all three adult children to house their aged mother and their reasons for not doing so. In this area, the basic motivating factor is that their mother is not wealthy, so they do not stand to gain much by having her live with one of them. Instead, they stand to lose their independent lifestyles, the approval of their spouses, or the small amount of free leisure time they have. What they say really justifies their interests.

The realm of legal behavior is reflected in her entitlements. Mrs. S is entitled to social security benefits, her husband's pension, and means-tested support for nursing home benefits. She has no right to be supported by her grown children.

Julia, the social worker, is being asked to give the scientific answer because she is in a business that has information on the subject of how to manage elderly persons in her culture. She suggests that this problem has no scientific solution, because no behavioral science has pronounced the final word about who should be the custodian of frail elderly people. In her profession, this problem is usually solved by local conventions, family resources, and support from the state. The problem is solved when Mrs. S goes into a private nursing home, supported by her small income that is then supplemented by the state.

In this case, political behavior is reflected in the interests of Mrs. S's three adult children and the excuses they offer. Moral behavior is manifested by the conflicts over who should take her in. Legal behavior is shown in the investigation of her entitlement from the state. Scientific behavior is reflected in the children's search for a scientific solution to the problem.

In social welfare, similar problems abound. A given problem may give rise to a set of interests and political positions, and given groups stand to lose or gain by supporting or opposing these political positions. The same problem may call for a moral solution, which may be embedded in local conventions and fortified by one or more religious traditions. In some cases, one political or moral solution of a predictable social problem is given legal sanction, and the issue becomes a matter of entitlement. It may be alleged that the problem can be solved by science, but science can only order the desirability of one solution over another on the basis of their cost–benefit ratio. Figures 10-1 and 10-2 depict these ways of approaching social welfare.

The question of whether there should be social welfare provisions for given groups can definitely be answered according to whether there is or is not a surplus. No transfer is possible if there is no surplus or there is no "culturally constructed" surplus. Once this question has been answered, then one can determine how the question is defined by a society's moral framework, by its political decision-making structure, by its legal foundation, and by its tradition of scientific investigation.

RIGHT VERSUS WRONG: THE MORAL JUSTIFICATION

Chapters 2, 4, and 5 examined several positions that form the moral basis of the welfare state. Marnell (1965) referred to such morality as "man-made," that is, socially constructed by human beings.

Perhaps the core of morality is how an individual, a group, a tribe, or a nation should behave toward another individual, group, tribe, or nation. This issue gets more complicated when it is reviewed across generational, gender, or privilege lines. I suggest that six conflicting norms have emerged from the past to deal with these issues because they contribute to the survival of the community, the clan, or the tribe: the norms of reciprocity, self-sufficiency, sources of income, adoption, tribalism, and commodification. When these norms are applied to the operation of the welfare state, they reflect some fundamental conflicts between the community, the clan, or the tribe, on the one hand, and the state on the other. Groups take positions about these norms and call them right or wrong positions. The resolution of the conflicts between these contradictory positions forms the moral basis of the welfare state.

The Norm of Reciprocity

Exchange theorists (see Blau, 1964; Gouldner, 1960) have pointed out that reciprocity is a fundamental norm in human behavior, from interpersonal behavior to international behavior. Reciprocity means that if A does a favor for B, then B should return the favor, either in the present or in the future. Compliance with this norm leads to social integration, whereas violation of it is often seen as deviance.

Two types of moral issues emerge in this regard: (1) What happens when B does not and cannot return the favor and (2) what happens when B is seen as able, but does not return the favor? If the payers are substituted for

Figure 10-1.

Approaches to the Welfare State: 1

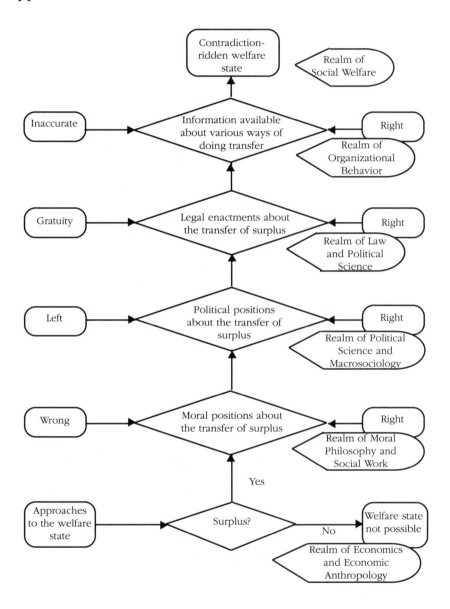

Figure 10-2.

Approaches to the Welfare State: 2

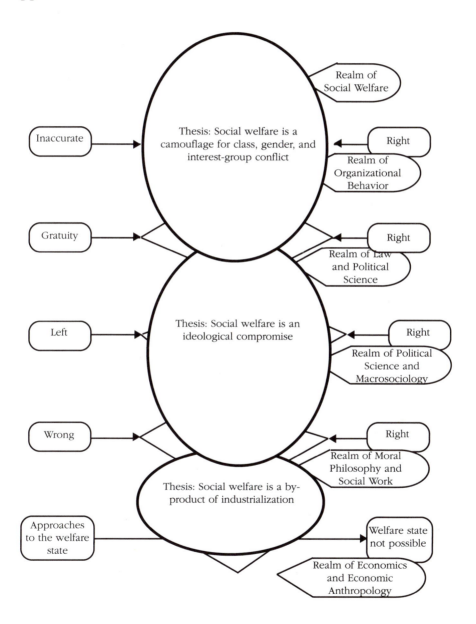

A, and the recipient is substituted for B, then one can envision the reciprocity dilemma in social welfare. Inherent in this dilemma, then, are two additional issues: (3) If B cannot return the favor, can it be construed that B did favors for A in the past and therefore is exempt from reciprocating now and (4) if B cannot return the favor and did not do any favors for A in the past, can it be construed that he or she is never likely to reciprocate in the future?

The moral issues in social welfare can now be posed as follows: What if Question 2 is seen as a situation in which B is a transgenerational poor person with no possibility of being employed in the labor force? What if Question 3 is seen as a situation in which B is an aged person who has retired from a modest job after lifelong participation in the labor force? What if Question 4 is seen as a situation in which B is a child with severe mental retardation?

Questions like these form one of the moral reasonings of a clan, a community, or a tribe. They also form moral questions for a state. The moral question can be framed as: How should the state deal with people (or categories of people) who (1) have been engaged in reciprocity in the past but cannot do so now (aged people and those who drop out of the labor force because of illness or changes in industries, for example), (2) have not been engaged in reciprocity in the past but are likely to do so in the future (children and people who need temporary assistance before they can return to the labor force), and (3) have not engaged in reciprocity in the past and are not likely to do so in the future (chronically ill people, mentally retarded people, and unskilled people who are not interested in skills training)?

The Norm of Self-Sufficiency

Almost all communities, clans, or tribes have a norm of self-sufficiency, which means that a dependent person should be educated, trained, and encouraged to become self-sufficient. Parents require this norm of their children, and clans and communities require it of their dependent populations. When it seems that a dependent person is not likely to achieve self-sufficiency, then the following questions emerge: (1) Has this person been self-sufficient before and, if so, did he or she engage in reciprocity with the community or the clan? (2) If this person has never been self-sufficient but is likely to become self-sufficient in the future, is he or she then likely to engage in reciprocity? Thus, a moral issue in social welfare is whether and to what extent the state (rather than the family, the clan, or the community) should become a transfer agent to foster the self-sufficiency of B now or in the future.

The Norm of Sources of Income

Yet another moral foundation is cultural views about sources of income. Should work be seen as the only means to gain income (as it was in

most Second World countries)? What sources of income have become culturally sanctioned as legitimate sources, as opposed to illegitimate sources (like
crime or transfer payments)? In most parts of the world, work for labor is
considered an important legitimate source of income, and capital is considered another legitimate source.

Often transfer payments made to individuals on the basis of past
reciprocity or past self-sufficiency or both are seen as deferred compen-
sation. They are made to appear as if they are delayed payments for
work done in the past. Transfer payments like these are called social
insurance and are given high legitimation (to become entitlements). In
contrast, transfer payments made to individuals who did not engage in
any clear past reciprocity are viewed as income that has low legitimation (to become gratuities).

The legitimacy of the source of income has long been a moral issue
in clans, tribes, and communities. It is often a moral issue in the welfare state
as well.

The Norm of Adoption

In most societies, being an orphan or a member of a dysfunctional
family (abusive family) is considered a reason for children to be adopted (by
another family in the clan, tribe, or community). When direct adoption is not
possible, communal institutions become the surrogate family. Most religious
ideologies prescribe procedures for adoption or its equivalent.

Throughout history, a serious problem has been what to do with
persons who are viewed as not readily adoptable (often people with no
promise of reciprocity or self-sufficiency). A moral issue emerges in the
modern welfare state when it is forced to become a surrogate parent or a
surrogate family member to such "unadoptable" people.

The Norm of Tribalism

Banfield (1958) coined the term *amoral familism* to describe the
moral basis of certain societies in which caregiving is extended only to members of the immediate family and the extended family. Requests to provide
care for persons who are not family members in such societies are met with
either hostility or avoidance. I call this the norm of tribalism, by which
caregiving is earmarked for members of the clan, the tribe, or the community. A clear example of this type of restricted transfer occurs in the voluntary sector of pluralist societies in which caregiving is restricted to members
of the payers' own ethnolingual, ethnoreligious, or ethnoracial groups.

The state, on the other hand, is caught between the norms of secularism and utilitarianism. Guided by the norm of secularism, it must become
a surrogate family and provide caregiving (the equivalent of adoption) to all

"unadoptable" individuals who are citizens of the state (regardless of their ethnic, clan, or tribal origin). Guided by the norm of utilitarianism, it must respond to the mandates of the majority (often the majority ethnic or tribal groups) and settle for the axiom of the maximal happiness for the maximal number of people. In the second case, members of a majority community, tribe, or clan sometimes refuse to pay taxes, vote for a levy, or otherwise support the state's efforts to adopt the unadoptable human beings.

The Norm of Commodification

Throughout the book, I have discussed how various goods and services become commodified in a market society and how different human beings take on commodified values. Although many moralists are uncomfortable with the idea of the commodification of human beings, it seems to be a natural by-product of capitalist societies. The Marxists made the condition visible and coined the term. In addition, Esping-Andersen (1990) argued in favor of the partial decommodification of certain goods and services to make the welfare state more viable.

Commodification occurs in market economies and is an outcome of human economic behavior. Revulsion toward commodification occurs in moral philosophy and the political ideology of egalitarianism. The conflict between the two poses another issue for the welfare state.

RIGHT VERSUS LEFT: THE POLITICAL BASIS

The position of the Right versus the Left in relation to social welfare is well established in the literature. Pinker (1979), for example, in discussing mercantile collectivism as a reason for social welfare, noted that it is neither a value-driven behavior nor an ideological position, but a means to an end. That is, the adoption of some concern for the collectivity may be good for business, can be used to show the merchants' sense of civic responsibility, and thus is multifunctional. Hence, it is a form of political behavior. Karger and Stoesz (1994) described at length how Left- or Right-oriented political behavior supports or opposes welfare spending in the United States. They also stated that in addition to being for or against a form of welfare spending, a Left or a Right political position is also for or against regulating labor costs, for or against taxing profits, for or against requiring employers to provide certain fringe benefits, and for or against the taxation of capital gains.

Given that political behavior is often interest driven, such interests are better served when an individual, a special-interest group, or a special-interest community builds alliances or coalitions. In social welfare development, political behavior is often a cleavage between pro-capital and pro-labor groups (Pierson, 1991; Rimlinger, 1971) that struggle to build alliances and coalitions and use various ideologies to justify their actions. Some components of such political behavior are as follows.

Capital versus labor. In some societies, such as the United States, pro-capital groups are called conservatives and pro-labor groups are called liberals (see Karger & Stoesz, 1994). The pro-labor groups are usually for social welfare spending, and the pro-capital groups are usually for cutbacks in spending. In some other societies, such as Germany, however, pro-capital groups have spearheaded welfare spending to appease people at the bottom of a social hierarchy or stratification system.

Elites versus the masses. The political traditions guiding the relationship between elites and the masses (see Kornhauser, 1959) contribute to welfare spending (Wilensky, 1975). Holders of capital can be thought of as economic elites, and their alliances and bargains with other types of elites (like political elites and intellectual elites) illustrate the political basis of the welfare state.

Ideologies. One school of thought may imply that the welfare state is ideology driven, and another may imply that the welfare state is ideology justified. Pro-capital groups more frequently use pro-market ideologies to reduce welfare spending, whereas pro-labor groups use ideologies in which the market is not considered important.

Without some form of political resolution, the welfare state is not possible. Each welfare state reflects a unique resolution of the ongoing tensions between capital and labor and between the elites and the masses and the political ideologies they use to legitimate their claims. These political interests are frequently disguised as moral positions.

RIGHT VERSUS GRATUITY: THE LEGAL CODIFICATION

The moral traditions of a culture, in combination with a society's capacity to make political decisions, become the basis of the legal codification of transfer by the formulation of rights (entitlements) and gratuities. Usually, entitlements are enacted for the middle- and working-class populations who are politically active, and gratuities are enacted for members of the underclass, or poverty class, who are not politically active. Borrowing a term from Wilensky (1975), the "middle masses" are given entitlements (which carry dignity), and the "lower masses" are given gratuities (which do not carry dignity). The entitlements are called social insurance, and the gratuities are called welfare. In many welfare states, several different transfer plans, each with its own administrative hierarchy, are instituted to manage different social insurance programs and welfare programs. The creation of all these different programs also gives the elites the opportunity to form a patronage system through which jobs are created for middle-class people, insurance programs are offered to middle- and working-class people, and welfare is given to poor people.

RIGHT VERSUS INACCURATE: THE SCIENTIFIC APPROACH

Once the ends (whether transfer should be made and to whom) are clearly established, questions about at least three sets of means become the reason to raise important scientific questions. The questions are these: (1) What are efficient organizational structures to deliver insurance or welfare programs? (2) What relative cost–benefit issues are raised by each organizational structure? (3) What, if any, social–psychological impact do these organizational structures have on the recipients of insurance or welfare programs?

The *organizational structure* refers to the design of a welfare state system for delivering services. The most frequent structure is a rational bureaucracy, in Weberian terms (see Weber, 1946). Mintzberg (1983) proposed five structures that reflect variations of this organizational design. Using Mintzberg's work as one model, one can raise the following questions: Is services delivery in the welfare state more efficient under one of these organizational designs and less efficient under the others? Is the quality of service better under one of these designs than under the others? Is there a conflict between what optimizes efficiency and what optimizes quality? Can program evaluation research (see Rossi & Freeman, 1985) shed any light on these questions?

The cost–benefit issue can be broken down into several questions. Is it possible to attach any cost–benefit model to the organizational studies to show that one type of organizational design is more cost-effective than the others? What happens when a cost-effective design is socially or politically undesirable?

The social–psychological issue can be framed as follows: What are the unintended consequences (see Merton, 1958) of a social welfare program? Does it destroy the incentive for self-sufficiency? Does it create mostly dependent personalities? Instead of giving dignity to human beings (as entitlements are supposed to do), does it erode human dignity in the long run? Does it create several recipient groups (with entitlements) who are engaged in keeping and enhancing their benefits, with no concern about the payers' ability to afford the benefits? What happens when these entitlements become transfers from future generations?

CONCLUDING REMARKS

At the beginning of this chapter, I noted that many scholars of the welfare state are either for or against the welfare state, in a manner comparable to attorneys who are for or against a defendant in a case. The ideologues discussed in chapters 4 and 5 can be seen from this perspective, and they contribute to the moral and political foundations of the welfare state (as shown in Figure 10-1). In contrast, the conflict theorists discussed in chapters

6 and 7 help one understand the political and legal foundations of the welfare state. And depending on their paradigmatic positions, the scholars of industrialization discussed in chapters 8 and 9 shed some lights on all the following three foundations of the welfare state: the political, the legal, and the scientific.

Furthermore, certain disciplines specialize in different approaches to the welfare state. Economics and economic anthropology help one understand the concept of surplus. Moral philosophy and social work contribute to the moral foundations of the welfare state. Political science and macrosociology foster an understanding of the political basis of the welfare state, as do law and political science with regard to the legal foundations and organizational behavior at the informational level. The field of social welfare, a multidisciplinary venture, reflects the problems and contradictions generated by the efforts of all these groups.

REFERENCES

Banfield, E. (1958). *The unheavenly city*. Boston: Little, Brown.

Blau, P. (1964). *Exchange and power in social life*. New York: John Wiley & Sons.

Esping-Andersen, G. (1990). *The three worlds of welfare capitalism*. Princeton, NJ: Princeton University Press.

Gouldner, A. (1960). The norm of reciprocity. *American Sociological Review, 25*, 161–178.

Karger, H. J., & Stoesz, D. (1994). *American social welfare policy*. New York: Longman.

Kornhauser, W. (1959). *The politics of mass society*. New York: Free Press.

Marnell, W. (1965). *Man-made morals: Four ideologies which shaped England and America*. Garden City, NY: Doubleday.

Merton, R. (1958). *Social theory and social structure*. Glencoe, IL: Free Press.

Mintzberg, H. (1983). *Structure in fives: Designing effective organizations*. Englewood Cliffs, NJ: Prentice Hall.

Pierson, C. (1991). *Beyond the welfare state?* University Park: University of Pennsylvania Press.

Pinker, R. (1979). *The idea of welfare*. London: Heinemann.

Rimlinger, G. (1971). *The welfare state and industrialization in Europe, America, and Russia*. New York: John Wiley & Sons.

Rossi, P., & Freeman, H. A. (1985). *Evaluation: A systematic approach*. Beverly Hills, CA: Sage Publications.

Tagore, R. (1973). *Kripon* [Miser]. In R. Tagore, *Rabindra-Rachanabali* [The works of Rabindra] (Vol. 5). Calcutta: Viswa-Bharati University Press.

Weber, M. (1946). *From Max Weber: Essays in sociology* (H. H. Gerth & C. W. Mills, Trans.). New York: Oxford University Press.

Wilensky, H. (1975). *The welfare state and equality.* Berkeley: University of California Press.

11

VISIONS OF THE WELFARE STATE: WHAT IS RIGHT?

You've added color and sound

to my dreams; a longing that lends

to a krait in the monsoon as it twists around

a banyan tree; a future that bends

through some mists unknown; eavesdropping nights

peering through the door; a wish to make sense

and sing it out in rhyme;

a wish to be a mime

and let go of my voice; a wish for the lights

of comets far away at elliptical heights.

You're the cries of a crocus in a darkness dense!

Chatterjee, *Reflections*

Given my knowledge of the welfare state, however partial it may be, what can I contribute to the vision of a future welfare state, or, for that matter, to the redirection of a present one? I attempt to answer these questions in this chapter.

IS THERE A SURPLUS?

I concluded that the prerequisite for a welfare state is a surplus. Thus, the first observation is that a welfare state is possible if, and only if, a surplus is available in the economic slope.

I realize that the concept of surplus can also be culturally constructed. A statement, attributed to Margaret Thatcher (prime minister of

England in the 1980s) was that those who generate wealth should be allowed to keep a higher share of it. In relation to Figure 9-1, Thatcher was trying to shift the location of the United Kingdom from box 6 (market production and distribution by both the market and the state) to box 9 (classic capitalism). The advantage of box 9 is that the producers of wealth have a greater incentive to produce wealth and hence to generate a higher surplus, which will benefit all. Therefore, Thatcher's position has substantial merit if one is interested in generating a decent surplus.

However, the position in box 9 rules out the welfare state. Leaving all distribution to the market can lead to disastrous results, as was seen during the Great Depression of the 1930s. Thus, distribution has to be partially controlled by the state, once free-market capitalist production has generated the needed surplus. In most parts of the First World today, boxes 2, 5, 3, and 6 are the only viable options.

In the Second World, the possession of capital (by individuals or families) was illegitimate. Only the state was allowed to accumulate capital (which, for most purposes, did not occur). The concept of surplus was whether there was a surplus in the country after the producers of wealth (the people who contributed labor) were allowed to retain a fair portion of it. In the Third World countries, the producers of wealth (both on farms and in the industries of the cities) do not produce enough for the state to tax them and transfer that income as welfare to groups who are not in the labor force.

With regard to surplus, two natural experiments have taken place. In the first, the capitalist industrialization of Hong Kong, South Korea, Taiwan, and Singapore (see chapters 8 and 9), the surplus was built by capitalist production and capitalist distribution (box 9 in Figure 9-1). Beginning in the 1990s, social policymakers in these four countries were moving toward capitalistic production and regulated distribution (box 6 in Figure 9-1).

The second experiment took place in five adjacent countries— Turkmenistan (GNP per capita in 1991–92 $3,435 in U.S. dollars), Kazakhstan (GNP per capita in 1991–92 $3,807), Tajikstan (GNP per capita in 1991–92 $2,434), Uzbekistan (GNP per capita in 1991–92 $2,798), and Afghanistan (GNP per capita in 1991–92, $192). In ethnoreligious origin, these five countries are very similar. However, Afghanistan (female life expectancy in 1991–92 was 43 years) was poor, preindustrial, and without a welfare state, whereas Turkmenistan, Kazakhstan, Tajikstan, and Uzbekistan were, in comparison, richer, selectively industrial, and offered some welfare state benefits (all four countries had female life expectancy around 74 years). Turkmenistan, Kazakhstan, Tajikstan, and Uzbekistan have been under industrial socialism for many years, since they were a part of the former Soviet Union. Afghanistan, on the other hand, is a Third World country. The concluding lesson, again, is that any form of industrialization is preferable for social and wealth development, but industrial capitalism is preferable.

A surplus increases the capacity of a centric agent (often the state) to tax the income of those in the labor force and to transfer some of that income to those who are not in the labor force. This concept has to be understood in combination with the dependency ratio. Are there enough people in the labor force from whom it is possible to transfer income to build a welfare state? Are those people from the next generation, and will they be able to receive transfer from a subsequent generation? What is the ratio of the dependent population to the population who is active in the labor force? In sum, the construction of a welfare state is possible when it has been ascertained that (1) there is a surplus available for transfer and that (2) the dependency ratio of the present and future populations is high enough for the society to contemplate building such a state.

THE MORAL FOUNDATION

If a welfare state is to be built, then what moral foundation should it have? The norm of reciprocity cannot be the sole guiding foundation in this respect. When a transfer plan is put in place, it reflects a one-way transaction from those who can pay to those who cannot. Among the recipients of transfer, there are four subgroups: those who have contributed to this process of reciprocity (by participating in the market) in the past and are likely to do so again in the future (Subgroup A), those who have done so in the past but are unlikely to do so in the future (Subgroup B), those who have not done so in the past but are likely to do so in the future (Subgroup C), and those who have not been able to do so in the past and are not likely to do so in the future (Subgroup D). People who are temporarily disabled or unemployed are examples of Subgroup A, and people who have retired from the labor force because of age, illness, or disability are examples of Subgroup B. Children, in general (and children from poor families, in particular), are exemplars of Subgroup C, and people who are developmentally disabled or born with severe handicaps and sometimes transgenerational poor people from a culture of poverty are exemplars of Subgroup D.

The challenge to the welfare state is that children from poor families should not be allowed to move from Subgroup C to Subgroup D. A welfare state based on a norm of reciprocity would mean that transfer would be permitted to flow to the first three groups and would not be given to the fourth group. As a result, those in Subgroup D would probably be homeless, on the streets, and a visible embarrassment (if not a guilt inducement) to many productive members of the state. A consequence of including Subgroup D in the transfer process is that the group would be relatively invisible, not on the streets, and a source of some political bickering.

The norm of self-sufficiency, like the norm of reciprocity, also cannot form the moral basis for the welfare state. The goal of self-sufficiency should be taught to all people in the family, the school, and other institutions of socialization. If a given institution fails to impart this value, then it may be thought of as dysfunctional and a cause for concern. The welfare state, however, is put in place to care for those who are not now and perhaps never will be capable of becoming self-sufficient. To blame the welfare state for supporting persons who are not and can never be self-sufficient is like blaming rain clouds for causing rain.

The norm of using either capital or labor as the only legitimate source of income also cannot form the moral basis of a welfare state. If one agrees that the norms of reciprocity and self-sufficiency cannot form the moral basis of the welfare state, then one also should agree that there is and is likely to be a third source of income that needs legitimation. That source is transfer payments.

The norm of adoption, or the state becoming a surrogate family, is an important moral foundation of the welfare state. It has been already established that because of industrialization and post-Fordism, it is likely that many people do not have the support of natural families and, sometimes, of natural communities. Consequently, there is practically no other choice but to vest a surrogate family function to the state. However, the state is not meant to do this job and, when required to do so, does it poorly.

The struggles against the norm of tribalism are another moral foundation of the welfare state. The welfare state should be prepared to extend its benefits to all its members, not just to the immediate kin and community of the payers. Thus, the norm of membership (citizenship)—not of tribalism—should be the guiding moral foundation of the welfare state. When citizenship becomes the basis of welfare state distributions, then a set of other moral questions need to be considered because in a global village (as the world has become), citizenship can sometimes restrict the humane treatment of people who are not citizens of a particular country. For example, the Netherlands extends its health care services to whoever requests them, including drug addicts from foreign countries, whereas the United States requires proof of insurance coverage. These two countries illustrate the moral dilemma: When should the welfare state provide transfer to noncitizens? I believe that the welfare state should be prepared to cover noncitizens as well as citizens because the increased movement of a large number of persons across national borders is a fact of life in a global village. Perhaps the issue could be resolved by treaties between two or more welfare states, and the provision of services to citizens of other countries could be part of an international reciprocity system.

The norm of commodification (what can be commodified and what cannot) has clear domains in gemeinschaft societies, but has an expansive domain in industrial capitalism. Although a person's age, appearance, body, and labor are subjected to commodification by a market economy, a welfare state cannot allow its moral foundation to rest on this norm. The first effort to achieve decommodification occurred when some states declared that people could not be bought or sold as slaves. An extension of that principle may be that people cannot be allowed to starve or to go untreated, unprotected, or uncared for because they are less valued as commodities.

Figure 11-1 summarizes the moral foundations of the welfare community and the welfare state. In this figure, the community reflects a gemeinschaft orientation, whereas the society reflects a gesellschaft orientation. The two different social organizations rest on different moral foundations. The basic argument behind Figure 11-1 is that if a neighborhood or village is an important way to assign geopolitical boundaries to a community, then the state is one important way to assign geopolitical boundaries to a society. The welfare community or the welfare state is the means by which these boundaries can be strengthened. The moral foundations of the two, however, are not necessarily the same.

THE POLITICAL FOUNDATION

Once the moral foundation of the welfare state is set (in relation to the norms of reciprocity, self-sufficiency, capital, or labor as the only acceptable source of income, tribalism, and commodification, adoption, and citizenship), then it is possible to look at the political foundation. If a welfare state is to be built, then a fundamental political principle must be established: to blame procedures rather than people. By procedures, I mean educational institutions that fail to educate some populations, health care institutions that fail to reach target populations, or the lack of agreement between pro-capital and pro-labor groups about these possibilities. When are these problems due to the escalation of costs or to inefficient management? Is there a political formula for making transfer to recipients without simultaneously enriching the transfer agents from the middle class? When does the building of a welfare state lead to the reduction of conflict between pro-capital and pro-labor groups and between the masses and the elites? What political strategies, if any, justify such a reduction of conflict and mutual payoffs?

THE LEGAL FOUNDATION

If a welfare state is to be built, then should the transfers be planned as entitlements for those who receive them? Or should they be considered gratuities that can be reduced at times or even eliminated? Should the benefits be indexed to the gross national product, the gross domestic product, or some measure of the dependency ratio? I think that a reduction of entitlements, coupled with benefits indexed to the gross domestic product, is a better solution. Increased entitlements pave the way for increased costs,

Figure 11-1.

The Moral Foundations of the Welfare Community and the Welfare State

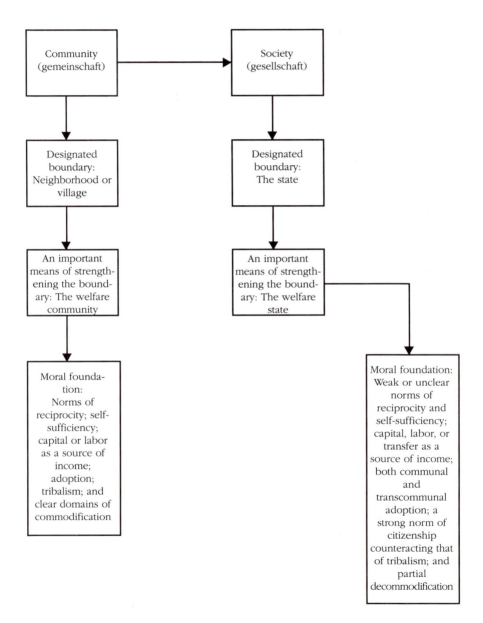

severe budget problems, borrowing from future generations, and the eventual loss of the surplus.

THE SCIENTIFIC FOUNDATION

If a welfare state is to be developed, then what kind of evaluation research
plan should be built into it to steer its course? Should it be program evaluation research, organizational design research, cost–benefit research, or out-
come-of-intervention research? What happens when the finding's of scientific research at one level contradict the findings at another level? For example, what happens when a given organizational design is found superior
for service delivery but inferior for cost-effectiveness? I think that the guiding principle should be survival of the state, its capacity to remain a welfare
state, and its capacity to maintain a surplus.

CONCLUSION

If a welfare state is to be built, then it has to be constructed on the premise
that it is morally desirable, politically feasible, legally enforceable, and scientifically testable. Once it has been built, the changing nature of surplus, moral
desirability, political feasibility, legal precedents, and scientific evidence steers
its path. The following eight statements summarize my thoughts about the
moral, political, economic, and scientific feasibility of the welfare state:

1. Without wealth building, the welfare state is not possible. Industrial capitalism is the best means of wealth building known
to date.
2. Those who produce wealth should have the right to keep a
greater share of it.
3. Wealth cannot be produced solely by capital; the cooperation
and collaboration of labor are necessary. Thus, labor's share of
the wealth that is produced is a natural and legitimate one. In
addition to direct recompensement, this share can be provided
in the form of social insurance.
4. The formula for both capital's and labor's share of the wealth
that is produced depends on the moral and political foundations of a culture.
5. People who have contributed to wealth building in the past
(such as aged people) or have the potential to contribute in the
future (like children or people who are temporarily ill or disabled) should be seen as claimants to a smaller share of the
wealth that is produced than should those who are active in
wealth building in the present. This is a moral foundation and is

operative in wealthy societies. This principle is the first major foundation of welfare state building.

6. Those who have not contributed and are not likely to contribute to wealth building can be supported by the state. This support can range from subsistence-level support to higher levels, depending on the political foundation of the state. It is desirable for the state to attempt to train or educate this group to become potential wealth builders. If it is not possible to do so, then this group's level of support continues to be set by the political foundation. This principle is the second major foundation of welfare state building.

7. The nonproductive populations (as in items 5 and 6) should be supported so they can live with dignity as much as possible (or as much as the state can afford). However, they have an obligation to continue to try to contribute to the production process as much as they can. This is a matter of rights (from the state) and obligations (to the state), and one cannot exist without the other. This principle is the third major foundation of welfare state building.

8. The state cannot be a substitute for the family or the community and must avoid the temptations to be so to populations who need protection (such as children, or ill or aged people). Its protective services arm should be designed to provide temporary services, and its taxation powers should create strong incentives in families and communities to adopt or provide foster care services to groups who need protection. This principle is the fourth major foundation of welfare state building.

Given these foundations, the following guidelines would make good templates for social welfare policy.

Income maintenance policy. First, all pension funds should be privatized under strict supervision and regulation. Contributions to such a privatized pool should be mandatory for all people in the labor force. They would become investments that people in Subgroup B could draw from when they retire from the labor force because of age, rather than depend on transfer payments from the state. Thus, on retirement, people would receive what they put in, plus any interest and appreciation of their input. This policy, which is true social insurance, not a transfer plan, has been implemented successfully in Chile, and is being introduced in Argentina, Australia, and Sweden (Klein, 1994; Ratan, 1995).

Second, all remaining plans should be means tested. This policy would cover members of Subgroup B who dropped out of the labor force because of illness or disability, as well as those in Subgroups A, C, and D.

(People who dropped out owing to work-related injuries should receive supplemental income from employers, who should carry mandatory insurance to cover this possibility.) If all these transfer plans were means tested, the stigma attached to using the state as a source of income (the norm of using either labor or capital as a source of income) would be reduced.

Third, over and above what may be available from means-tested transfer, supplementary provisions should be made for people in Subgroup C. In addition to income maintenance policy, education and health care policies must also be firmly supportive of this group. Fourth, members of Subgroup D should be given transfers at the level of basic necessities.

Health policy. No satisfactory organizational structure has yet been devised that can deliver an unlimited amount of high-quality health care to all citizens. If the goal is to provide health care services for all citizens, then a package of *rationed and basic care* must be developed that covers only survival needs. It may be cheaper to deliver such rationed basic health care through one tier of a two-tier system as is done in many capitalist countries. In such a system, one tier is operated by the state, and the other tier is operated by the market. Furthermore, the state must impose strict quality-control measures for the daily functioning of the state-operated tier.

Protective services. The protective services policy of the modern welfare state is based on the norm of adoption. However, as was mentioned earlier, the state is not capable of performing this task well. Therefore, the state should provide only policing and crisis care, including foster care for children of parents with problems, and offer strong tax incentives to encourage adults to adopt children and other persons in need.

Housing policy. The state should not be in the housing-construction business. The U.S. experience is enough of an example of the poor job the state does of developing housing for poor people and of subsidizing middle-class interests through construction contracts and employment of housing officials. Instead, housing programs should be privatized and left to market development. The state must set strict housing codes through its regulatory powers and offer tax incentives for builders of housing for poor people. One important goal of housing policy should be *ownership* of homes by people. Thus, the state could issue mortgage (or rent) supplements as part of its income maintenance program.

Education policy. Because education is a part of cultural capital, to use Bourdieu's (1977, 1984, 1989) term, the state should maximize its efforts to provide decent education. As with health care, there should be a two-tier educational system. The first tier should provide primary and secondary education to all under the auspices of a central (rather than a local or regional) government, to ensure a consistent level of education across the country, and university-level education for those who are able and want to continue their schooling. The state-run educational services should aspire to be as good as reasonably possible. The second tier should provide private, for-profit, and nonprofit education at all levels, from primary school to the university.

In the United States, the public–private mix has been greatly successful in higher education, but a dismal failure in primary and secondary education. One reason for the extreme unevenness of primary and secondary education in that country is the dependence of school systems on local taxes and local politics. Education is a precious resource and should not be left in the hands of diverse and feuding local groups who may not have enough resources and are committed to the norm of tribalism.

Except for education, the welfare state should be engineered to meet basic survival needs, not the higher-order needs of those who have neither capital nor the capacity for labor. Its preferences should be for investments, rather than for a patchwork of transfer payments. Its mission should be to build a better tomorrow and not to spend beyond its means today.

REFERENCES

Bourdieu, P. (1977). *Outline of a theory of practice.* Cambridge, England: Cambridge University Press.

Bourdieu, P. (1984). *Distinction: A social critique of the judgment of taste.* Cambridge, MA: Harvard University Press.

Bourdieu, P. (1989). Social space and symbolic power. *Sociological Theory, 7,* 14–25.

Chatterjee, P. (1995). The color and sound of dreams. *Reflections, 1,* 25.

Klein, J. (1994, December 12). If Chile can do it. *Newsweek,* p. 50.

Ratan, S. (1995, March 20). How Chile got it right. *Time,* p. 30.

GLOSSARY

Acceptable deviant. A recipient (such as a person who is poor because of a physical disability) who is in a socially unacceptable role but whose deviance can be tolerated.

Adoption, norm of. *See* **Norm of adoption.**

Alienated labor. The process resulting from the conflict between the human need to find meaning and creativity in one's work and an economic ideology that converts that work or labor into only an economic exchange. Also, human labor sold as a commodity without any meaningful attachment to the products generated by that labor.

Alienation. *See* **Economic alienation, Political alienation,** and **Religious alienation.**

Allocations. Goods or services that are transferred either in a cash or a cash equivalent or in kind. Transfers that go directly to the recipient or to a third party who provides certain goods and services to the recipient.

Anarchists. Those who believe in the formation of natural communities as a way to achieve a just society.

Anticollectivism. A typology of the welfare state in which redistribution is seen as unwelcome, liberty and individualism are supported, the free market is considered the organizing principle of society, and the state thought to facilitate the operation of the free market. It views capitalism as

---

Note: I wish to thank Barbara Wester and Theresa Wilson for their help in developing this glossary.

self-regulating, supports a market economy, and is hostile to the ideal of a welfare state.

Capitalism, ideology of. *See* **Ideology of capitalism.**

Cash transfer. A transfer in the form of a check or money, a tax credit or tax deduction, or vouchers that are redeemable for a set of named goods and services.

Centric transfer. A transfer from one party or group to another through a central collection or clearing agent.

Class analysis. A theory of the impact of class position or stratification on such outcomes as health or mental health condition, life expectancy and life choices, political participation, and ways of thinking.

Class conflict. A conflict between interest groups that are organized to represent class interests and that have class consciousness.

Collectivism. The commitment to collective interests. *See also* **Anticollectivism** and **Reluctant collectivism.**

Commodification, norm of. *See* **Norm of commodification.**

Comprehensive social welfare. The transfer of several items to a given person or population at one time and perhaps through the same agent.

Comprehensive transfer. A transfer administered by one set of offices or agencies.

Conduit capitalism. The process by which forms of transfer and services aimed at poor people provide hidden benefits to upper-class people.

Conflict. A hostile encounter or struggle that originates in an existing order, either within or between persons, roles, or groups, because of actual or perceived differences in the possession of status, resources, or opportunities. *See also* **Class conflict, Gender-oppression conflict, Ideological conflict, Knowledge-base conflict, Macrolevel conflict, Microlevel conflict, Role-interest conflict,** and **Technological-change conflict.**

Contract-oriented societies. Societies in which the rights and obligations of parties are defined by custom and law. When a conflict between custom and law occurs, law prevails. Term introduced by Henry Maine. *See also* **Status-oriented societies.**

Corporate–individual payers. Individuals and their employer corporations who provide voluntary payments to transfer agent.

Cultural capital. A composite of linguistic, aesthetic, normative, and behavioral preferences in a given situation and knowledge that originate from the familiarity of higher social classes with such preferences.

Decommodification. The ability of a society to liberate its employees' basic requirements of living independent of the market structure.

Deism, ideology of. *See* **Ideology of deism.**

Demand-and-supply matrix. A theory that income derived from a wage–labor exchange depends on the productivity of labor. Labor and commodities produced with labor are valued according to their demand in the marketplace. When demand and supply are balanced, that is, when there is perfect competition and individuals and groups maximize their choices under these circumstances, there is market equilibrium.

Democracy, ideology of. *See* **Ideology of democracy.**

Demographic analysis. The identification and precise measurement of the influences that underlie population changes.

Dependency ratio. A ratio in which the numerator is one unit of benefit paid to a recipient and the denominator is the number of persons taxed from the labor force to provide this unit of benefit.

Differentiated welfare state. A welfare state that is relatively autonomous and emerges as a response to the demand side of the economy.

Direct transfer. A transaction between a recipient and a centric agent (including groups and organizations employed by the transfer agent to provide services).

Diversified transfer. A transfer administered by many sets of agencies and offices.

Dual labor market theory. A theory that there is a strong association between stratification and market structure. The primary market offers high wages, fringe benefits, employment security, and due process and consists of members of the middle class and some selected members of the working class. The secondary market offers low wages, no or few fringe benefits, no job security, and no due process and consists of members of the poor or lower class.

Economic alienation. A Marxist theory that explains how humanity becomes alienated from human labor. Certain socioeconomic conditions, legitimated by accompanying ideologies, transform labor into a commodity to be sold in the marketplace.

Economic welfare. An individual's well-being as a function of that person's income, holdings, tax status, and the like.

Elites. Groups at the top of the social-class hierarchy of an industrialized society.

Elitism. Autocracy of the elites.

Exchange system. A two-way transaction, in which one party provides some goods or services to another and is recompensed for doing so.

Exchange theory. A theory that all interactions between persons, groups, communities, organizations, and nations are transactions. All transactions are exchanges guided by conscious rationality. Many involve material resources, information, role, attractiveness, and the ability to commit violence and are even or uneven; uneven exchanges lead to power imbalances.

Fabianism. A typology of the welfare state in which redistribution is welcomed incrementally and freedom and fellowship are supported, as are purposeful government action and regulated markets as the organizing principle of society. It recommends that the state should build institutions to deal with market failure on a planned basis; views capitalism as generating and perpetuating most inequalities; and supports a mixed economy and state-supported and administered social services, which incrementally move the state toward a total welfare state. A form of socialism popular in Britain from the 1890s onward.

False consciousness. A consciousness alien to one's struggle for freedom.

Field. A network of relations that exist apart from individual consciousness and will.

First World. The rich, capitalist, industrialized, and (mostly) white nations of North America, western Europe, Australia, and Japan that are based on the traditions of a market economy and individualism.

Fordism. An economic system whose basic idea is derived from Henry Ford's mass manufacturing of automobiles on an assembly line, coupled with Frederick Taylor's "scientific management" of the assembly line. Its attributes include mass-produced and homogenized products, assembly-line technology, time management, quota-per-time-unit productivity, homogenized workers' skills, unionization, and a market for homogenized products and services. *See also* **Post-Fordism.**

Gemeinschaft societies. Small communal or tribal groups in which most human relationships (between friends or those involving face-to-face affective interactions) are an end in themselves. A term popularized by Ferdinand Tonnies.

Gender-oppression conflict. A form of conflict in a social system in which women are controlled or subjected. The conflict becomes more prominent when women become aware of this subjected status and attempt to change it.

Gesellschaft societies. Large industrial societies in which many forms of human relations (such as lawyer–client, salesperson–customer relationships) are a means to an end, and many transactions are between secondary, rather than within primary, groups. A term popularized by Ferdinand Tonnies and Max Weber.

Gross domestic product (GDP). The measure of all goods and services produced in a nation.

Gross national product (GNP). The total income of all residents of a nation, regardless of where it comes from. A measure that is equal to the GDP, plus all income, profits, and so on from outside the nation, minus income, profits, and so forth payable to other nations.

Guild socialism. The belief in workers' control, instead of state control, of industry without direct action or selective violence.

Habitus. The cognitive structure through which people deal with the social world.

Human Development Index (HDI). A composite measure of human development containing indicators representing three equally weighted dimensions for human development: longevity, knowledge, and income.

Human relations, ideology of. *See* **Ideology of human relations.**

Ideological conflict. A conflict between interest groups that are organized to represent ideological positions.

Ideology. A system of thought that prescribes the relationship among people and between people and their culturally produced artifacts or services.

Ideology of capitalism. A system of thought that assumes that human needs can be understood only as individual needs, not as needs of the members of the community.

Ideology of deism. A system of thought that holds that the preferred way of organizing the family, religious institutions, and the relationships between the governor and governed is for authority to follow from a male God to a male head of state and then to a male head of a household.

Ideology of democracy. A system of thought that advocates self-rule by popular participation in decision making.

Ideology of human relations. A system of thought that states that laboring groups are to be treated with dignity and equality.

Ideology of inheritance. A system of thought that prescribes the way by which the genders and generations can be entitled to land, artifacts, and ideas owned by previous generations.

Ideology of laissez-faire. The belief that laboring poor people should be left alone, as should rich people.

Ideology of ownership. A system of thought that prescribes the way by which the genders and generations can own land, artifacts, and ideas.

Ideology of patriarchy. A system of thought that prescribes a hierarchical relationship between the genders that leads to a preferred way of identifying generational relationships.

Ideology of pragmatism. The belief that truth is successful experience.

Ideology of social Darwinism. The belief that only the "fit" or the "able" species, capable of adapting to the environment, survive.

Ideology of socialism. A system of thought that assumes that human needs can be understood as being on a continuum between individual needs and the needs of members of the community.

Ideology of utilitarianism. The belief in the maximal happiness of the maximal number.

Income transfer. The part of the income of those who are in the marketplace that is transferred to those who are not, or the part of the income of all people that is transferred to those who are relatively privileged.

Indexed transfer. A form of transfer that may increase or decrease with a nationally standardized scale (such as the income needed by a family of four to survive at a subsistence level during a given year) and is adjusted for inflation periodically thereafter.

Indirect transfer. A transaction between independent providers who are reimbursed by a transfer agent and a recipient.

Industrial society. A society whose economic sector produces mostly secondary goods (manufacturing and processing), whose occupational slope leads to skilled labor and engineering and management skills to oversee skilled labor, which is dependent on energy to convert raw materials into secondary goods, and which requires capital and skilled labor.

Industrialization. A technological process involving the large-scale manufacturing of goods by machines.

Inheritance, ideology of. *See* **Ideology of inheritance.**

In-kind transfer. A transfer that occurs when an agent of transfer employs a group or develops an organization to provide certain services or purchases those services from independent providers.

Institutional social welfare. A form of social welfare in which planned intervention structures are in place to manage vulnerable populations and it is assumed social welfare is the first line of defense against calamities.

Integrated welfare state. A welfare state that is responsive to both demand and supply and in which welfare expenditures are indexed to the spending capacity of the state and the purchasing capacity of the currency.

Involuntary payer. A taxpayer who pays money, in the form of taxes, that provides income to the state to pay for social and other services.

Item-focused social welfare. A form of social welfare that focuses on one item at a time and in which transfers of only one item at a time take place.

Knowledge-base conflict. A conflict between groups that represent different knowledge structures and interests generated from these structures.

Labor force replacement ratio. A ratio that is calculated as the population under age 15 divided by one-third of the present population aged 15 to 59.

Laissez-faire, ideology of. *See* **Ideology of laissez-faire.**

Liaison elite. Appointed rulers from the mother country and their agents, a local elite of a colonized country.

Liberal tradition. A tradition in which the community and state intervene to support marginal and vulnerable groups.

Limits on transfer. The rationing of income, goods, or services to recipients.

Macrolevel conflict. A conflict within and between large groups like communities; organizations; interest groups; ethnoracial, ethnolingual, ethnoreligious groups; social classes within a nation; and nations themselves.

Maoism. The Chinese interpretation and adaptation of Marxism by Mao Tse-tung that focuses on rural populations and farmworkers promoting community-based social welfare.

Market exchange. A transaction by the rules of supply and demand.

Marxism. A typology of the welfare state within which redistribution is immediately welcomed, freedom and collectivism are supported, free markets are viewed as the source of all evil, the state is considered the main or only player in a controlled market, capitalism is thought of as an alien ideology that corrupts all people, a planned economy is supported, and the welfare state is a socialist state.

Means-tested transfer. A transfer available only to those of modest social position or economic status.

Medicalization. The definition of somatic, aesthetic, psychological, interpersonal, and social problems as problems in the individual that can be dealt with by the medical metaphors of diagnosis and treatment.

Membership. The concept that a recipient is entitled to certain goods or services by virtue of his or her belonging to a specific group (such as a church or a state).

Microlevel conflict. A conflict within or between persons, roles, and small groups.

Modernization theory. A theory that the problems of Third World nations are due to the values, attitudes, and behavior of the people in these countries. Modernization (resocialization) of Third World countries with the values, information, and institutions of the First World countries would lead to industrialization and the development of wealth.

Monopoly capital. A situation in which the owners of capital (upper-class people and their agents, who are mostly from the upper middle class) are always in pursuit of further capital accumulation by gaining a monopoly in the marketplace.

Neutral transfer. A transfer situation that cannot be identified as either progressive or regressive.

Noncentric transfer. The absence of a central agent in the transfer situation.

Noneconomic welfare. An individual's well-being that is due to biological, spiritual, emotional, or normative conditions.

Nonmarket exchange. A transaction by social norms and emotional bonds.

Norm of adoption. The view that not having a family or having a dysfunctional family is a reason for adoption (by another family in the clan, tribe, or community). At times, the state serves as a surrogate family.

Norm of commodification. The process by which goods and services are commodified in a market society. The concept can apply to the assignment of commodified values to individuals or groups.

Norm of reciprocity. If A does B a favor, then B should return the favor either in the present or in the future.

Norm of self-sufficiency. The belief that a dependent person should be educated, trained, and encouraged to become self-sufficient.

Norm of tribalism. The belief that caregiving should be extended only to members of the family and the extended family.

Normative theory. A formalized position (a prescriptive action scheme) about what should be done under given circumstances.

Ownership, ideology of. *See* **Ideology of ownership.**

Panoptican. A device that permits the complete observation of subjects in a knowledge-seeking endeavor.

Patriarchy, ideology of. *See* **Ideology of patriarchy.**

Payers. *See* **Corporate–individual payers, Involuntary payers, Public–private payers,** and **Voluntary payers.**

Performance principle. A process by which the body and mind are made into instruments of alienated labor.

Political alienation. A Marxist theory portraying the human need to escape the demand for loyalty to and the pretentious promise of a political system. Those at the bottom of a stratification ladder surrender their labor and life to serve the interests of those on higher rungs.

Postfisc welfare state. A welfare state in which benefits to a given population are itemized after the state's taxation capacity and budgetary provisions are ascertained.

Post-Fordism. An economic system whose attributes include the individualized and specialized production of products, small and diversified technological processes, output management, total-quality-per-product productivity, diversified and flexible workers' skills, ineffective unionization, and a market for specialized products and services.

Postindustrial society. A society whose economic sector is dependent on services and information (trade, finance, health, research, insurance, and recreation), whose occupational slope leads to knowledge and information processing, which is dependent on knowledge and information to produce services, and which requires capital and knowledge.

Postmodernism. A theory that assumes that cultural occurrences are bound by language, and are specific to given localities and not necessarily a part of either universal or unilinear patterns of development.

Pragmatism, ideology of. *See* **Ideology of pragmatism.**

Prefisc welfare state. A welfare state in which benefits to given population groups are promised before the taxation capacity of the state is ascertained and a budget is in place.

Preindustrial society. A society whose economic sector is extractive (agriculture, mining, fishing, timber); whose occupational slope leads to farming, mining, and fishing; which is dependent on the availability of raw materials; and which requires expanses of land and relatively unskilled labor.

Privatization. The shift of production and transfer activities from the state to private entrepreneurs.

Progressive social welfare. A form of social welfare in which transfers are made from well-to-do people or groups to those who are not or from those who are successful in the marketplace to those who are not.

Progressive transfer. A transfer between a payer who is a well-to-do person or group and a recipient who is a person or group of modest means.

Proletariat. A term derived from the Greek word *proles,* which means prolific, that originally referred to people who had many children. Marxists use it to refer to persons who have no property or other capital and depend on the wages they receive from the sale of their labor.

Protected entrepreneurs. Powerful individuals and corporations who receive large amounts of transfer from the state.

Provider. A person, group, or organization that has important skills and "provides" important in-kind services to recipients.

Public–private payers. Individuals and nonprofit organizations whose voluntary donations are combined with matching public funds collected by the state acting as a transfer agent.

Rational choice theory. A theory that states that an important function of any cultural group is production and assumes that there are likely to be persons who may avoid any role in the production of public goods. Thus, the problem for the state is who, if any one, should be allowed to avoid this role in the production of public goods.

Reciprocal altruism. A situation in which unrelated members of a community tacitly provide mutual support.

Reciprocity, norm of. *See* **Norm of reciprocity.**

Reciprocity network. A system in which workers provide productive labor during some time of their lives and are protected when they can no longer provide this labor.

Regressive social welfare. A form of social welfare in which transfer flows either uniformly from everyone to the privileged and the successful in the marketplace or from the less privileged and those who are not engaged in market exchange to those who are.

Regressive transfer. A transfer from a person or group of modest means to well-to-do person or group.

Religious alienation. The Marxist theory that people at the bottom of a stratification ladder find justification of their misery in a religious ideology and that religion is an instrument of social control by the upper stratum of society.

Reluctant collectivism. A typology of the welfare state within which redistribution is selectively tolerated; liberty and pragmatism are supported; somewhat regulated markets are viewed as the organizing principle of society; it is believed that the state should leave the free market alone but remedy the impact of market failure and that capitalism, though not self-regulating, is the best foundation for society; and a mixed economy and privatization of social welfare, sometimes with state support, are supported.

Residual social welfare. Based on the assumption that social welfare policy applies only to those who cannot be supported by family or market systems, and no planned intervention structure is in place to manage vulnerable populations.

Role-interest conflict. A conflict between groups that represent interests inherent in certain roles.

Second World. Cuba and countries in Eastern Europe and central and northern Asia that are or were socialist, selectively industrial, neither rich nor poor, and based on the traditions of a planned economy and collectivism.

Self-sufficiency, norm of. *See* **Norm of self-sufficiency.**

Social Darwinism, ideology of. *See* **Ideology of social Darwinism.**

Social welfare. A transfer system through goods and services are allocated to individuals and groups through a given unit of social organization, such as the family, the church, the guild, the state, or the corporate group, under a set of rules and with a set of reciprocal roles. *See also* **Comprehensive social welfare, Institutional social welfare, Item-focused social welfare, Progressive social welfare, Regressive social welfare,** and **Residual social welfare.**

Social welfare policy. The ensemble of concrete plans by which social welfare is implemented. At times, some of these plans may be in conflict with each other.

Socialism, ideology of. *See* **Ideology of socialism.**

Societies. *See* **Contract-oriented societies** and **Status-oriented societies.**

Society. *See* **Industrial society, Postindustrial society,** and **Preindustrial society.**

Status-oriented societies. Societies in which the rights and obligations of parties are defined by traditions and legitimated by ideology. A term introduced by Henry Maine. *See also* **Contract-oriented societies.**

Structural-functionalism. A theory that all societies or national cultures must perform certain key functions to survive as cultural entities. These functions are universal regardless of where societies are located. However, the macrostructures that perform these functions may take different shapes in different cultures.

Surplus repression. An intrapsychic process by which repression is used to justify the domination of one group (class) over another.

Syndicalism. The belief that incremental and selective violence against dominant groups is a way to bring about a better and just society in which ownership and control of industries would rest in the hands of workers' unions, rather than the state.

System. *See* **Exchange system** and **Transfer system.**

Technological-change conflict. A conflict between two or more parties, one of which has access to improved, developed, or superior technology and the others do not.

Theory. *See* **Dual labor market theory, Exchange theory, Normative theory, Rational choice theory,** and **Theory of dependence.**

Theory of dependence. The theory that laboring poor people need to be treated like children and to be protected from themselves.

Third-party payment system. A system in which the transfer agent pays the provider to render services to the recipient.

Third World. Mostly nonwhite, poor, preindustrial, developing countries located in Africa, southern and Southeast Asia, and South America that are often nationalistic, selectively industrial to preindustrial, and based on a mixed economy and regional loyalties.

Transfer. *See* **Cash transfer, Centric transfer, Comprehensive transfer, Direct transfer, Diversified transfer, Income transfer, Indirect transfer, In-kind transfer, Means-tested transfer, Neutral transfer, Noncentric transfer, Progressive transfer, Regressive transfer,** and **Universal transfer.**

Transfer system. A one-way transaction in which income, wealth, or some other item is transferred from one person or group to another or in which there is no identifiable recompense to the party originating the transfer.

Transgenerational poor. A group of poor people in the First World, primarily in the United States, who remain poor generation after generation, trapped in a "culture of poverty," a term introduced by Oscar Lewis.

Tribalism, norm of. *See* **Norm of tribalism.**

Universal transfer. A transfer in the form of a basic floor of income and services to all in a society, regardless of their social position or economic status.

Utilitarianism, ideology of. *See* **Ideology of utilitarianism.**

Utopia. An unattainable community in which all rules, artifacts, and human relationships are perfect.

Value-orientation analysis. A theory that human values are enduring beliefs that a specific mode of conduct or end-state of existence is personally or socially preferable to an opposite or converse mode of conduct or end-state of existence.

Value system. An enduring organization of beliefs concerning preferable modes of conduct or end-states of existence along a continuum of relative importance.

Voluntary payer. A payer who voluntarily gives funds through private contributions.

Welfare church. The church acting as a transfer agent.

Welfare community. The community as a second-line provider of transfers to persons in need.

Welfare family. A family in which those who earn income transfer it to those who do not.

Welfare state. The state as a provider of transfers to persons in need. *See also* **Differentiated welfare state, Integrated welfare state, Postfisc welfare state,** and **Prefisc welfare state.**

Zero transfer. No transfer.

INDEX

A

Acceptable deviance, 20, 236, 283
Addams, Jane, 103–104, 121
Adoption, norm of, 267, 276, 291
African Americans, community
    conflict regarding, 156–157
Aggressors, 98
Agricultural societies, 9–10
Alauddin, sultan of Delhi, 225–226
Alienated labor, 283
Alienation
    economic, 142, 143, 285
    Marxist sources of, 95, 142
    political, 142–143, 291
    religious, 142, 143, 293
Alinsky, S., 96
Allocations
    cash vs. kind, 6, 7
    direct vs. indirect, 6–7
    explanation of, 6, 283
    as right or gratuity, 12, 269
    types of, 7
Althusser, A., 97
Amoral familism, 267
Anarchists, 95–96, 283
Anticollectivism
    capitalism and, 120
    explanation of, 283–284
    welfare state and, 120, 122–123
Appold, S. J., 49
Aron, R., 102
Atherton, C. R., 214
Authoritarianism, 101

B

Bailey, D., 126
Bandung Conference (1955), 45

Banfield, E., 267
Barry, N., 39, 222
Beeghley, L., 215–216
Bell, D., 48, 102
Bendix, R., 101, 102
Bentham, Jeremy, 102
Berger, P., 46, 48, 99, 189, 247, 248
Bernstein, B. J., 165
Beveridge, W. H., 124, 246
Billingsley, A., 157
Blumer, H., 188
Bollen, K., 49
Bourdieu, P., 145

C

Capitalism
    conduit, 164, 284
    education under, 93
    health care under, 92
    housing under, 93–94
    human needs and, 105–106
    ideology of, 88–90, 129, 287
    income sources under, 91
    industrialization and, 189–191
    Protestant ethic and, 101, 108
    technocratic consciousness in,
       143
Cash transfer, 6, 7, 284
Centric transfer
    explanation of, 5, 284
    in First World, 68
Chapin, M., 175
Chatterjee, P., 4, 125, 126, 159, 273
Children
    income-support policy for, 167,
      168
    vulnerability of, 32–33
Choi, I., 125

Church, as form of social organization, 9
Civil disobedience, 145–146
Clarke, S., 149
Class analysis
    explanation of, 284
    industrialization and, 215–216
Class conflict
    explanation of, 141–143, 284
    Pohlmann paradigm of, 164–165
Cloward, R., 161
Collectivism
    anti-, 283–284
    explanation of, 284
    mercantile, 125
    reluctant, 293
    socialism and, 88
Commodification
    of education, 93
    of human vulnerability, 249
    of illness, 124
    norm of, 268, 276–277, 291
    technocratic consciousness in
        capitalism leading to, 143
Communities
    conflict between, 140, 155–159
    as form of social organization, 9
    impact of industrialization on,
        188–189
Community Development Corporation (CDC), 157–158
Comprehensive social welfare, 284
Comprehensive transfer, 7, 284
Conduit capitalism, 164, 284
Conflict. *See also specific types of
    conflict*
    civil disobedience and, 145–146
    class, 164–166
    community-level, 140, 155–159
    ethnic, 140, 162–163, 179
    explanation of, 137–139, 284
    functions of, 143–144
    from gender-based oppression,
        148–150, 175–177, 287

generated by technology,
    177–178
ideological, 166–170, 288
interest-group, 163–164
international, 178–180
of knowledge, 144–145,
    170–174, 289
organizational, 140, 159–161
parties to, 139–141
in production styles, 148
in role interests, 174–175
social welfare and, 150–151
theories of, 141–143, 150
welfare infrastructure and,
    180–183
in world systems, 146–148
Contract-oriented societies, 206,
    284
Corporate social responsibility,
    67–68
Corporate–individual payers, 30,
    284
Coser, L., 87, 143–144, 162
Cost containment
    as managed better by indexing
        welfare expenditure than by
        deficit financing, 246–247
    as problem in industrial capitalism, 245–246
Courtney, M. E., 123, 175
Cree tribe, 158
Cultural capital, 285

D

Dahrendorf, R., 144
Darwin, Charles, 102
Decommodification, 41, 285
Deism
    basic assumptions of, 102
    ideology of, 88, 89, 287
Demand-and-supply matrix, 214,
    285

Democracy
  background of, 89
  development of American, 106
  development of western
      Europe, 106
  ideology of, 89, 90, 288
Demographic analysis, 213, 285
Dependency ratio, 194, 285
Dependency theory
  explanation of, 101, 295
  international conflict and, 180
  modernization theory vs., 218
Deregulation, 60
Dewey, John, 102
Differentiated welfare state, 21, 285
Direct transfer, 6–7, 285
Divale, W. T., 162
Diversified transfer, 7, 285
Dual labor market theory
  explanation of, 285
  industrialization and, 214–215

E

Economic alienation
  effects of, 143
  explanation of, 142–143, 285
Economic welfare, 3, 286
Economy, impact of industrializa-
      tion on, 189–196
Education
  ideology and, 93
  percentage of GNP for, 60, 61
  policy guidelines for, 281–282
Elderly individuals, income-
      support policy for, 167, 169,
      170
Elites
  explanation of, 108, 286
  industrialization of society and
      influence of industrializing,
      117–118
  liaison, 118

relationship between masses
      and, 269
  types of, 108
Elitism, 286
Employees, providers as, 35
Ephross, P., 125
Esping-Andersen, G., 237, 238, 244
Ethnic groups, 140, 162–163, 179
Eulau, H., 124
Exchange. *See* Market exchange;
      Nonmarket exchange
Exchange system, 286
Exchange theory
  explanation of, 286
  industrialization and, 220–221

F

Fabianism
  explanation of, 40–41, 106, 286
  impact of Marxist thought on,
      95
  U.S. social workers and, 121
  welfare state and, 120, 122–123
False consciousness, 98, 286
Family
  as form of social organization,
      8–9
  ideologies of, 89
  impact of industrialization on,
      188
Females. *See* Women
Feminism/feminist groups
  gender-oppression conflict and,
      148–150, 175–177, 287
  ideology of, 88
  as parties to conflict, 141
  radical, 149–150
  in Third World, 77
  view of family wage concept,
      226
Feminization of poverty, 64
Feuer, L., 102–103

Field, 145, 286
First World
    community-based social inter-
        vention in, 104
    conflict and, 183
    contemporary definition of, 49
    development of democracy in,
        106
    explanation of, 46, 286
    female life expectancy in, 56, 58
    functions of poverty in, 242–243
    future for, 251
    growth in GNP in, 56, 57
    ideology in, 132–133
    impact of 1980s on, 60, 63–64
    in 1992, 50
    per capita GNP in, 53, 55
    percentage of GNP for educa-
        tion in, 60, 61
    population of, 53, 54
    population per hospital bed in,
        56, 59
    relevance of ideology in, 102
    social welfare provisions in,
        71–72
    welfare infrastructure in, 67–70,
        130
    welfare trends in, 62–63
Ford, Henry, 148
Fordism
    conflict and, 148, 149, 177
    explanation of, 286
    post-, 148, 177, 178, 291–292
For-profit organizations, providers
    as, 36
Foucault, M., 144
Frankfurt school, 98–100
Free World. *See* First World
Freud, A., 101
Freud, Sigmund, 98
Friedman, K. V., 125
Friedman, Milton, 117, 120, 214,
    243
Friere, P., 97, 143

Fromm, Erich, 99
Fundamentalism, 162

G

Game theory, 220–221
Gandhi, Mohandas K., 104, 145,
    146
Gans, H., 108, 240, 243
Gemeinschaft societies, 286–287
Gender-oppression conflict
    examples of, 176–177
    explanation of, 148–150,
        175–176, 287
George, V., 119–122, 124, 125
Gesellschaft societies, 287
Gilbert, N., 236
Gilly, Adolfo, 115
Goodin, R. E., 15
Gordon, D., 214
Gould, A., 176, 238–240
Gouldner, Alvin, 100
Gramsci, A., 97
Gross domestic product (GDP),
    287
Gross national product (GNP)
    explanation of, 287
    growth in, 56, 57
    per capita, 53, 55
    percentage for education, 60, 61
Guild socialism, 96, 287
Gypsy communities, 157

H

Habermas, J., 100, 143
Habitus, 145, 287
Harris, M., 162
Hayek, Friederich, 243
Health care
    expenditures for, 196, 198
    guidelines for, 281

ideology and, 91–92
views of sick role and, 124
Hechter, M., 221
Heilbronner, R., 155
Help
  model of ideologies of,
    126–129
  role of state and market in
    ideologies of, 130
Hesse, H., 45
Hobhouse, L. T., 39
Hofstede, G., 103
Holland, T., 125
Housing policy
  guidelines for, 281
  ideology and, 93–94
Human Development Index (HDI)
  explanation of, 287
  industrialization and, 194–196
Human needs
  ideology and, 105–107
  prescriptions for meeting,
    105–107
  vulnerability of, 105
Human relations, 102, 288

I

Ideological conflict
  examples of, 167–170
  explanation of, 166–167, 288
Ideology
  of capitalism, 88–90, 288
  of deism, 88, 89, 102, 287
  of democracy, 89, 90, 288
  education and, 93
  explanation of, 87, 90, 107–108,
    288
  of feminism, 88
  Frankfurt school and, 98–100
  health care and, 91–92
  housing and, 93–94
  human needs and, 105–107

of human relations, 102, 288
income and, 91
of inheritance, 88, 288
Marxist tradition and, 95–98
methodology and, 107
non-Marxist tradition and,
    100–103
of ownership, 88, 288
of patriarchy, 88–90, 288
personal social service and,
    94–95
of pragmatism, 102, 288
as reason and justification,
    115–116
of social Darwinism, 102, 288.
    See also Social Darwinism
social welfare and, 103–104,
    108–109
of socialism, 88–90, 288
of utilitarianism, 102, 288
variations among national
    systems justified by,
    124–125
variations between national
    systems due to, 116–121
variations within national
    systems due to, 121, 123–124
variations within national
    systems justified by, 125–130
welfare infrastructure and, 129,
    131–132
IK tribe (Kenya), 155–156
Income
  ideology and, 91
  norm of sources of, 266–267
  sources of U.S., 199
Income maintenance plans. *See*
    Income supplement plans
Income maintenance policy
  guidelines for, 280
  ways of defining, 171, 173, 174
Income supplement plans, 7
Income transfer
  explanation of, 7, 288

in Second World, 73
wealth vs., 13, 193–194
Independent contractors, 35–36
Indexed transfer, 7, 288
Indirect transfer, 288
Individualism, 88
Industrial society
    explanation of, 48, 288–289
    providers in, 212
    state in, 10
Industrialization
    explanation of, 187–188, 289
    groups that sponsor, 202, 207
    impact of, 188–189, 191–200
    pre- and post-, 201–202
    role of industrializing elites in,
        117–118
    social welfare and, 227
    welfare infrastructure and,
        207–212
    welfare state as by-product of,
        233–240
Industrialization paradigms
    class analysis and, 215–216
    demand-and-supply matrix and,
        214
    demographic analysis and, 213
    dual labor market theory and,
        214–215
    exchange and game theory and,
        220–221
    explanation of, 212–213
    modernization theory and,
        218–220
    monopoly capital and, 215
    normative theory and, 222
    ontological issues and, 222–226
    postmodernism and, 220
    rational choice theory and,
        221–222
    structural functionalism and,
        217–218
    value-orientation analysis and,
        216

Inheritance, ideology of, 88, 288
In-kind transfer, 6, 7, 289
Institutional social welfare, 19, 289
Insurance, 6
Integrated welfare state (IWS), 21,
    289
Interest groups, conflict between,
    140–141, 163–164, 206
International conflict, 178–180
Interorganizational conflict, 140
Intraorganizational conflict, 140
Involuntary payers, 28, 289
Item-focused social welfare, 289

J, K

Janowitz, M., 188, 245–246
Karger, H. J., 123, 216, 268
Katz, M. B., 237
Kautilya, 222
Kerr, C., 118
Keyes, John Maynard, 246
Kick, E., 48, 49
King, Martin Luther, Jr., 145–146
Knowledge-base conflict
    examples of, 171–174
    explanation of, 144–145,
        170–171, 289
Kropotkin, Peter, 96, 117
Kuznets, S., 191, 192
Kuznets curve, 191–192

L

Labor
    under capitalism, 95
    as source of income, 91
Labor force attachment, 191
Labor force replacement ratio, 194,
    289
Ladestro, D., 163
Laissez-faire, 101, 288

Laski, Harold, 46
Lenin, Vladimir, 96
Levine, R., 165
Lewin, K., 150
Liaison elite, 289
Liberal tradition, 104, 289
Limits on transfer
   conflict and, 183
   explanation of, 37, 289
   industrialization and, 212
   in Third World, 77
   welfare society infrastructure
     and, 38
Lipsky, M., 160
Lohmann, R., 187
Luckman, T., 99
Lukacs, G., 97, 143

M

Machiavelli, Niccolo, 222
Macrolevel conflict. *See also*
   Conflict
  at community level, 140
  between ethnic groups, 140
  explanation of, 139, 289
  between interest groups,
    140–141
  between nations, 141
  at organizational level, 140
Maine, Sir Henry, 206, 284
Malinowski, B., 217
Mannheim, K., 98, 143
Mao Tse-tung, 96–97
Maoism, 96–97, 290
Marcuse, Herbert, 98–99
Market, industrialization and,
   224–225
Market exchange, 5, 290
Market rationing, 93
Marnell, W., 101, 102
Marshall, T. H., 119, 243
Martin, E., 125

Marx, Karl, 98, 116, 137, 141–142, 147
Marxism
  explanation of, 290
  ideology of, 95–98
  welfare state and, 120, 122–123
Maslow, Abraham, 105
Master–subject conflict, 141
Mauss, M., 3
Means-tested transfer, 7, 8, 290
Medicalization
  under capitalism and patriarchy,
    92
  explanation of, 290
Membership, 290
Mercantile collectivism, 125, 268
Merton, R., 218
Microlending, 67
Microlevel conflict. *See also*
   Conflict
  explanation of, 139, 290
  studies for, 139–140
Midgley, J., 219
Mill, John Stuart, 39, 101
Mills, C. W., 108
Mintzberg, H., 270
Mishra, R., 246
Modernization theory
  explanation of, 290
  industrialization and, 218–220
Monopoly capital
  explanation of, 290
  industrialization and, 215
Moore, B., Jr., 233
More, Sir Thomas, 222
Mo-tzu, 222
Moynihan, D. P., 156–157
Moynihan report, 156–157

N

Nationalization, 36
Nations, conflict between, 141,
   146–148

Needs. *See* Human needs
Nehru, Jawaharlal, 45, 46
Neutral transfer, 5, 290
New Deal, 165–166, 204
Nkrumah, Kwame, 45
Noncentric transfer
    explanation of, 5, 290
    in First World, 68
    in Third World, 76, 77
Noneconomic welfare, 3, 290
Nonmarket exchange, 5, 291
Non-Marxist tradition, 100–103
Nonprofit organizations, 36
Normative theory, 222, 291
Norms
    of adoption, 267, 276, 291
    of commodification, 268,
        276–277, 291
    of reciprocity, 263, 266, 291
    of self-sufficiency, 266, 275–276,
        291
    of sources of income, 266–267
    of tribalism, 267–268, 276, 291
    of utilitarianism, 267, 268
Nozick, R., 222, 243

O

Oakshott, Michael, 102
Offe, C., 16
Offe, C., 216
Organizational conflict, 140,
    159–161
Orloff, A. S., 175, 176
Ownership, 88, 288

P

Panoptican, 144–145, 291
Parsons, T., 217–218
Patriarchy
    capitalism, social Darwinism,
        and, 91, 92

    health care under, 92
    ideology of, 88–90, 288
    personal social service and,
        94–95
Payers. *See also specific types of*
        payers
    conflict and, 181
    in First World, 67–68
    industrialization and, 207
    involuntary, 28
    in Second World, 70, 72–73
    in Third World, 76
    voluntary, 29
    in welfare society, 28–30
Performance principle, 98, 291
Personal social service, 94–95
Pierson, C., 238–240
Pinker, R., 125, 268
Piven, F. F., 161
Pohlmann, M., 164–165
Political alienation
    effects of, 143
    explanation of, 142, 291
Political behavior, 268–269
Politician alienation, 291
Population
    per hospital bed, 56, 59
    in Three Worlds, 53, 54
Postfisc welfare states
    as better than prefisc welfare
        states, 245
    characteristics of, 244
    explanation of, 291
    industrial capitalism leading to,
        240, 243–245
Post-Fordism
    conflict and, 148, 149, 177, 178
    explanation of, 291–292
Postindustrial society
    explanation of, 48, 292
    social welfare programs and,
        201–202
    status orientation of, 206
Postmodernism, 220, 292

Poverty
  exploitation due to, 176–177
  feminization of, 64
  functions in First World of,
    242–243
  industrial capitalism and, 240
  transgeneralization, 64, 295
Powell, B., 200
Pragmatism, 102, 288
Prefisc welfare states
  characteristics of, 244
  explanation of, 191, 292
  industrial socialism leading to,
    240, 243–245
  postfisc welfare states as better
    than, 245
Preindustrial society
  community in, 188–189
  explanation of, 48, 292
  providers in, 212
  social welfare programs and,
    201–202
  status orientation of, 206
Privatization
  explanation of, 60, 292
  recent trends toward, 36
  of social welfare, 104, 120
Production, conflict in styles of,
  148
Professionalized psychology, 249
Profit motive, 223
Progressive social welfare
  explanation of, 13, 292
  model for, 14
Progressive transfer, 4, 5, 292
Proletariat, 292
Protected entrepreneurs, 33, 292
Protective services, 281
Protestant ethic, 101, 108
Proudhon, Pierre-Joseph, 96, 117,
  119
Providers
  conflict and, 182–183
  explanation of, 10, 34–35, 292

in First World, 69–70
in Second World, 73–74, 76
in Third World, 77
in welfare society, 35–36
Pryor, F. L., 4, 5
Public–private payers, 30, 293

R

Rational choice theory
  explanation of, 293
  industrialization and, 221–222
Rationalism
  ideology of, 102
  industrialization and, 225–226
Rationing, 93, 246
Rawls, J., 222, 243
Reagan, Ronald
  privatization and, 36, 60
  social policy and, 121
Recipients
  acceptance of welfare benefits
    by, 224
  allocations for, 12
  categories of, 32–34, 208–210
  conflict and, 182
  deserving status of, 12
  in First World, 68–69
  industrialization and, 208–211
  membership status of, 10
  in Second World, 73
  self-appointed advocates for,
    36, 70
  vulnerability of, 12, 32
Reciprocal altruism, 140, 293
Reciprocity
  industrialization and, 223
  norm of, 263–266, 291
Regressive social welfare
  explanation of, 13, 293
  model for, 15
Regressive transfer, 4, 293
Reisch, M., 125

Rejai, M., 89
Religious alienation
    effects of, 143
    explanation of, 142, 293
Reluctant collectivism
    explanation of, 293
    welfare state and, 120, 122–123
Repression, surplus, 98, 294
Residual social welfare, 19, 293
Richmond, Mary, 103–104
Rimlinger, G., 125, 162, 236, 237
Rokeach, M., 216
Role-interest conflict, 293
Rural Reconstruction project
    (Sriniketan, India), 104

S

Samuelsson, K., 101
Schoor, A., 126
Schumpeter, J., 233–234
Second World
    conflict and, 183
    contemporary definition of, 49
    explanation of, 46, 294
    female life expectancy in, 56, 58
    growth in GNP in, 56, 57
    historic functions of, 250–251
    ideology in, 132
    impact of 1980s on, 65
    in 1992, 51
    per capita GNP in, 53, 55
    percentage of GNP for educa-
        tion in, 60, 61
    population of, 53, 54
    population per hospital bed in,
        56, 59
    relevance of ideology in, 102
    social welfare provisions in, 75
    state-sponsored, community-
        based social intervention in,
        104

welfare infrastructure in, 70,
    72–74, 76, 129
welfare trends in, 62–63
Secularism, 162, 267–268
Self-appointed advocates, 36, 70
Self-sufficiency, norm of, 266,
    275–276, 291
Sen, A., 224–225
Shah, I., 27
Shils, E., 48
Sick role
    development of concept of,
        217–218
    differences in concept of, 171
    health care and view of, 124
    impact of professionalized
        psychological orientation on,
        249
Skocpol, T., 147–148, 237
Smith, Adam, 116–117, 214
Snyder, D., 48, 49
Social class, 108
Social Darwinism
    capitalism, patriarchy and, 91,
        92
    human needs and, 106
    ideology of, 102, 123, 288
Social insurance, 6, 8
Social organization
    church as form of, 9
    community as form of, 9
    family as form of, 8–9
    society as form of, 10
    state as form of, 9–10
    units of, 11
Social security expenditures, 196,
    197
Social service, ideology and
    personal, 94–95
Social welfare
    as camouflage for conflict. *See*
        Conflict
    components of, 4–13

comprehensive, 284
explanation of, 3–4, 6, 8, 18,
    294
ideology and, 103–104, 108–110
institutional, 289
item-focused, 289
origins of, 21–22
political ideologies and, 89–90
progressive, 13, 14, 292
regressive, 13, 15, 293
residual, 293
set of rules for, 10, 12
variations in, 19
for well-to-do, 12–13
Social welfare policy
    explanation of, 13–14
    orientations to study of, 17–18
    from social science perspective,
        15–17
    social work perspective of,
        16–17
    taxonomies of, 19–20
Social welfare programs, 121
Social welfare systems
    variations among national
        systems justified by ideology,
        124–125
    variations between national
        systems due to ideology,
        116–121
    variations within national
        systems due to ideology, 121,
        123–124
    variations within national
        systems justified by ideology,
        125–130
Social work
    First World professionalization
        of, 70
    ideologies held by, 95, 103–104,
        125–126
    in Third World, 77
    trends in 1980s in, 64

view of human needs by,
    105–107
Socialism
    guild, 96, 287
    health care under, 92
    housing under, 94
    human needs and, 107
    ideology of, 88–90, 106, 129,
        131, 288
    industrialization and, 189–191
    patriarchal, 91
Society
    concept of sick, 99
    contract-oriented, 284
    as form of social organization,
        10
    gemeinschaft, 286–287
    gesellschaft, 287
    industrial. *See* Industrial society
    postindustrial. *See* Postindustrial
        society
    preindustrial. *See* Preindustrial
        society
    status-oriented, 294
Sosrodihardjo, Sukarno, 45
Specht, H., 123, 175, 236
State
    as agent of centric transfer, 10
    as form of social organization,
        9–10
    impact of industrialization on,
        189
    as provider in First World, 70
    as transfer agent in First World,
        68
    as transfer agent in Second
        World, 73
Status-oriented societies, 206, 294
Steward, J. H., 219
Stoesz, D., 123, 126, 216, 268
Structural functionalism
    explanation of, 294
    industrialization and, 217–218

intended and unintended
consequences of welfare
state, 241
unintended consequences and,
226
Surplus repression, 98, 294
Syndicalism, 95, 294
System. *See* Exchange system;
Transfer system

T

Tagore, Rabindranath, 104, 258
Tawney, R. H., 101
Technological-change conflict,
177–178, 294
Thatcher, Margaret
privatization and, 36, 60
social policy and, 121
on wealth generation, 273–274
Third World
brain drain from, 69
community-based social intervention in, 104
conflict and, 183
contemporary definition of, 49
development of, 147
explanation of, 46, 48, 295
female life expectancy in, 56, 58
growth in GNP in, 56, 57
housing in, 94
ideology in, 132
impact of 1980s on, 65–67
industrialization and, 250
meeting human needs in, 107
natural experiments in social
development in, 248
in 1964, 47
in 1992, 52
per capita GNP in, 53, 55
percentage of GNP for education in, 60, 61
population of, 53, 54

population per hospital bed in,
56, 59
relevance of ideology in, 102
social welfare provisions in, 79
welfare infrastructure in, 76–78
welfare trends in, 62–63
Third-party payment system, 7, 295
Three concentric worlds model,
48–49
Three discrete worlds model,
45–48
Three Worlds. *See* First World;
Second World; Third World;
World system
Titmuss, Richard M., 118–120, 175,
243
Towle, Charlotte, 104, 105, 121
Trader–captive client conflict, 141
Trader–independent client conflict,
141
Transfer. *See also specific types of
transfer*
conflict and, 181–182
explanation of, 4
in First World, 68
limits on, 37, 38, 77, 183, 289
in Second World, 73
social insurance as form of, 6
in Third World, 76–77
Type 1, Type 2, and Type 3,
30–32
types of, 4–8
welfare as form of, 6
Transfer agents
conflict and, 182
in First World, 68
industrialization and, 207–208
rules for, 12
in Second World, 73
in Third World, 76–77
types of, 32, 207–208
Transfer system, 4–6, 295
Transgenerational poor, 64, 295
Triage rationing, 93

Tribal societies, 9
Tribalism, norm of, 267–268,
    276, 291
Tropman, J. E., 216
Trotsky, Leon, 96

U

Unacceptable deviance, 20
Unintended consequences, 226
Universal transfer, 7, 8, 295
Utilitarianism
    ideology of, 102, 288
    norm of, 267, 268
Utopia, 98, 295

V

Value system, 295
Value-orientation analysis, 216, 295
Victims, 34
Voluntary payers
    explanation of, 29, 296
    in First World, 67–68
    transfers from, 29–30
von Hayek, Friedrich A., 120
Vulnerability
    of children, 32–33
    commodified, 249
    definition of, 32
    of human needs, 105

W, Z

Wallerstein, I., 48, 146, 147
Wealth, income transfer vs., 13,
    193–194
Weber, Max, 98, 100–101, 103, 108,
    219, 225
Welfare church, 9, 18, 296
Welfare community, 9, 18, 296

Welfare family, 18, 296
Welfare society, 10, 18
Welfare society infrastructure
    categories of recipients in,
        32–34, 68–69
    limits on transfer in, 37, 38,
        77–78, 183, 289
    payers in, 28–30, 67–68, 70,
        72–73, 76
    providers in, 34–36, 69–70,
        73–74, 76, 77
    types of transfer agents in, 32,
        33, 68, 73, 76–77
    types of transfer in, 30–32,
        68, 73
Welfare state
    as by-product of industrializa-
        tion, 233–236
    as by-product of industrializa-
        tion, but justified by ideol-
        ogy, 236–240
    classification systems used for,
        20–21
    comparison of 11 variables in,
        80
    conflict and development of,
        137. *See also* Conflict
    differentiated, 285
    explanation of, 10, 18, 296
    ideological orientations to
        British, 120, 122–123
    industrialization and, 196,
        199–200
    integrated, 289
    intellectual foundations of,
        37, 39, 40–41
    legal foundation for, 277, 279
    levels of right and, 261–270
    moral foundation for, 263,
        266–268, 275–278
    origins of, 22
    points of agreement on,
        259–260
    points of disagreement on, 260

political foundation for, 277
postfisc. *See* Postfisc welfare
    states
prefisc. *See* Prefisc welfare
    states
relationship between market
    economy and, 16
scientific foundation for, 279
surplus as prerequisite for,
    273–275
Wilding, P., 119–122, 124, 125
Wilensky, H., 108, 235, 236
Wilson, W. J., 157
Wolins, M., 236

Women
    devaluation of labor of, 93
    life expectancy of, 56, 58
    as vulnerable group, 64
World system
    convergence of views on, 49
    impact of 1980s on, 60, 62–67
    three concentric worlds model
        of, 48–49
    three discrete worlds model of,
        45–48
    trends in, 49–63
    welfare infrastructure in, 67–80
Zero transfer, 296

About the Author

P ranab Chatterjee received his undergraduate education from Viswa-Bharati University, India. He subsequently earned a master's degree in social work from the University of Tennessee and master's and doctoral degrees in sociology from the University of Chicago. Currently he is professor of social work at Case Western Reserve University in Cleveland. His academic interests are in comparative studies of the welfare state, technology transfer, and organizational behavior. He is also a bilingual poet and has published several volumes of poetry.

Approaches to the Welfare State

Cover design by The Watermark Design Office.

Composed by Wolf Publications, Inc., in Garamond and Bauer Bodini.

Printed by Graphic Communications, Inc., on 60# Finch Opaque.

Related Titles from the NASW Press

Approaches to the Welfare State, *by Pranab Chatterjee.* Examines the contradictions and conflicts that characterize the welfare state. Offers solid information for beginning comparative social policy, sociology, and political science courses as well as advanced courses. 1996.

ISBN: 0-87101-262-6, Item #2626, $34.95.

Women & Social Change, *by Felice Davidson Perlmutter.* Provides an insightful look at the global women's movement and how it cuts across social, cultural, and economic lines to improve women's lives. An eye-opening text for anyone interested in women's issues, social policy, management, and alternative or nonprofit organizations. 1994.

ISBN: 0-87101-239-1, Item #2391, $24.95.

How People Get Power, by Si Kahn. Describes how an effective organizer enables others to improve their lives—by convincing naysayers, persuading policymakers, and using self-determination to create change. 1994.

ISBN: 0-87101-236-7, Item #2367, $18.95.

Profiles in International Social Work, *edited by M. C. Hokenstad, S. K. Khinduka, and James Midgley.* Looks at the social work profession in 13 countries. Examines how social work is defined in different countries and how differing levels of prestige and professional respect for social workers affect work on behalf of their clients. 1992.

ISBN: 0-87101-215-4, Item #2154, $24.95.

(order form on reverse side)

ORDER FORM

Title	Item #	Price	Total
__ Approaches to the Welfare State	__ Item 2626	__ $34.95	_____
__ Women & Social Change	__ Item 2391	__ $24.95	_____
__ How People Get Power	__ Item 2367	__ $18.95	_____
__ Profiles in International Social Work	__ Item 2154	__ $24.95	_____
	+ 10% postage and handling		_____
		Total	_____

❏ I've enclosed my check or money order for $_____.

❏ Please charge my   ❏ NASW Visa*   ❏ Other Visa   ❏ MasterCard

Credit Card No. _____ Exp. Date _____

Signature _____
Use of this card generates funds in support of the social work profession.

Name _____

Address_____

_____

City _____ State/Province _____

Country _____ Zip _____

Phone _____

NASW Member # (if applicable) _____

(Make checks payable to NASW Press. Prices are subject to change.)

NASW PRESS

NASW Distribution Center
P.O. Box 431
Annapolis JCT, MD 20701
USA

Credit card orders call
1-800-227-3590
(In metro Wash., DC, call 301-317-8688)
Or fax your order to
301-206-7989

*AWSz 1/96